Climbing a Broken Ladder

The American Campus

Founded by Harold S. Wechsler

The books in the American Campus series explore recent developments and public policy issues in higher education in the United States. Topics of interest include access to college and college affordability; college retention; tenure and academic freedom; campus labor; the expansion and evolution of administrative posts and salaries; the crisis in the humanities and the arts; the corporate university and for-profit colleges; online education; controversy in sport programs; and gender, ethnic, racial, religious, and class dynamics and diversity. Books feature scholarship from a variety of disciplines in the humanities and social sciences.

Climbing a Broken Ladder

Contributors of College Success for Youth in Foster Care

NATHANAEL J. OKPYCH

Rutgers University Press

New Brunswick, Camden, and Newark, New Jersey, and London

Library of Congress Cataloging-in-Publication Data

Names: Okpych, Nathanael J., author.
Title: Climbing a broken ladder : contributors of college success for youth in foster care /
    Nathanael J. Okpych.
Description: New Brunswick : Rutgers University Press, [2021] | Series: The American
    campus | Includes bibliographical references and index.
Identifiers: LCCN 2020020456 | ISBN 9781978809178 (hardcover) |
    ISBN 9781978809161 (paperback) | ISBN 9781978809185 (epub) |
    ISBN 9781978809192 (mobi) | ISBN 9781978809208 (pdf)
Subjects: LCSH: Foster children—Education (Higher)—United States—Case studies. |
    College attendance—United States—Case studies. | Foster children—United States—
    Social conditions.
Classification: LCC LC4091 .O394 2021 | DDC 362.73/30973—dc23
LC record available at https://lccn.loc.gov/2020020456

A British Cataloging-in-Publication record for this book is available from the British Library.

www.rutgersuniversitypress.org

Manufactured in the United States of America

This book is dedicated to Andy Zinn

Contents

Climbing a Broken Ladder

Part I

Background

_____

Introduction

Baseball and Broken Ladders

While writing this book, my mother was in the process of moving out of the house she had lived in for thirty-seven years. Her attic was cluttered with enough stuff to fill a small museum. My Little League baseball trophies were on the chopping block. Most of the trophies did not hold much sentimental value, but there was one that I struggled to part with. I was around ten years old that season, and things looked grim from the start. Several players on the team had minimal exposure to baseball. As other teams were practicing hook slides and turning double plays, we were working on the mechanics of a proper throw.

One saving grace was the coaches. They saw something in us that was blocked from our view by doubt and frustration. What they saw was not where we were, but what we could become. They had us practice, far more than other teams. The coaches drove from neighborhood to neighborhood to pick up players who could not get to practice. Even on game days we were catching pop flies an hour before the first player of the opposing team showed up. Instead of giving players equal time or even devoting more time to the standouts, players who needed the most help got the most practice. The coaches showed a genuine interest in us. This rubbed off on the players, and a strong bond started to form.

At first, we had to weather hard losses, but we were not allowed to beat up on ourselves, blame each other, or wallow in our mistakes. Instead we continued to practice and improve. Eventually the hard work started to pay off. On the field, we began to look like other teams that were loaded with seasoned players, and eventually we won enough games to land a spot in the playoffs. One playoff game in particular is etched in my memory. We had made it to the quarter-finals and were facing one of the toughest teams in the league. In the last inning we were down by a run with a couple of our players on base. With two outs, the one player on our team who had never gotten a hit the entire season stepped up to the plate. The pitcher threw a hard fastball, and the batter cracked a line drive deep into the outfield that left the fielders scrambling. He made it to third base, driving in the winning run. I remember the roar that erupted from the crowd, the disbelief on the other team's faces, and the tears that filled his father's eyes. We went on to win the league championship, with each of us sent home with a big goofy-looking trophy.

My trophy, which was now sandwiched between a Singer sewing machine and outdated New Jersey road maps in my mother's attic, was so meaningful not because of anything I personally achieved but because of the transformation that occurred in our team. Although the comparison is far from perfect, I think some parallels exist between the turnaround baseball story and the college completion gap for foster youth. One statistic that drew me to this area of research is that less than 10 percent of foster youth complete college, despite the fact that the overwhelming majority aspire to do so. Like some of the players on the team, life circumstances leave many foster youth behind their peers in how prepared they are for college. This is due to a variety of reasons, such as gaps in educational opportunities, frequent school changes that derail learning, and the emotional toll of maltreatment and separation from one's family. However, there is also good reason for hope. Similar to the baseball story, with the right mix of relationships, resources, and support, which are undergirded by effective policies, I believe it is possible to increase the number of foster youth who enter and finish college. The transformation will not happen overnight. There is no magic bullet. And similar to the way in which the coaches sized up the challenges at the beginning of the season, what is needed is a frank account of the challenges that lie ahead for foster youth in pursuit of college degrees.

In my years as a therapist, counselor, care coordinator, middle school teacher, Upward Bound SAT instructor, college residence life building director, and researcher, I have had the opportunity to work with many young people who had to face considerable obstacles standing between them and a college degree. One foster youth compared her experience of making it through college to that of climbing a broken ladder.[1] Take a moment to picture this image in your mind. On the one hand, there is the insistent climber. Youth with foster care backgrounds have made it through extremely trying circumstances. They know how to fight and survive, to persevere through material and emotional hardships, and they draw on this strength when faced with challenges. However, on the other hand, before them are ladders that are missing rungs, that have unsteady side rails, or that stop halfway to the top. The ladder placed before each youth is a little bit different. The broken pieces symbolize the impediments each foster youth will face on the climb into and through college, both personal and systemic. What are the common impediments? This is an important question for child welfare and education professionals, advocates, foster parents, foster care alumni, scholars, and anyone else invested in improving college outcomes for youth with care histories. Having a clearer picture of the impediments will put us in a better position to develop effective responses. This book illuminates pieces of the broken ladder based on rigorous analyses of data and presents practical suggestions about challenges to target.

Purpose of This Book

The central purpose of this book is to investigate a wide range of factors that influence the chances of college success of young people with foster care backgrounds. It examines three principal outcomes: college enrollment, persistence, and degree completion. Each outcome is an important marker on the road from secondary school to finishing college. Additionally, the book probes a number of special topics, such as identifying enrollment patterns through college, investigating the role that trauma plays in college success, and evaluating the impact of a policy that increased the age limit youth can remain in foster care by three years.

This book focuses on a small but understudied group of students: adolescents and young adults who are in foster care. More than seven decades of theory building and empirical research have been conducted on students entering and attending college. This research has pointed to a number of background characteristics, experiences while in college, and institutional factors that influence persistence and degree completion for students (e.g., Mayhew et al., 2016). Importantly, there is the widespread recognition that different sets of risks may be at play for certain subgroups of college students, which challenges a one-size-fits-all explanation of college completion (Perna, 2013). Young people with foster care histories are an important subgroup. Compared to the massive amount of research on the general college student body, theoretical and empirical research on factors influencing college success for foster youth is thin.

In higher education, foster youth are considered one of the "hidden" student populations. They are not easily identified on campus and face a particular set of challenges unlike those encountered by most college students. Most have experienced maltreatment severe enough to require separation from family and being taken into the care of "the system." While in foster care, bouncing from placement to placement and school to school causes further disruption and academic setbacks. The turnstile of relationships leaves many foster youth understandably wary of trusting others, including those who genuinely want to help. Food scarcity, economic hardships, housing instability, and needing to work are common burdens that bear down on foster youth who make it to college. Some foster youth reach the age limit of foster care while they are in college, which means they then must survive in an adult world without the material and symbolic safety net that foster care afforded them. Often, family members are not there to fall back on. This early, forced transition to adulthood occurs without a pause in the academic clock—tuition bills are due, classes must be attended, and exams must be passed.

Contribution of This Book

This book is written at a time when there is a growing momentum around initiatives to improve college outcomes for youth who are or were in foster care. Several federal laws in this area were passed in the last two decades, as well as varying state laws that specifically address foster youth who pursue higher education. There has also been an uptick in the number of programs offered by nonprofit agencies and programs, both in the community and on college campuses. It is exciting and promising that more laws, resources, and services are being directed toward a population that for years largely fell under the radar (Barth, 1990). However, despite the policy and service advances, the amount and rigor of quantitative research presently available to guide these initiatives are limited. Several qualitative studies, which are based on in-depth interviews with foster youth and professionals who serve foster youth, have provided rich descriptions of barriers to and promoters of college success (e.g., Batsche et al., 2014; Hines, Merdinger, & Wyatt, 2005; Salazar, Jones, Emerson, & Mucha, 2016; Salazar, Roe, Ulrich, & Haggerty, 2016). However, these studies tend to be small and are not designed to provide generalizable findings.[2] Quantitative analyses, like the ones in this book, build on these earlier qualitative studies by rigorously analyzing data collected from a large, representative sample of foster youth. Their findings will help meet the need for research to inform our laws and services, ensuring that our initiatives affect factors that will be most influential in improving the chances that foster youth succeed in college. In the absence of such research, even well-intentioned policies and programs can wind up expending money, time, and effort that could have been used more effectively.

Although the volume of postsecondary education research on foster youth is growing (see Geiger & Beltran, 2017a, 2017b), more research is needed to understand which factors influence foster youths' likelihood of enrolling in college, persisting through the first few semesters, and completing a degree.[3] This book is one of the most extensive and data-driven investigations of college outcomes of foster youth to date. The findings are based on data collected by the Midwest Evaluation of Adult Functioning of Former Foster Youth (hereafter, Midwest Study), a seminal study of transition-age foster youth, which followed more than 700 young people for nearly a decade from 2002 to 2011 (Courtney,

Terao, & Bost, 2004). When considered together, the five waves of interviews conducted as part of the Midwest Study provide a moving picture of the transition that foster youth made from late adolescence to early adulthood. College records for Midwest Study participants were obtained from the National Student Clearinghouse (NSC) in 2015, which provided information on college enrollment, persistence, and completion. The data collected from Midwest Study interviews combined with NSC college records provided an unprecedented opportunity to examine factors that influence college outcomes for foster youth.

This book moves the field forward in several important ways. First, the breadth of predictors is wider than those examined in most studies: predictors include characteristics of the youth, their academic backgrounds, and their foster care histories, as well as life circumstances at play before and after they enroll in college and characteristics of the colleges they attend. Second, contributors of college persistence and degree completion are particularly understudied outcomes for foster youth. In this book, these college outcomes are assessed up to about age thirty, which is important because foster youth tend to enroll in college later and progress through college slower than their peers. Having data on foster care youth into their late twenties captures achievements missed by other studies that end earlier. Third, the book uses a range of advanced statistical methods to increase the rigor of the analyses and confidence in the results. This is complemented by the high quality of the data. The Midwest Study is a representative sample of foster youth in three states and has high participation rates at each interview wave. Finally, the book adds to emerging research on the impact of the extended foster care policy on college outcomes. This is a timely issue, because only about three-fifths of U.S. states have extended the foster care age limit beyond age 18. Findings from this study can be used to inform states taking a wait-and-see approach to extending care.

Straddling the Child Welfare and Education Systems

This book focuses on young people who have been in foster care in their late adolescence, roughly on or after their sixteenth birthday. The period of time between the late teenage years and the mid-twenties provides a window of opportunity in which we can potentially intervene and move the needle on college outcomes for foster youth. Within this window, college-bound foster youth are involved with at least three systems: the foster care system, the secondary education system, and the higher education system. Although college preparation and support have become an increasingly important focus of child welfare departments, and secondary and postsecondary education systems are beginning to recognize foster youth as a distinguishable student subgroup, these systems too seldom interact in planned and coordinated ways. With a growing number of states signing on to extended foster care, supporting college success is a new reality that child welfare departments need to grapple with. Conversely, students with foster care histories are among the college students at greatest risk of dropping out, and higher education institutions need to be better attuned to and equipped to address the needs of this student population.

This book straddles these two professional fields: education and child welfare. Some parts of the book may be well known by those on the child welfare side but new to those in education. Conversely, other parts will be familiar to those in education but new to child welfare professionals. An aim of this book is to provide information and recommendations that are useful to both fields.

Why We Need to Study Youth with Foster Care Histories

Young people in foster care make up a small fraction of the population of youth in the United States and a small fraction of the college student body. This begs the question: Why devote so much attention to such a small group? There are many good reasons, and in this section I present a few of them. First and foremost, rates of educational attainment are demonstrably lower for youth with care histories than for their peers. Among those who make it to college, foster youth are in greater danger of dropping out than other high-risk groups, such as first-generation low-income students without foster care involvement (Day, Dworsky, Fogarty, & Damashek, 2011; Frerer, Sosenko, & Henke, 2013; John Burton Advocates for Youth, 2015, 2017). For example, the fifth wave of the Midwest Study reported that foster youth were about five times less likely than their peers to have earned a college degree by their mid-twenties (Courtney et al., 2011). These disparities are especially concerning because children of color are disproportionately involved in foster care. Increasing the rate of college success for foster youth is one avenue for addressing inequities in higher education access and completion among African American, Hispanic, and Native American young adults. On the flipside, failing to adequately support college success for youth with care histories disproportionately hurts children of color.

Second, the consequences of not going to college or leaving college without a degree are arguably more severe for youth with care histories than for their peers. When young people reach their state's foster care age limit, foster youth are expected to transition to adult independence and financial self-sufficiency without necessarily having the safety net of family support. As would be the case for many youth who had to fend for themselves, many foster care alumni experience bouts of economic hardship, homelessness, unemployment, need for public assistance benefits, and justice system involvement (Courtney et al.,

2007, 2016). Having a college degree can help avert these difficulties. For example, an earlier analysis of Midwest Study data found that the annual earnings of youth with care histories were about half that of young adults in the United States—$14,148 versus $28,105—and they were employed at much lower rates (48.7% versus 70.0%; Okpych & Courtney, 2014). However, the earnings and employment rate gaps narrowed substantially for youth who had completed at least some college (Okpych & Courtney, 2014). This is an important but not surprising finding. Voluminous research has demonstrated the benefits of higher education. We know that having a college degree increases the chances of getting a job with higher wages and more stability, of saving more, of relying less on public welfare benefits, of and attaining higher levels of physical and psychological health and civic engagement, and lower levels of family stress (for reviews see Ma et al., 2016; Mayhew et al., 2016; Tinto, 2012). If we are able to effectively intervene with foster youth, the course of their lives could be fundamentally altered.

Third, as a society, we should be profoundly troubled by the stark disparities in higher education outcomes between youth with care histories and their peers. When young people are placed in foster care, the state essentially becomes legally responsible for their protection and well-being (Courtney, 2009). We need to ensure that foster youth are afforded the opportunity to lead safe, healthy, and productive lives, just as we want our own children, nieces, nephews, and other young loved ones to do. This includes supporting their pursuit of a college degree. It also means that we may need to invest more resources and services in youth with care histories than in other young people to address the oversized challenges they face. The fact that foster youth make up a relatively small fraction of the youth and college student populations means that targeted, tailored services to support college success can be provided without exorbitant cost.

To be sure, college is not the only path to economic security, and this book certainly does not take the position that it is college or bust. However, the overwhelming majority of foster youth say that they want to go to college, so helping them get there aligns with their hopes and intentions. Moreover, although there are certainly good jobs that do not require postsecondary education, the employment landscape has been shifting over the last few decades. The proportion of jobs that require analytic skills and higher-level social skills has increased, while jobs in manufacturing and physically intensive sectors have declined. Moreover, wages have also increased for jobs that require high levels of social and analytic skills but have remained stagnant for jobs that require more physically intensive skills (Pew Research Center, 2016). This means that jobs that pay a living wage are increasingly going to workers who have education beyond high school.

Book's Audience and Organization

This book comprises two background chapters followed by several empirical chapters and a concluding chapter. The empirical chapters present findings from a variety of quantitative analyses. Although some of these analyses are quite sophisticated, the book is written to be accessible to a broad audience. For readers who may not have been exposed to the types of analyses in the book or for those who need a refresher, several appendices explain the statistical methods underlying the analyses and how to interpret the results. For readers with stronger statistical backgrounds, additional details about some of the analyses are provided in technical appendices. Given its interdisciplinary and practical focus, the book will serve as a useful resource for bachelor's- to doctoral-level students, policy makers, advocates, higher education administrators, child welfare professionals, youth-serving organizations and programs, foster parents and other caregivers, youth with care histories, and researchers.

This book has three parts: Background, Findings, and Recommendations. The first part has two chapters. Chapter 1 summarizes information on the foster care system, relevant federal laws pertinent to foster youth and college, and the programs designed to support foster youth into and through college. The chapter also presents a conceptual framework for the book. Chapter 2 introduces readers to the Midwest Study, explaining the study design and describing its participants.

The Findings section includes seven empirical chapters, each with a different purpose. Chapter 3 summarizes the main outcomes examined in this book: the percentages of youth enrolled in college, who persisted, and who earned a degree. College persistence and degree completion outcomes are compared to a nationally representative sample of low-income first-generation students. The chapter also describes the types of colleges that foster youth commonly attend and analyzes the extent to which foster youth enroll in colleges that match their academic credentials. Chapter 4 describes semester-by-semester enrollment trends of youth in the study who made it to college. This analysis identifies four common enrollment patterns and describes the types of students who fit into each pattern.

The next three chapters investigate predictors of the three key outcomes of this book: enrollment (chapter 5), persistence (chapter 6), and degree completion (chapter 7). These chapters draw on rich data collected from the Midwest Study on foster youth's background characteristics and experiences. The analyses of persistence and completion also examine characteristics of the colleges that youth attended.

Having examined general sets of predictors of the three college outcomes, the final two empirical chapters examine topics particularly important to practice and policy audiences. Chapter 8 investigates the relationship between avoidant attachment and college persistence and degree completion. Avoidant attachment stems from high exposure to past maltreatment and relationship instability and is characterized by emotional guardedness and a disavowal of the need to depend on others for help. Findings from this chapter have relevance for programs and professionals who work directly with foster youth in college. Chapter 9 is a policy analysis of extended foster care. Does extra time in foster care affect foster youths' likelihood of entering college, persisting, and earning a degree?

Part III includes a single chapter that synthesizes the findings from the empirical chapters and presents practical, actionable next steps (Chapter 10). Recommendations are organized around two critical tasks: increasing college enrollment and promoting college persistence to degree completion.

Foster Youth Terminology

The terms "youth with foster care histories/background/experience/involvement," "foster youth," and "transition-age foster youth" are used interchangeably throughout this book. The first set of terms is preferred, because it captures the fact that being in foster care is a part of a young person's life and experiences but does not define who they are.

It is important to note that, in the research literature, the term "foster youth" does not have a clear and consistent definition. Some studies denote "foster youth" to include young people who were in foster care after a certain age (e.g., their thirteenth birthday), whereas other studies use a more expansive definition that includes young people who were in foster care at any point in their lives. A major drawback of such expansive definitions is that they group together youth with fundamentally different life experiences and types of engagement with the foster care system. A seventeen-year-old who was in care for just the first six months of her life differs in fundamental ways from a seventeen-year-old who is currently in care and is preparing to age out of the system. As with young children in foster care, the primary goal for older adolescents in care is to safely return them to their family or to another permanent placement (i.e., adoption or guardianship), if returning home is not possible. However, for older adolescents in care, there is the distinct possibility that they may exit not to permanency but instead to independence (i.e., legal emancipation or reaching their state's foster care age limit). Child welfare departments are charged with preparing these youth to live independently should they exit to independence. This includes equipping them with independent living skills and providing them with opportunities to complete education and obtain employment. As is reviewed in chapter 1, a constellation of child welfare policies and services are designed for older adolescents in care who may exit to independence.

In this book, "youth with foster care histories," "foster youth," and the other terms noted earlier include young people who were in foster care in their late adolescence. This reflects the sampling strategy of the Midwest Study and captures a meaningful subgroup of young people with foster care involvement.

1

Framework for the Book

This chapter provides key background information that puts the rest of the book in context. First, a brief overview of the foster care system is provided, followed by a summary of federal child welfare and education laws that pertain to foster youth and higher education. The second section summarizes a widely used theory of college student departure and presents critiques that push back on the theory's applicability to underrepresented students (including foster youth). This critique draws attention to factors that need to be considered when thinking about promoting college success for foster youth. The third section builds on this critique by describing a distinct set of challenges and circumstances faced by college students with foster care histories. These challenges and circumstances are important for professionals to be aware of, whether they work on a college campus, in child welfare, with a nonprofit agency, or in some other capacity. The chapter closes with a summary of studies that describe the resilience of foster youth as a contributor to their college success.

Background Information

About Foster Care

Foster care is intended to be a temporary solution when children must be removed from their family because of concerns about their safety or well-being. Although local communities and states have long histories of creating systems for protecting vulnerable children, a federally funded system of foster care was not established in the United States until 1961 (Myers, 2006; U.S. Department of Health and Human Services, 2005). Since then, federal laws have expanded and formalized the system of child protection and foster care. They have established mandated reporting laws, increased the states' accountability for ensuring safety and stability, reduced the amount of time children can stay in care, and allocated resources that help families avoid formal involvement in foster care (Myers, 2006). The patchwork of federal laws provides an overarching framework, but variation exists among states in how the federal statues are codified into polices and implemented. It is beyond the scope of this book to review the evolution of the modern-day foster care system, but those interested in learning more can read Myers's (2006) excellent book on the topic.

Only about 0.5 percent of U.S. children are in foster care on any given day (Child Trends, 2018). Given that most young people in care are under the age of ten (Adoption and Foster Care Analysis and Reporting System [AFCARS], 2019), older foster youth constitute a small slice of our nation's foster population. On September 30, 2018, there were about 59,300 young people between the ages of sixteen and twenty-one in care, comprising roughly 13.5% of the national foster care population of 437,000 (AFCARS, 2019).

The majority of adolescents in foster care first enter care during their elementary through high school years; the most common reasons precipitating removal from their home are neglect and youth behavioral problems, followed by physical abuse, sexual abuse, and parental drug problems or incarceration (Okpych, 2015). Removing a child from their family is a serious matter and only occurs under extreme circumstances, such as the presence of harm that has been substantiated by a child welfare investigation, death or incapacitation of their caregiver, or a parent or guardian voluntarily turning over the child because he or she is unable to care for them. When a child is placed into foster care, the family court and child protection agency take an *in loco parentis* (in place of the parent) role, assuming responsibility for legal decisions. While children or adolescents are in foster care, the primary goal is to safely return them to their families. However, this is not always feasible, and in some cases older adolescents exit foster care to adoption or a guardianship arrangement, through a petition to be emancipated, or by reaching the state's foster care age limit ("aging out").

While in foster care, efforts are made to place youth in family-like settings with relatives or with a nonrelative foster family. Some foster families have undergone special training and receive extra support to care for children with emotional disturbances or special needs. As a last resort, if family-like placements are not appropriate or were previously unsuccessful, young people are placed in more restrictive settings, such as group homes or residential treatment centers. These placements are generally used when there are significant mental health, behavioral, or substance use problems that need more intensive care than what is provided in family-like settings.

In states that have extended the foster care age limit beyond age eighteen, additional placement options are available after youth reach their eighteenth birthdays. These placement types reflect the shift into a developmental phase with increased independence and serve as stepping-stones that prepare youth to live on their own. Supported independent placements (SILPs) are living arrangements such as apartment units and college dorms. To be allowed to live in a SILP, youth have to be assessed by their child welfare worker to be capable of living on their own. They still meet with their caseworker once per month and receive a monthly living subsidy to pay for rent and other living expenses (e.g., utility bills). For youth who may not be ready for the level of independence of a SILP, another placement option is a transitional housing placement (THP). These are apartment units that have staff on-site and provide a range of programs and services to meet the needs of the youth and help them develop independent living skills. In addition to SILPs and THPs, foster youth older than age eighteen can live in traditional foster care placements (e.g., foster homes with relatives, nonrelative foster homes), although there has been a shift away from placing youth in congregate care settings, such as group homes and residential treatment centers.

It is common for adolescents in care to have lived in multiple foster care placements (Courtney et al., 2004, 2014). For example, in a national sample of foster youths age sixteen or older, the average number of placements that they had lived in was 5.4 (Okpych, 2015). Each placement change means breaking ties with a caregiver, neighborhood, and sometimes a school, and then starting fresh in a new environment with a new cast of people. Sometimes fresh starts are beneficial, but frequent changes can take a toll on the trust that young people place in relationships (Morton, 2018; Perry, 2006; Seita et al., 2016).

As will become clear in the next section, several federal laws fund services and supports to help adolescents in care make the transition to adulthood. This was certainly not always the case. For nearly two decades after the federal government began to fund foster care, little attention was paid to the tens of thousands of adolescents in care who had to fend for themselves on reaching age eighteen. In the late 1980s and 1990s, with few exceptions, most states required foster youth to exit care at the age of majority (typically age eighteen).[1] Few specialized services were in place to help them with the transition (Barth, 1986), and as one can imagine, these young people faced a jarring transition to adulthood (Festinger, 1983). This changed beginning with a 1986 federal child welfare law that was followed by a series of other federal laws described in the next section.

Overview of Federal Laws Pertaining to Foster Youth Pursuing College

This section reviews several federals laws enacted over the past three decades that have direct bearing on postsecondary education for youth with care histories. It provides an overview of the current legislative landscape designed to support foster youth into and through college.

The *Independent Living Initiative* (ILI), which was passed by Congress in 1986, was one of the first laws to address older adolescents in care who were unlikely to find a permanent placement before aging out of care. This law set aside a modest amount of funding—$70M per year to be divvyed up among all fifty states. This allocation funded programs that were designed to equip foster youth and foster care alumni ages sixteen to twenty-one with skills in areas such as job preparation, daily living skills, and financial literacy. Although its funding was modest, the ILI was significant because it drew attention to a formerly hidden population and paved the way for future legislation that was more expansive and substantial.

The ILI was passed during a time when researchers and advocates were bringing to light some of the challenges that foster youth encountered during their transition to adulthood (Barth, 1990). Early studies of foster care alumni focused on disrupted and missed opportunities in educational attainment (Barth, 1986, 1990; Festinger, 1983; Jones & Moses, 1983); their findings provided the impetus to legislative and programmatic efforts to increase the proportion of foster care youth who would enter and complete college. Figure 1.1 displays a timeline of the principal federal laws that followed the 1986 ILI.

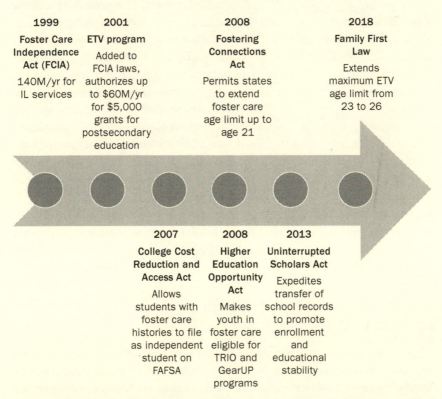

1999	2001	2008	2018
Foster Care Independence Act (FCIA)	ETV program	Fostering Connections Act	Family First Law
140M/yr for IL services	Added to FCIA laws, authorizes up to $60M/yr for $5,000 grants for postsecondary education	Permits states to extend foster care age limit up to age 21	Extends maximum ETV age limit from 23 to 26

2007	2008	2013
College Cost Reduction and Access Act	Higher Education Opportunity Act	Uninterrupted Scholars Act
Allows students with foster care histories to file as independent student on FAFSA	Makes youth in foster care eligible for TRIO and GearUP programs	Expedites transfer of school records to promote enrollment and educational stability

FIG. 1.1 Federal child welfare and education laws pertinent to foster youth pursuing college

Following a few minor amendments to the ILI in 1990 and 1993, the *John H. Chafee Foster Care to Independence Act of 1999* (FCIA) substantially improved the ILI by creating the John Chafee Foster Care Independence Program. First, it doubled the annual amount allocated to states to develop and deliver independent living (IL) services (sometimes called "Chafee services") for youth expected to remain in foster care. These services were typically directed to young people in care between the ages of sixteen to twenty-one, but states had flexibility in expanding the age range. Thirteen categories of independent living services are covered under FCIA, such as housing subsidies, mentoring, employment preparation, financial literacy, health education, career preparation, and postsecondary education support. Not all foster youth receive IL services. In a 2015 study, it was estimated that just about half (50.2%) of youth in care age sixteen or older received any one of FCIA's thirteen service areas (Okpych, 2015). Second, FCIA increased flexibility in how states could use the funding. For example, states could now use up to 30 percent of their IL funding on housing assistance (e.g., a security deposit for an apartment, money for furniture). Third, the FCIA also gave states the option to extend Medicaid coverage beyond age eighteen so that foster youth would still have health insurance for a few years after exiting care. Since then, the Affordable Care Act permits youth who are in foster care on their eighteenth birthday to receive Medicaid coverage up to age twenty-six.

The final improvement ushered in by the FCIA involves program evaluation and data collection. A small portion of the $140M annual allotment (1.5%) is dedicated to evaluating IL programs that are "innovative or of potential national significance." A grant was used to fund the Multisite Evaluation, which was the first rigorous evaluation of IL programs and was conducted between 2001 and 2010 (OPRE, 2011). The FCIA also requires states to systematically collect data on transition-age foster youth. Beginning in 2010, states have to (a) track receipt of IL services funded by the FCIA and (b) conduct longitudinal studies that follow cohorts of seventeen-year-olds in care up through age twenty-one. These two sources of data make up the National Youth in Transition Database (NYTD). When data from all states are combined, NYTD provides a national picture of the inventory of IL services funded by the FCIA and of key outcomes of foster youth as they transition to adulthood.[2] NYTD is pivotal in making more visible a population that largely fell under the radar just a few decades ago.

In 2001, the FCIA was amended with the *Education and Training Voucher* (ETV) program, which provides youth enrolled in college or vocational training programs up to $5,000 annually toward educational expenses. This money can be used to pay for tuition, fees, books, supplies for college, and other related expenses. When combined with other sources of financial aid, ETVs can help reduce the financial burden of college. To receive an ETV, students usually have to make satisfactory academic progress, which typically requires completing a certain number of credits and earning a GPA of 2.0 or higher. Qualifying youth can receive an ETV for up to five years, with the current maximum age limit set at age twenty-six.[3] The ETV program is discretionary and must be approved by Congress to receive funding. Up to $60M per year can be allocated for the program, but it has been funded at annual levels closer to $40M (e.g., $43.3M was allocated in 2019 [Fernandes-Alcantara, 2019]). As with IL services, there is variability among states in the proportion of eligible youth who receive an ETV (Fernandes-Alcantara, 2017). Since ETV is not an entitlement program, some qualifying youth living in states with funding shortfalls may not receive an ETV or may receive less than what they qualify for (Kelly, 2015; Tureck, 2016). Tens of thousands of ETVs are disbursed each year. For example, between 16,514 and 17,100 youths received an ETV each year in the years 2011 to 2014 (Fernandes-Alcantara, 2019).

Two pieces of higher education legislation enacted in 2007 and 2008 are relevant to students with foster care histories. First, the 2007 *College Cost Reduction and Access Act* permits youth who were in foster care on or after their thirteenth birthday to file as an independent student on their Free Application for Federal Student Aid (FAFSA).[4] This means that the income of a foster youth's parent or guardian is not included when determining the types and amount of financial aid they receive. Independent student status is particularly important for need-based funding that does not have to be repaid, such as Pell Grants. Second, the *Higher Education Opportunities Act of 2008* reauthorized a 1965 version of the law to render youth with foster care histories eligible for federal programs that target low-income and underrepresented students. This includes TRIO Programs such as Upward Bound and Student Support Services, as well as Gaining Early Awareness and Readiness for Undergraduate Programs (GEAR UP).

The year 2008 was also a watershed moment for child welfare legislation. Under the 2008 *Fostering Connections to Success and Increasing Adoptions Act* (Fostering Connections), states were given the option to extend the age limit of foster care from eighteen to twenty-one. Fostering Connections changed the architecture of the foster care system by increasing the maximum age limit that federal dollars could be used to pay for foster care. Before it was implemented in 2010, two states—Illinois and New York—and Washington, DC, had raised the age limit of foster care beyond age eighteen. Other states allowed some youth to remain in care past age eighteen (but usually not past age nineteen) while they were finishing high school or if they were pregnant or parenting. Fostering Connections is pertinent to college access and persistence because it meets the basic needs of youth in care; it gives them a roof over their head, food on the table, and shoes on their feet during the ages that many young people enroll in college. It also keeps youth connected to child welfare professionals who can link them to resources and information that are instrumental to getting them into college and through college (Okpych & Courtney, 2017). Yet not all states have adopted extended foster care. At the time this book was written, twenty-nine U.S. states and territories had an approved extended foster care law (Heath, 2019). Importantly, this includes the states with the largest shares of the foster care population such as California, New York, Illinois, Pennsylvania, and Texas (Kids Count, 2018).

The 2013 *Uninterrupted Scholars Act* was another important law that helped ensure educational stability for youth in foster care when then enter care or change placements. One of the provisions of the 2008 Fostering Connections Act requires child welfare agencies to work with school systems to ensure that the child either remains in the same school or is quickly transferred to a new school. However, this process was sometimes impeded by difficulties that child welfare agencies encountered when trying to access the child's educational records, which are protected by privacy laws under the Family Educational Rights and Privacy Act (FERPA). The Uninterrupted Scholars Act created an exception for child welfare agencies so that they do not have to obtain parental permission to receive a child's educational records. In effect, by not holding up necessary paperwork, this law allows child welfare agencies to more effectively ensure that children in care are enrolled in school and do not experience lengthy gaps when changing schools.

Finally, a few provisions in the 2018 *Family First Prevention Services Act* (Family First) made some notable changes to the 1999 FCIA law and the ETV program. First, it raised the age limit of youth who could receive independent living services from twenty-one to twenty-three.[5] Second, it increased the ETV age limit from twenty-three to twenty-six. These changes are important because they provide more realistic time frames of support for foster care alumni pursuing postsecondary education. Third, the Family First law made a nominal change in the name of the FCIA: it is now called the John Chafee Foster Care Program for Successful Transition to Adulthood Program.

Taken together, this patchwork of federal child welfare and education laws has the potential to provide considerable support for foster youth who are pursuing college. However, two points are important to keep in mind. First, the cost of college and the cost of administering and delivering IL services have increased dramatically since the early 2000s, yet funding for the FCIA and the ETV programs have not substantially changed.[6] This means that financial shortfalls either fall on states to meet or else fewer benefits are provided. Second, state variability can be a blessing and a curse. On the one hand, it allows states to try out bold innovations to meeting the needs of its young people in care. On the other hand, it also creates the potential for extreme disparities in available supports. Depending on where youth live, they could be eligible for extended foster care to age twenty-one, receive an ETV, qualify for a state tuition waiver for foster youth, and benefit from a robust system of independent living services. However, foster care youth living one state over may have to exit care at age eighteen, be unlikely to get an ETV, not have access to a tuition waiver, and receive few IL services to prepare them for college.[7]

Programs Supporting College Students with Foster Care Histories

Increased funding for IL services has led to the development of programs that target educational outcomes of foster youth. These programs aim to equip them with the knowledge, skills, and resources that will prepare them for college entry and success. These supports generally fall into three baskets: high school completion programs, college access programs, and college success programs (Dworsky et al., 2014). However, some programs target more than one of these three educational outcomes, especially those in the first two baskets that help foster youth finish high school and enroll in college. Thus, the first two baskets are discussed together.

Typical services provided by programs that support high school completion and college access include academic support (e.g., tutoring, supplemental instruction, study skills training), preparation for standardized tests like the SAT or ACT, guidance with college selection, and assistance with college and financial aid applications. Treehouse's Graduation Success program (Washington State), First Place for Youth (California and Mississippi), and First Star Academies (locations across the United States) are three prominent examples. Both First Place and Treehouse couch postsecondary education support within a broader mission of equipping foster youth to make a smooth transition to adulthood, and they therefore address housing and employment needs. All three programs offer services that can stretch over several months or years. Other programs are more targeted and time limited. For example, the Better Futures program is a ten-month program developed for foster youth with mental health challenges (Geenen et al., 2015). It provides one-on-one bimonthly peer coaching, a four-day intensive summer institute, and four themed mentoring workshops (e.g., writing your college admissions essay).

The second group of programs target college persistence and completion for foster youth enrolled in higher education. Campus support programs for foster youth (CSPs) have flourished in the past decade. CSPs are distinct from broader programs that serve low-income and underrepresented college students (e.g., Extended Opportunity Programs and Services [EOPS], Student Support Services, McNair Scholars) in that they are specifically attuned to the challenges and circumstances of students with foster care histories. Some CSPs also serve other vulnerable student groups, such as students who are homeless. CSP participants are typically assigned a coach or advisor (some also incorporate peer mentoring) whom they meet with regularly. This advisor helps students acclimate to college and navigate logistical tasks, provides services and referrals, offers emotional support, and advocates for the student (Dworsky & Peréz, 2010). Some CSPs offer workshops and first-year seminar courses and provide financial assistance such as scholarships and a small fund for emergencies. An important component of CSPs is the community that develops among participants, which has been described as family-like (Unrau et al., 2017). One of the earliest CPSs was founded in 1998 at the University of California, Fullerton; the Guardian Scholars Program is still in operation today. The last ten years have seen prolific growth in CSPs across the United States, mostly in four-year colleges but increasingly in two-year colleges. As part of my work on a California-based study on transition-age foster youth, we counted 122 two-year and four-year colleges in the state that housed a CSP (Okpych et al., 2020).

In addition to CSPs, other programs that are not located on college campuses provide support to foster youth in college. For example, Beyond the Safety Net is a program that is being piloted in California in more than three dozen THPs (Lemly et al., 2019). These programs incorporate a strong postsecondary education emphasis into the culture, aims, and services offered. Some of their principal program components provide intensive academic-focused case management, foster access to academic supports, develop a college-going culture, reduce work obligations, ensure that youth apply for financial aid, and establish close relationships with local colleges and CSPs.

Although the college access and completion programs for foster youth are promising, a major limitation is that we have little evidence about their effectiveness (Miller et al., 2017). A recent analysis in California found that youth involved in a CSP were significantly more likely than youth who were not involved to persist through two semesters in college, after statistically controlling for a range of youth and college characteristics (Okpych et al., 2020). However, these findings were an early look at the impact of CSPs, and more rigorous evaluation studies are needed. A related caveat is that there is much variation in the types, quality, and breadth of services that different CSPs offer. As the cooking saying goes, the secret may be in the sauce. Just having a CSP program available may not automatically mean that foster youth will fare better, and it may come down to providing the right ingredients, in the right amounts, at the right time for the right amount of time. Third, particularly for CSPs, funding remains a challenge. Many CSPs are funded by private dollars or a mix of public and private dollars (Geiger et al., 2018). Because funding is not guaranteed, a program that is up and running one year may have to scale back or even close shop within a few years if a reliable funding source is not established.

With this broad overview of the laws and programs in place to support higher education attainment among foster youth, we now turn to the conceptual framework for this book.

Tinto's Theory of Student Departure

Over the past half-century, more than a dozen psychological, economic, and sociological theories have been introduced to explain why students leave college (e.g., Astin, 1977; Bean, 1980; Braxton et al., 2013; Seidman, 2005; Summerskill, 1962; for review, see Melguizo, 2011). Many of the early theories have since been critiqued, particularly for their lack of relevance to nontraditional students, low-income students, nonwhite students, and students in two-year institutions (Melguizo, 2011; Metz, 2004; Tierney, 1999). One of the most widely cited of these early theories is Vincent Tinto's theory of college student departure, which grew out of his dissertation work (1975) and was fully explained in the 1987 and 1993 editions of his book *Leaving College: Rethinking the Causes and Cures of Student Attrition*. I first summarize the main tenets of his and then present several prominent critiques.

Tinto proposed that students enter college with a wide range of pre-entry characteristics that will influence their college experience and performance. These include personal attributes (e.g., gender, race, physical disabilities), characteristics of their family background (e.g., family socioeconomic status, parental education), skills and abilities (e.g., aptitude in different subjects, social skills), and prior schooling (e.g., quality of schooling, high school grades, school mobility). These sets of factors also shape students' goals and commitment to the institution that they bring to their college experience. At the heart of Tinto's theory is a process of sociocultural integration into communities within the college. By focusing on the interaction between students and institutional communities, Tinto broke from previous psychological theories that emphasized characteristics of the students (e.g., personality traits, academic drive) as key drivers of student departure.

The process of students evolving from outsiders to members of the college community does not happen automatically or immediately. It is a gradual process of loosening ties with their old community and becoming ensconced in the norms, behaviors, and life of the college. Tinto identifies two distinguishable but interrelated spheres of the college in which students can experience varying degrees of integration. *Academic integration* is when students possess the skills and knowledge needed to succeed academically, along with a feeling that they belong in academic contexts (e.g., classes, study groups, feeling part of a major or department). In his later work, Tinto (1993) succinctly defines academic integration as "competent membership" (p. 208). *Social integration* is when students feel a sense of membership in the larger college community by, for example, establishing a network of friends, joining clubs or groups, or participating in social events. Integrating into the academic and social spheres of college leads students to feel like they belong at college and are capable of succeeding, and enables them to access resources that can help them persist. As students adopt the institution's normative values and behaviors, their commitment to their own goals about completing college (intentions) and their effort in carrying out necessary tasks (commitment) are reinforced.

Ideally, students would experience integration in both the academic and social spheres, but Tinto emphasized that integration into both is not a necessary condition for persistence (1993, p. 120). When there is a misalignment or disconnection between the student and these two spheres of the college experience, it ultimately leads to a diminution of the student's desires, expectations, and directed efforts to remain at the college. Although Tinto acknowledged that external influences such as work or family commitments may pull students away from engagement with the institution, he maintained that they play a secondary role for most students: their experience on campus is the primary driver of whether they stay or leave.

Tinto's (1993) theory has been critiqued on many fronts, including its applicability to students who do not follow the "traditional" college route (i.e., enter a four-year college directly after high school) and who come from underrepresented racial and ethnic groups, are the first in their families to attend college, and have low-income backgrounds. These critiques are relevant to students with foster care histories. Black and Hispanic youth are overrepresented in the foster care population, and foster youth tend to come from low-income families and communities, more commonly enter two-year colleges than four-year colleges, and are typically the first in the family to go to college (Frerer et al., 2013; Fries et al., 2014; Gross et al., 2019; Summers et al., 2012; Wildeman & Emanuel, 2014). Three critiques are discussed next that are applicable to students with foster care backgrounds.

First, some scholars take issue with Tinto's separation phase, which involves severing or loosening ties to past communities to make way for the adoption of norms and behaviors of the college (Fischer, 2007; Guiffrida, 2006; Nora & Crisp, 2009; Tierney, 1999). Continuing relationships with home communities may be particularly important for students who are underrepresented on college campuses, and scholars have proposed that a more appropriate goal for such students entails the formation of mutual identities and maintenance of connections to both outside communities and college communities. This likely applies to students with foster care histories who may look for support from existing and long-standing relationships as they make the transition into the new college environment.

Second, scholars have critiqued Tinto's conceptualization of integration as the process of students acculturating to the institution's prevailing norms and patterns of behavior (Longwell-Grice & Longwell-Grice, 2008; Rendón et al., 2000). They have argued that Tinto's concept of "integration" should be replaced by "connectedness." The latter concept more explicitly acknowledges the institution's responsibility to create campus environments that are welcoming to and supportive of the diversity of its student body. Given that many colleges mirror the social and economic inequalities prevalent in the United States, framing the path to success as eschewing one's own values and customs and adopting those of the dominant culture places the responsibility of adaptation on the student (Carter et al., 2013; Núñez, 2014; Smerek, 2010; Tierney, 1999). Doing so can lead to a failure to dismantle structures of campus culture that actually harm underrepresented students' chances to achieve college success. This can play out in pervasive but unrecognized ways. In his compelling book, Anthony Abraham Jack (2019) details the many ways elite colleges are structured to serve students from privileged backgrounds, but do not meet the needs of students from disadvantaged backgrounds so that they fall behind. Working multiple jobs to pay bills, taking on responsibilities of family members back home, having to decode unfamiliar practices not explicitly taught but that are necessary for survival (e.g., what "office hours" are), and not having a place to stay during campus breaks are experiences that more privileged students rarely have to think about. When campuses are unaware of and underresponsive to these extra demands, this lack of attention wears on students' bodies, minds, and hearts.

More insidious are influences of cultural values that pervade college messaging, norms, and expectations. For example, Stephens and colleagues (2012) found that when students from working-class backgrounds were given a welcome packet that emphasized individualism and carving out one's own path (middle- and upper-class values), low-income students performed significantly worse on cognitive tests than when they were presented materials that aligned with communalism and learning together (traditional working-class values). The performance of middle- and upper-income students was unaffected by the cultural norm messaging they received.

Unexamined cultural norms on campus can also negatively influence the academic identity and performance of racial, ethnic, and gender groups that are underrepresented on campuses and in departments. This situation often plays out in unintended slights that reinforce negative stereotypes and lead students to question their academic ability and belongingness at college (Nadal et al., 2014; Steele, 1997). Research suggests that institutions of higher education must be attentive to and intentional about cultural norms that may marginalize underrepresented students.

A third critique of Tinto's model is that it places too little emphasis on the weighty influence that external demands like financial hardships, the need to work, and family and child care responsibilities exert on students' ability to remain in college (Braxton et al., 2013; Cabrera et al., 1992; Davidson & Wilson, 2016; Goldrick-Rab et al., 2009; Hossler et al., 2009; Melguizo, 2011; Ozaki, 2016). Given that the looming responsibilities posed by these external demands may be more the rule than the exception for low-income students, a theory of college departure needs to emphasize their regularity and potentially disruptive influence.

If there is greater acknowledgement of the role of external demands on college departure, we may also want to rethink the way in which the departure decision is framed. Often, that decision is implicitly conceptualized from a "rational actor" model, which assumes that a student decides whether to stay or leave college based on a calculus of the costs and benefits of different scenarios. In this conceptualization, the student tries to optimize the return on investment of time, energy, and resources. Tinto writes, "Like all decisions, individual judgments concerning continued participation in college may be viewed as weighing the costs and benefits of college persistence relative to alternative forms of investment of one's time, energies, and scarce resources" (1993, p. 128). Perhaps a more fitting way to think about a student's departure decision, as well as the many important decisions that come up along the way, is in terms of constrained choice. For low-income students, the departure decision often involves choosing between meeting basic needs or not (e.g., pay utilities bill or purchase books), rather than optimizing their return on investment. The constrained nature of the choices needs to be more explicitly acknowledged in models of student departure, or else we risk inadvertently blaming their dropping out on students' faulty optimizing, rather than on the realities they are dealing with.

Another consequence of giving more weight to the role of external demands in student departure is a more explicit recognition of the importance of the larger policy context, particularly higher education policies and other policies that affect students' ability to pay for college (St. John et al., 2000). This consideration does not loom as large for students who have families that can pay for or at least pitch in for college, but it is foundational for low-income students. It may be particularly important for foster youth, whose funding for college is heavily dependent on the patchwork of provisions made available through federal and state policies, rather than on family contributions or personal savings. Thus, for youth whose primary caregiver is the government, federal and state policy play a central role in their ability to afford college, which in turn affects the likelihood that they will stay in college.

The critical points just raised—replacing the concept of integration with connectedness, preserving rather than severing ties to one's home community, acknowledging the powerful influence of external circumstances, viewing decisions as constrained choices, and foregrounding relevant policy—are applicable to college students with foster care histories. These critical points do not discredit Tinto's theory; indeed, foster youth may still drop out of college because they did not make strong, meaningful, and lasting connections to people and places at college. Rather, they point to a set of factors present for a subset of college students who face different realities than most.

Distinct Challenges and Circumstances of College Students with Foster Care Histories

The previous section drew attention to considerations that are important for underrepresented, low-income, and first-generation students and touched on their relevance to foster youth. This section highlights several challenges and circumstances that are unique to or more pervasive among college students with foster care histories. To bring to life each of these challenges, I draw heavily from studies based on interviews with foster youth and the professionals who serve them.

Frequent Placement Changes and School Mobility

Placement changes and enrolling in different schools, which disrupt learning and leave students academically behind when they enter college, are common experiences among foster youth.

On average, young people in foster care will enter college less prepared for college-level work than their peers. This is in part a consequence of poverty, which limits resources and educational opportunities in the communities and homes where foster youth grow up (Frerer et al., 2013). In addition, many move around a lot while in foster care. Unlike some of their peers, for whom residential moves and school changes are timed during the summer or breaks so that disruption to education is minimized, school changes for foster youth often occur in the middle of the school year. As we will see in the next chapter, Midwest Study youth reported changing schools an average of 2.8 times. The repeated changes in homes and schools can severely disrupt learning (Clemens et al., 2016; Courtney et al., 2004; Fawley-King et al., 2017; Strolin-Goltzman et al., 2016; Sullivan et al., 2010). Frequent school changes mean that students must acclimate to a new school, often move to different tracks in different curricula, and have breaks in the accumulation of knowledge and skills. As described by a foster youth who changed high schools five times, "You are trying to learn something but you are constantly moving, so now you are getting sidetracked from the main goal that you had which is succeeding in school" (Batsche et al., 2014, p.178). Another youth described failing to learn basic math functions, because "each school I've moved to has taught me just multiplication" (Clemens et al., 2016, p. 72). Misalignment in curricula can also derail learning. One student described the misalignment between the chemistry class in her old and new school: students "are learning two completely different things at two completely different levels" (p. 72). In addition to missed concepts and curriculum misalignment, school changes can also result in students being retaught the same concepts again and again: "so when I went to the new school, I was already relearning what I had already learned the first semester, so it was always just like repeat. So I went through the American Revolution probably like 13 times" (p. 72).

Practically speaking, frequent school changes can also make it harder for foster youth to accumulate the required credit hours needed to earn a high school diploma. They may lose days of school attendance during school transfers, have trouble passing a course they joined mid-marking period, and be unable to complete a class because their new school does not offer the course.

Constantly being shuffled from school to school can also take a psychological toll. One youth put it this way: "it is really, really, really hard going from one school to another to another, and especially if nobody's preparing you for it . . . and then you're just kind of lost in the dust. You're just another particle that is just there. Nobody really knows what to do with you, but it's just there" (Clemens et al., 2016, p. 72). Feeling like a dust particle blowing in the wind can certainly affect students' investment in trying to do good in school. One student reflected on how school mobility affected her motivation and behavior: "It causes you not to care about school. I might care about school. I ain't here to learn, I'm here to make new friends. I mean, I'm not going to be here long enough to see what I can do, so I have fun as opposed to learn. I don't care to learn. I'm not even going to have the chance to learn. . . . Why should I care to graduate when you're not caring to keep me on a stable level so that I can get that education I need?" (p. 72). Educational stability is something that most students in school take for granted and many foster youth yearn for: "Stability is the biggest issue, because that's your main issue in life and that's the biggest [thing] that you desire. And school is like the most normal it gets for stability" (p. 72).

It is thus not surprising that many young people in foster care are academically behind in the years leading up to college. The Midwest Study found that, at age seventeen to eighteen, when most youth should be reading at an eleventh- or twelfth-grade level, 56 percent were reading below a ninth-grade level (Courtney et al., 2004). Similarly, a more recent California study found that more than half (51%) of seventeen- and eighteen-year-olds were reading below a ninth-grade level (Courtney et al., 2014).

One marker of students' preparedness for college-level work is whether they have to take noncredit remedial courses on entering college. Research suggests that remedial course taking is high for foster youth, especially youth in two-year colleges. Youth attending five California state universities were almost twice as likely than their peers to require a remedial English course (46% vs. 25%) and were more than twice as likely to require a remedial math course (43%

vs. 21%; John Burton Advocates for Youth [JBAY], 2015). Foster youth entering California community colleges were also more likely than other students to have their first course be a remedial course (88% vs. 80%; JBAY, 2015). What this means is that more foster youth will require extra support to get them on the same academic level as other college freshmen.

Stigma Associated with Foster Care

Studies in which youth were interviewed about their high school experience also find that some youth experience stigma due to being in foster care. As one youth put it when talking about moving to a new school, "You're flagged as foster care, and they know. Like, they have the mentality, and most of your teachers will kind of act like that towards you, too. But every time you switch a school, the new counselor is like, 'Oh, they're in foster care'" (Clemens et al., 2016, p. 71). Another student said that once she was "branded as a foster youth" the teachers and school personnel saw her as not being college material (Batsche et al., 2014, p. 178). This is significant because young students can internalize the messages they get from others, which affect their aspirations, expectations, and beliefs they have about their own ability to do well in school and go to college (Clemens et al., 2016; Tobolowsky et al., 2019). These stereotypes can deflate youths' motivation and self-confidence. Stigma can also come from peers at school (Tobolowsky et al., 2019). When other students learn that a youth is in foster care, this can lead to judgments about their character:

> As soon as I told one person, "Hey, I'm in foster care," kids over here, they made judgments automatically, which can lead to youth disengaging from school. "Oh, she's in foster care because she's a bad kid. I don't want to hang out with her. I don't want to be friends with her. I don't even want to get to know her." Then there's this social barrier that's like, I don't really want to be at school. (Clemens et al., 2016, p. 72)

Stigma also arises after foster youth enroll in college. Frequently they require support from college administrators to help them navigate logistical aspects of college, such as registering for classes and processing financial aid. To receive some of these benefits, students are required to disclose their foster care background. In one study, all twelve participants said that they had been given the "runaround," needing to talk to several different college administrators before they received the assistance they needed: "for these students there was additional pain and shame in having to share their challenging backgrounds with different anonymous staff members" (Tobolowsky et al., 2019, p. 8). Several participants in the study said that they encountered higher education staff who were unfamiliar with programs or benefits specific to foster youth and at times were given incorrect information that resulted in their failing to receive an

ETV. Many of the participants wished that there was a single person they could speak to, who was knowledgeable about foster care-related benefits, so that they could get the help they needed and also avoid feeling stigmatized by not having to repeat their story (Tobolowsky et al., 2019).

Vestiges of Past Maltreatment: Behavioral Health Problems

A third distinguishing feature of youth with care histories is that they are likely to have higher rates of behavioral health problems than their peers. Most foster youth have experienced maltreatment that was severe enough to require removal from their family. Some youth also experience further maltreatment, bullying, instability, and other psychologically harmful experiences after entering foster care. Understandably, some emotional and behavioral problems manifest at higher rates in youth with care histories than in same-age peers (Deutsch et al., 2015; Havlicek et al., 2013). Depression, post-traumatic stress disorder, and alcohol and substance use problems are the most prevalent disorders that foster youth grapple with (Havlicek et al., 2013). A recent study of California foster youth found that more than half (53%) of the seventeen-year-olds presented with at least one behavioral health disorder (Courtney et al., 2014). In an analysis by Gross and colleagues (2019, p. 93) of first-time students enrolled in four-year colleges, former foster youth were nearly twice as likely to report having a psychological disorder than their peers without foster care involvement (21.5% vs. 11.1%). A substantial body of research has also shown that the experience of childhood maltreatment disrupts cognitive functioning (e.g., sustaining attention and processing information) and emotional regulation, which are important for learning (Cicchetti, 2016; Klein et al., 2015; Romano et al., 2015).

Qualitative studies of college students found that many foster youth reported grappling with depression that stemmed from a loss of childhood, not being able to participate in normative events, and guilt about their past, as well as anxiety induced by past trauma (Day et al., 2012; Hines et al., 2005; Salazar, Jones, 2016). Because behavioral health problems can affect self-confidence, motivation, and the ability to sustain attention and retain information, handle multiple tasks and time pressures, and stick with a planned course of action, young people with care histories will have a greater need for psychological services in college than their peers (Hogan, 2018). As one foster youth described the emotional consequences of past trauma and being in foster care, "It slows down the learning process because you're sitting here dealing with so much that you don't even know how to deal with your own mind" (Clemens et al., 2016, p. 70). Similarly, another foster youth described how vestiges of past trauma come to bear on her college success: "I feel like my biggest obstacle is myself. . . . I think a lot that has to do with me having lack of motivation or it's mainly me with a lot of my emotional things in the past that interfere with where I am now on unresolved issues" (Franco & Durdella, 2018, p. 76).

Vestiges of Past Trauma and Instability: Vigilant Self-Reliance

In addition to leading to diagnosable behavioral health problems, experiences of trauma and relational disruption can also affect youths' ability to form relationships on campus with resourceful individuals. A core feature of Tinto's theory and similar theories is the importance of connections that students make to people, places, and things at their college. However, many foster youth have experienced considerable trauma in their lives that leave them understandably distrusting of relationships. Several qualitative studies have described how histories of trauma and loss leave youth guarded, distant, and vigilantly self-reliant (e.g., Kools, 1999; Morton, 2018; Samuels & Pryce, 2008; Unrau et al., 2008). Rigidity was one of the themes identified among interviews with fourteen students enrolled in a four-year college, where youth found it hard to change their old way of doing things, to adopt new ways of being, and to find balance in their lives (Hines et al., 2005).

Thinking back to Tinto's model, this means that vigilant self-reliance will be an additional barrier for some foster youth to getting plugged into the social and academic spheres of college. Some students with foster care histories may be particularly unreceptive or resistant to using support services available on campus, even if they recognize that those services could help them succeed in college.

Family May Not Be a Fallback

Most young people in college have biological family members to turn to for support. They have a bed waiting for them during campus breaks. They have money deposited in their account if their meal plan runs out or they get a flat tire. If they are having relationship problems or just bombed an exam, there is someone who will listen. As a child welfare worker explained, "When I went to college, I had somebody to go home to. If things got rough, I had somebody that I could call. [Former foster youth] don't" (Tobolowsky et al., 2019, p. 8). Although many foster youth do stay connected to family members in their late teenage years (Courtney et al., 2016), others have family members who passed away, moved away, became incarcerated, or fell out of their lives. Some foster youth do have family safety nets, but they are dotted with holes, hooks, and thorns. Understandably, foster youths' relationships with family can be complicated and trying. There can be intense conflict, criticism, anger, resentment, rejection, and expectations that the youth should sacrifice for the family (Curry & Abrams, 2015; Salazar, Jones, 2016; Samuels, 2009; Wojciak, 2017). Thus, unlike many young people in college whose biological families have an important and substantial influence on their continued success (Kriegbaum et al., 2016), foster youth do not always have biological family members they can reliably fall back on.

The presence of family is important both in a material and emotional sense. One study in *Forbes* (Eisenberg, 2018) found that about 80 percent of parents provide financial support to their adult children (aged 18–34) to the tune of about $7,000 per year. One foster youth compared his own abrupt and trying transition to adulthood to his peers: "people with families have [parents] to get them cars, buy their books, feed them, put a roof over their head, [and] help them with homework" (Batsche et al., 2014). Parents also play an important role emotionally. Having a family creates an unspoken assurance that there is someone who care about you, believes in you, and will be there should you need them. As Margaret Mead once said, "One of the oldest human needs is having someone to wonder where you are when you don't come home at night." Lacking this assurance can lead to feelings of isolation and anxiety. In a survey of foster youth in college, some students reflected on the feeling of being alone and on their own as one of the biggest challenges when transitioning to college: "not knowing what to do and knowing that I was going to be alone" and "not having anybody to help or someplace to be in the transition" were realities they felt in their bones (Dworsky & Pérez, 2010).

Looming External Demands, Responsibilities, and Unmet Needs

Foster youth are more likely than their peers to grapple with challenging life circumstances that can undermine their pursuit of a college degree. These challenges, which include financial hardships and food insecurity, needing to work, and having to care for a child, have been identified as barriers to success by foster youth (Batsche et al., 2014; Courtney et al., 2011; Goldrick-Rab et al., 2018; Salazar, Jones, 2016; Skobba et al., 2018; Svoboda et al., 2012) and professionals serving foster youth (Tobolowsky et al., 2019). Youth with care histories are highly vulnerable to economic emergencies such as running out of food and becoming homeless. In a study of 123 two- and four-year colleges across the United States, Goldrick-Rabb and colleagues (2019) found that students with foster care histories were at greater risk to experience food insecurity, housing insecurity, and homelessness than any other student group they examined. Nearly two-thirds of foster youth had been food insecure in the past month, and about one-quarter four had experienced homelessness in the past year. Not only does meeting basic needs consume a good deal of time and energy but it is also on the forefront of students' minds (Tobolowsky et al., 2019). As a former foster youth put it, "A lot of people are oblivious to youth homelessness, and as soon as you leave foster care, I feel like that's what happens" (Clemens et al., 2016, p. 71). Another youth conveyed the constant worry that accompanies housing insecurity: "I think that for me feeling secure about where I'm going to live is always in the back of my head. . . . I don't know if I'll have a roof over my head. And that is very scary to think about" (Dworsky & Peréz, 2010, p. 261).

Taking care of children, siblings, and others is an additional responsibility that some foster youth have. Caring for children may be an especially prevalent challenge for students enrolled in two-year colleges (Gross et al. 2019). One foster youth who had a child commented, "The only thing I could focus on was where I am going to live, how I am going to eat, how I am going to feed my baby, stuff like that" (Batsche et al., 2015, p. 179).

Support and Resources That Are Time Limited and Have Strings Attached

A final feature of foster youths' experiences is that many of the supports they receive for postsecondary education are contingent on maintaining satisfactory academic progress (SAP). This usually means that youth must enroll in a certain number of credits and must maintain at least a 2.0 GPA. Youth who fail to make SAP may lose their state tuition waivers, Pell Grants, and $5,000 ETV and potentially may be forced to leave foster care (if they do not meet one of the other EFC eligibility requirements). A catch-22 is that succeeding academically is all the more important for foster youth, but they enter college with less preparation, less family support, and more disruptive life events. If foster youth dip below the academic threshold, they could enter an economic death spiral that makes continuing in college untenable.

Even if a youth does fulfill the academic requirements and does remain in foster care past age eighteen, foster care abruptly ends on the day they turn twenty-one. I remember sitting in a meeting with a young student in her last semester of two-year college. She was just several weeks away from completing her associate's degree. This was a success story in the making—she had entered college soon after finishing high school, enrolled full-time and did well in her classes, and was on track to graduate. The unfortunate thing was that her twenty-first birthday happened to fall in the middle of her last semester of college. For most young people, their twenty-first birthday is something to look forward to and to celebrate, but for this young woman the date circled on the calendar signaled dread and the need to scramble for money. On her mind was figuring out if she could work extra hours to pay rent or find someone to live with until she finished college. In addition to concrete concerns about food and shelter, leaving foster care can have a profound psychological toll. It means crossing a precipice with no option to turn back. On some level youth may feel excited or relieved not to be "in the system" any longer, but on another level, this means that they are truly on their own. One day the guard rails are there in case the bridge gets shaky, but the next day they are gone.

Resilience in Foster Youth

Although this chapter has focused on the considerable challenges and circumstances that foster youth face on their journey into and through college, their experiences have also taught many of them to be fighters. Some of the foundational studies of foster youth in college are qualitative, and the theme of resilience comes up again and again. Resilience is commonly thought of as an ability to perform well despite unfavorable circumstances, or to bounce back from adversity (Fraser et al., 1999). In the qualitative interviews, resilience was cited both as personal attributes of the youth (e.g., strong-mindedness, maintaining a positive outlook) and as resources present in their environment that could be tapped in the face of adversity (e.g., family, school, and community).

In terms of individual attributes, analyses of interview transcripts find that foster youth tend to be goal oriented, assertive, driven, and persevering (Hass et al., 2014; Hines et al., 2005; Morton, 2015; Neal, 2017; Rios & Rocco, 2014; Salazar, Jones, 2016). Learning from past mistakes and making intentional changes to better themselves and their future were reported in several studies (Batsche et al., 2014; Rios & Rocco, 2014; Salazar, Jones, 2016), as well as possessing a resolve to create a future that was different from their past life (Hines et al., 2005; Morton, 2015; Neal, 2017; Tobolowsky et al., 2019). Study participants were optimistic and hopeful about their future and had plans to succeed in school, work, and establishing a home and family (Batsche et al., 2014; Hines et al., 2005; Morton, 2015; Neal, 2017). Even though youth faced considerable obstacles, hardships, and disappointments, they were resourceful and became adept at advocating for themselves to get what they needed (Batsche et al., 2014; Morton, 2015; Rios & Rocco, 2014), sometimes using others' doubts as fuel to prove them wrong (Rios & Rocco, 2014; Salazar, Jones, 2016).

In terms of resources in their environment, connections to socially supportive individuals were a source of resilience found in several studies. Because many youth lacked stable and meaningful connections to parents, their relationships with older siblings, friends, significant others, mentors, teachers, counselors, and nonparent adults were especially important (Batsche et al., 2014; Hass et al., 2014; Hass & Graydon, 2009; Hines et al., 2005; Merdinger et al., 2005; Morton, 2015; Neal, 2017; Rios & Rocco, 2014; Salazar, Jones, 2016; Skobba et al., 2018; Strolin-Goltzman et al., 2016; Tobolowsky et al., 2019). These individuals became like family to the youth, and youth often referred to individuals they were not biologically related to as "like my dad" or "auntie." Some studies found that the education system plays a positive role. It served as a safe haven from the troubles of life and enabled foster youth to feel good about themselves (Hass et al., 2014; Hines et al., 2005; Morton, 2015; Neal, 2017; Rios & Rocco, 2014; Skobba et al., 2018). Not all studies found school to be a safe haven, however. Participants in some studies complained that stereotypes and a lack of empathy and understanding by teachers made school an unwelcoming environment (Batsche et al., 2014; Rios & Rocco, 2014).

Some studies report that the foster care system also provides an important opportunity for youth to further their education and develop important relationships (Hines et al., 2005). However, not all youth had such positive experiences, and some felt a lack of support and genuine care (Batsche et al., 2014) or that their experiences depended on the specific foster home or caseworker they were placed in the care of (Morton, 2015; Rios & Rocco, 2014). Participating in extracurricular activities and programs also provided positive outlets for negative energy, serving as a distraction from and a coping mechanism with stress and providing something positive to focus on that enhanced their experience in school (Neal, 2017; Skobba et al., 2018).

These qualitative studies are important because they challenge the all-too-common narrative of imperiled foster youth overrun by obstacles. They show that foster youth possess grit and rely on available support, and many thrive despite the barriers they encounter. At the same time, it is also important to recognize that these studies do not represent the experiences of *all* foster youth in colleges. The foster youth who wound up participating in these studies, and thus whose accounts were heard, tend to be on high end of academic success. Nearly all of the studies recruited participants through convenience sampling, which entails getting participants who are easy to access. The samples typically included foster youth who were still enrolled in college or who graduated from college, and who were willing to take part in a study that asked about their experiences in college and foster care. Many studies interviewed only youth in four-year colleges, which is problematic because the majority of foster youth enroll in two-year colleges. Consequently, most of these studies wound up with young people who were academically successful and willing participants. Underrepresented in these studies are foster youth who had dropped out of college or who wanted no part of a study about their experiences in college.

One qualitative study lends support to this assertion. Rather than recruiting just academically successful foster youth, the study included both young people who had finished high school and others who had dropped out (Clemens et al., 2016). They were asked to reflect on different educational statistics about foster youth in their state, such as why smaller percentages of foster youth graduated high school and why larger percentages of foster youth earned a GED relative to other students. One of the study findings is that the group was polarized on the topic of resilience. Youth who had earned a high school diploma or GED were more driven, showed a strong motivation to succeed, and reframed past struggles as experiences that made them stronger (Clemens et al., 2016). The authors characterized this group as applying a "resilience lens" to their experiences. This was a stark contrast to the students who had dropped out of high school, who tended to disengage from school rather than lean into challenges.

The failure to get a complete picture of the range of experiences of foster youth in college is not limited to qualitative studies. It can also occur in larger quantitative studies with low participation rates. For example, a highly cited study by Merdinger and colleagues (2005) did not use a convenience sample, but instead sent surveys to more than 800 foster youths enrolled in eleven California four-year colleges. In this study, the response rate was just 28 percent, which means that only about one in four youth took part. Which youth were less likely to return the survey? My hunch would be youth who were struggling in school. Indeed, more than half of the youth who did participate were either juniors or seniors in college (53%), which means that they had defied the odds and had made it into their advanced years in college. The average GPA for the total sample was about 3.0 (Merdinger et al., 2005).

I raise these points so that you may interpret the findings of qualitative studies and other studies with questionable representativeness with an appropriate degree of caution. They certainly capture the experiences of a segment of foster youth in college. Yet they also miss or underrepresent other students, particularly youth who struggle and drop out, as well as youth in two-year colleges. If we are to develop effective polices, programs, and practices to support foster youth through college, we need to understand the full range of experiences of the youth we are targeting. This includes the voices of those who, arguably, are at greatest risk of not succeeding in college.

Chapter Summary

This chapter summarized federal education and child welfare laws that provide important resources to support foster youth into and through college. Depending on where a foster youth happens to live, considerably different types and amounts of support are available. A prominent theory of student departure was presented, followed by critiques of the model that pertain to students with foster care histories. The chapter identified several challenges and circumstances that distinguish college students with care histories. Foster youth are typically further academically behind than their peers, may be grappling with the reverberations of past trauma, do not necessarily have biological family to fall back on, are pulled away from college by external demands, and have access to support that has requirements attached or looming expiration dates. The chapter concluded with a summary of studies on resilience in students with care histories. The next chapter introduces the Midwest Study, which is the group of 732 youths followed for about a decade that animate the analyses in the rest of this book.

2

Description of the Midwest Study

Midwest Study Background

The Midwest Evaluation of Adult Functioning of Former Foster Youth (Midwest Study) was launched in 2002 with an ambitious goal: to follow more than 700 young people in foster care in three Midwestern states as they made the transition into their early twenties. The study was original slated for three waves of data collection, interviewing participants at ages seventeen, nineteen, and twenty-one (Courtney et al., 2004). However, because of the considerable interest that the study generated, it was funded for an additional two rounds of interviews at ages twenty-three and twenty-five. Over the course of nine years and five interview waves, a total of 3,124 interviews were completed. Assuming each interview lasted about 75 minutes (which is a conservative estimate), this adds up to nearly 4,000 hours of gathering information and learning about the lives of young people in the study.

At the time the Midwest Study was initiated, few longitudinal studies of this size had been conducted with transition-age foster youth (e.g., Courtney et al., 2001; McMillen et al., 2004), and none had followed a cohort for such a long period of time. It was the first study to provide a moving picture of the lives of these young people as they moved out of foster care and into the rest of their lives. The Midwest Study was conducted under the direction of Dr. Mark Courtney, a child welfare scholar and professor at University of Chicago's School of Social Service Administration (SSA).

An important feature of the study's design is that it served as a natural experiment. The foster care age limit was age eighteen in two of the Midwest Study states (Wisconsin and Iowa) and age twenty-one in the third state (Illinois). Thus, depending on the state in which study participants happened to reside, they would be forced to leave foster care as early as their eighteenth birthday or as late as their twenty-first birthday. The Midwest Study was an opportunity to examine whether the extra three years in foster care helped youth better land on their feet in early adulthood. This was an important issue in the early 2000s, because the overwhelming majority of states required youth to exit care when they turned eighteen. In a few places, such as Illinois, New York, and Washington, DC, state and city funding was used to extend the foster care age limit to twenty-one. Nationally, however, there was growing recognition that age eighteen may be too young to expect youth in care to be on their own.

The Midwest Study had a profound impact on child welfare. The five descriptive reports released after each interview wave, in addition to the dozens of articles and brief reports on special topics, have been cited thousands of times in books, academic journals, newspapers, and federal and state legislation. Importantly, study findings were instrumental in the passage of the 2008 Fostering Connections law. Many of the questions used in the Midwest Study informed the development of National Youth in Transition Database (NYTD) questions, which, beginning in 2010, required all fifty states and U.S. territories to track outcomes of transition-age foster youth.

Over the course of the Midwest Study, a small army of scholars and students developed and pretested the survey instruments, analyzed the data, wrote and edited descriptive reports, and disseminated the findings. Several individuals were faculty members or doctoral students at the time of their involvement (e.g., Noel Bost, Adam Brown, Colleen Cary-Katz, Judy Havlicek, Tom Keller, JoAnn Lee, Kara Love, Gretchen Ruth Cusick, Alfred Peréz, Melissa Raap, Sherri Terao, and Vanessa Vorhies). Amy Dworsky joined as the project director between the second and third interview waves to manage the day-to-day operations of the project under Dr. Courtney's leadership.

My involvement in the Midwest Study came late in the game. I joined the study when I started a PhD program at SSA in the fall of 2011. By that time, the fifth wave of interviews had been completed, and the team was finalizing the accompanying descriptive report. I worked with Midwest Study data over the next few years as I became a research assistant and then the project director for Dr. Courtney's California Youth Transitions to Adulthood Study (CalYOUTH; Courtney et al., 2014). When it was time to begin my dissertation, I knew that the Midwest Study would provide an unprecedented opportunity to study college outcomes for foster youth. Moreover, obtaining National Student Clearinghouse (NSC) data for participants would provide an extra four years of college outcome information beyond the last Midwest Study interview. The NSC records would also fill in missing college information for participants who missed follow-up interviews. Thus, in May 2015, I began a two-year dissertation trek that involved many long days crunching numbers and drafting chapters in an unused classroom in the basement of SSA. Another year was spent converting the stuffy dissertation tome into the book you now hold.

With this background, the next section provides details about the Midwest Study and the other data sources used in this book. The chapter closes with a description of the Midwest Study participants based on data from the baseline interview.

Data Sources

Data Collection and Response Rates

The population of interest for the Midwest Study included young people in foster care in three Midwestern states: Illinois, Wisconsin, and Iowa. Youth were eligible to participate if they were between seventeen and seventeen and a half years old in 2002 and had been in foster care for at least one year. The entire populations of eligible youth in Wisconsin and Iowa were included in the study, as well as a random sample of two-thirds of the population of Illinois youth. Of the 767 adolescents who were fielded for interviews, a total of 732 participated in the study (95% response rate). The overwhelming majority of interviews were completed in person, although some were completed over the telephone. As displayed in Table 2.1, response rates for the follow-up interviews were consistently high. Of the original 732 participants, more than 80 percent participated in each of the follow-up interviews. In total, 435 of 732 youths (59.4%) participated in all five interview waves. By the end of Wave 5, twelve participants were known to be deceased.

Table 2.1
Response Rates of the Five Midwest Study Interviews

Interview Wave	Interview Field Period	Age of Respondents	Number of Respondents	Response Rate
Wave 1	May 2002–March 2003	17–18	732	95.4%
Wave 2	March 2004–December 2004	19	603	82.4%
Wave 3	March 2006–January 2007	21	591	80.7%
Wave 4	July 2008–April 2009	23–24	602	82.2%
Wave 5	October 2010–May 2011	25–26	596	81.4%

NOTE: Response rates for Waves 2–5 are calculated as the percentage of the baseline participants.

The University of Wisconsin Survey Center (UWSC) was contracted to conduct the field interviews with study participants. UWSC had experience interviewing transition-age foster youth, a population that is sometimes difficult to track down because of frequent moves and changing contact information. At each wave, trained interviewers met with the young person in a location that was convenient and private. The interviewer read most questions aloud and recorded responses on a laptop computer. For questions that were sensitive in nature, participants were given the computer and a set of headphones, and they listened to and answered the questions on their own. At the end of the interview, youth were given a monetary incentive for participating in the study.

Survey Instrument

The instrument used during the interviews was created from existing scales and questions from other reputable studies; it also included questions that were developed specifically for the Midwest Study. Information on a broad range of topics—youths' living arrangements, mental health, education and employment, parental status, social support, and delinquency—was collected during each interview wave. Later interview waves dropped some questions that were no longer relevant (e.g., experiences in foster care) and added other ones that were relevant to participants who were now older and out of foster care (e.g., experiences of financial hardships). Many of the factors investigated as contributors to college outcomes in this book come from Midwest Study data. These data were used to construct measures of youth's demographic characteristics, education background, foster care history, risk and protective factors, and other characteristics.

National Student Clearinghouse Records

The NSC data were used to create measures of the main outcomes of the study (i.e., enrollment, persistence, and completion) and to identify enrollment trends. After receiving approval from the School of Social Service Administration/Chapin Hall Institutional Review Board in May 2015, NSC data were requested for the 732 Midwest Study participants. NSC is a 501(c)(6) nonprofit and nongovernmental organization that provides enrollment and degree records for more than 3,600 public and private U.S. postsecondary institutions (National Student Clearinghouse [NSC], 2019a). NSC records account for about 97 percent of all currently enrolled students and almost 99 percent of all postsecondary education institutions (NSC, 2019b), including in-state and out-of-state schools; vocational, two-year, and four-year schools; and public and private schools.

NSC provides the following types of information for each marking period during which youth were enrolled: name of the institution, characteristics of the institution (i.e., two year or four year, private or public), enrollment start date and end date, enrollment status (full-time, part-time, and less than part-time), class level (e.g., freshman), major, graduation date, degree title, and degree major. NSC records were requested from the date of participants' sixteenth birthdays to May 2015. At the time of the NSC data draw, Midwest Study participants were twenty-nine or thirty years old.

NSC data are not without limitations. There are likely some Midwest Study participants who appeared in NSC records but should not have been counted as enrolled in college, such as youth who were just taking noncredit adult basic education classes. In other instances, there were participants who enrolled in college but did not appear in NSC records. If not corrected, these issues could lead to inaccurate estimates of college enrollment, persistence, and completion rates. Fortunately, self-report information on high school completion, college enrollment, and college degree completion was gathered at each of the five Midwest Study interview waves and used to address limitations of the NSC data. The NSC data were carefully cross-checked with Midwest Study data to identify (a) youths who enrolled in college but did not appear in NSC records and (b) youths in NSC records who should not be counted as having enrolled in college. Readers interested in learning more about the strategy used to address NSC limitations can read the appendix to this chapter.

Barron's Profiles of American Colleges

Barron's Profiles of American Colleges was used to create a measure of the selectivity level of the colleges in which Midwest Study participants were enrolled. *Barron's* classifies four-year institutions into six categories based on factors such as admission rates and characteristics of the incoming student body (e.g., standardized test scores). In this book, the six categories were collapsed into two categories: nonselective (*Barron's* noncompetitive and less competitive colleges) and selective (*Barron's* competitive, very competitive, highly competitive, and most competitive colleges). A third category was added for two-year colleges. Electronic copies of *Barron's Profiles* were not available for most years between 2002 and 2015, and thus paperback books had to be purchased and manually searched. Consequently, college selectivity ratings were obtained for three years: 2003, 2007, and 2011. The selectivity score of a college was based on the year closest to the start date of the marking period in which the youth was enrolled. For example, if a youth enrolled in a college from 2003 to 2007, the 2003 *Barron's* score was used for the semesters in 2003 and 2004, and the 2007 Barron's score was used for the semesters in 2005 and 2006.

Integrated Postsecondary Education Data System (IPEDS)

The second source of data used to construct institution-level variables was IPEDS. Administered by the National Center for Education Statistics within the U.S. Department of Education's Institute for Education Sciences, IPEDS collects data from all institutions of higher education that participate in any federal Title IV financial assistance program. Data are collected annually on institutional characteristics, costs, admissions, enrollment, student financial aid, degrees and certificates conferred, student retention, and institutional resources. Similar to the strategy used with *Barron's* data, measures created from IPEDS were obtained for the 2003, 2007, and 2011 academic years, and the year closest to the students' enrollment dates were used. Several measures were created that captured aspects of the institution's study body and expenditures.

Study Measures

This section provides a broad overview of the measures analyzed in this book. Readers interested in more specific information can refer to Appendix D at the end of the book for a complete list of variables.

Outcome Measures

College enrollment. As described earlier, participants were classified as being enrolled in college based on data from the NSC and supplemented by self-report data from the Midwest Study. Only youth who had attained a secondary credential (high school diploma, GED, or certificate of completion) by the time they entered college were counted as having enrolled in college. Of the 402 youths who enrolled in college, 331 were identified by NSC records (82.3%) and 71 were identified by Midwest Study data (17.7%).

College persistence. Persistence is measured by completion of the first three consecutive non-summer semesters, either on a full-time or part-time basis. Students were counted as not persisting if they failed to enroll for three consecutive semesters or to complete one of the first three semesters (e.g., they withdrew). Because this measure requires semester-by-semester data, only youth appearing in NSC records ($n = 331$) were included in the analyses of college persistence.

Degree completion. A binary variable was constructed to indicate whether a youth earned a college degree (i.e., two-year degree/four-year degree vs. no degree) by the time of the NSC data draw in May 2015. Self-report data from the Midwest Study were used for the college students not identified in the NSC record. Of the fifty-six youths who earned a college degree, forty-five were identified from NSC data and eleven were identified from Midwest Study data.

Characteristics of the Study Participants

Youth Characteristics Measured Only at Age 17 (Wave 1). The first set of youth characteristics was taken from the baseline interview, when most participants were seventeen years old. These measures capture different aspects of youths' background that could be associated with their later college outcomes. They include demographic characteristics (age, gender, race/ethnicity) and measures of their academic background (self-reported high school math and English grades, reading proficiency, highest completed grade, ever repeating a grade, ever in special education, ever expelled from school, and activities they participated in to prepare for college). They also include foster care history characteristics (ever placed in a group home or residential treatment center, number of foster care placements, number of school changes, physical abuse, sexual abuse, and neglect) and other risk and protective factors (e.g., had a living child, amount of social support).

Pre-entry and Post-entry Characteristics. For youth who enrolled in college ($n = 402$), several measures were created to capture characteristics and life circumstances in the time period before they enrolled (pre-entry) and the time after they enrolled (post-entry). These measures drew on data from multiple Midwest Study interview waves and were used in the analyses that investigated predictors of persistence and degree completion. More information about how the pre-entry and post-entry variables were created is presented in the appendix to this chapter.

A pre-entry measure and a post-entry measure were created for several characteristics. Seven measures were expected to decrease the likelihood that youth persisted and completed a degree: presence of a mental health problem, presence of an alcohol or substance use problem, number of economic hardships, experiencing food insecurity, engagement in delinquent behavior, parental status, and being employed for many hours. Three measures were expected to increase the likelihood of persistence and degree completion: amount of social support, educational aspirations, and marital status.

Other youth characteristics of special interest are included in this book. Two chapters focus on youth characteristics that are of special interest: avoidant attachment (chapter 8) and the number of years youth spent in foster care past age eighteen (chapter 9).

Characteristics of the Colleges

Several institutional-level variables were created to capture aspects of the colleges in which Midwest Study participants were enrolled. These measures were used to investigate predictors of persistence and degree completion. Two versions of each variable were created. The first version pertained to the first institution that participants attended. However, because some participants attended more than one college, a second variable was created for the institution at which the youth spent the most time (as measured by the number of semesters at each institution). In cases where they spent an equal amount of time at two institutions, the more selective college was chosen. The first institution measures are reported in the analyses throughout this book. There were very few differences when the modal institution measure was used, and those differences are noted in the endnotes when present. As noted earlier, institutional variables were created for three years (2003, 2007, and 2011), and information from the year closest to their enrollment was used to input data about the institution in which youth was enrolled.

One main institution-level variable captured the type and selectivity of the college. Colleges were classified into one of three categories: two-year college, nonselective/minimally selective four-year college, and selective/highly selective four-year college. Because four-year college attendance was relatively uncommon, it was not possible to break four-year institutions into more refined categories based on their selectivity. Some other college-level measures included sector and control (public, private for-profit, and private nonprofit), size of undergraduate enrollment, and average cost of in-state tuition and fees. A few measures captured characteristics of the undergraduate student body, including the percentage of students enrolled in college part-time, the percentage of first-year students who returned for a second year, and the percentage of students who received a Pell Grant (a need-based grant for low-income students). Finally, three measures captured the average per-student expenditures in three areas: instruction, academic support services, and student services.

Approach to Addressing Missing Data

Some participants were missing information either because they did not answer every interview question (e.g., a respondent answered "don't know" or "refused") or did not participate in an interview wave. The proportion of data missing on individual items was small, typically below 5 percent. Missingness due to skipped survey waves was larger. Additionally, IPEDS data were missing for seventy-one individuals identified as college entrants from Midwest Study data, because the specific college(s) they attended was not known. If these missing data were not addressed, then statistical packages used to analyze the data would exclude youth from the analyses by default. This would cause a number of problems. Fewer youth means less statistical power to detect significant associations. More troubling, excluding youth with missing data could bias the results, leading to inaccurate estimates and conclusions.

A first step used to address missing information was to exploit data collected across survey waves. For example, if a youth did not participate in Waves 3 and 4 interviews, but indicated at Wave 5 that they were not a parent, then information on parental status was filled in for Waves 3 and 4. We then used an advanced statistical method—multiple imputation by chained equations—to address the remaining missing data (Azur et al., 2011; White et al., 2011). Multiple imputation is a sophisticated statistical method that uses existing data to impute (i.e., fill in) the missing values with plausible estimates. During the analyses, multiple imputation also takes into account the fact that there is uncertainty around the imputed values by creating multiple versions of the datasets with different imputed values, and then adjusts the tests of statistical significance accordingly. See Appendix C at the end of this chapter for more information on multiple imputation.

Description of the Midwest Study Participants at Age Seventeen

The remainder of this chapter presents information gathered from the baseline interview on the 732 Midwest Study participants. This will give readers a sense of the young people who took part in the study. As seen in Table 2.2, there was a slightly higher percentage of females than males, and the sample was racially and ethnically diverse. Several measures provide a sense of the academic history of the participants at age seventeen. The highest completed grade for more than one-third of the sample was tenth grade or less. On average, participants were more than three-quarters of a standard deviation below their same-aged peers in reading level. On a 0–4 GPA scale, the average GPA in math and English for youths' most recent marking period was 2.47, or about a C+. Nontrivial proportions of youth encountered difficulties in school. More than one-third reported being held back a grade, about one-sixth had been expelled from school, and nearly half said that they had ever been in a special education classroom. Despite these signs of difficulties, three-quarters of the youth aspired to earn a college degree or more, whereas the other quarter indicated that they aspired to complete just some college or less. In terms of youths' participation in four types of college-preparatory activities (e.g., attending college fairs, taking SAT courses), youth reported partaking in an average of less than one activity (median = 0).

Several additional measures described participants' foster care histories and experiences with maltreatment. Placement changes and school mobility were prevalent. On average, youth had been in just under six foster care placements (median = 4) and had experienced a little under three school changes for a foster-care–related reason or a family move (median = 3). About two in five youth had ever been placed in a group home or residential treatment center. During the interview, youth were asked eighteen questions about specific acts of neglect, physical abuse, and sexual abuse (see Appendix D at the end of the book). Youth reported experiencing an average of 3.2 different acts ($SD = 3.7$, median = 2). Based on the number of acts they reported, youth were divided into low, medium, and high maltreatment groups.

The bottom part of Table 2.2 presents characteristics of the youth that were suspected to promote or hinder their college outcomes. At age seventeen, about one in seven youth had a living child. On a scale from 0–4, the average social support score was 2.9 (median = 3.1), corresponding with the response option of feeling supported "most of the time" across four types of support: emotional/informational, tangible, positive social interaction, and companionship. Nearly three-quarters of youth had ever worked for pay. Delinquency scores

Table 2.2

Characteristics of Study Participants at Age 17 (Wave 1)

	% / Mean (SD)
DEMOGRAPHIC CHARACTERISTICS	
Gender	
Female (%)	51.5
Male (%)	48.5
Race/ethnicity (%)	
White	28.8
African American	55.3
Hispanic	8.6
Other race	7.2
Age at baseline interview (mean/SD)	17.9 (.4)
State (%)	
Illinois	64.8
Wisconsin	26.6
Iowa	8.6
ACADEMIC HISTORY	
Highest completed grade (%)	
Tenth grade or lower	35.6
Eleventh grade	52.6
Twelfth grade	11.8
Reading level, standardized (mean/SD)	−.83 (1.18)
High school math and English GPA (mean/SD)	2.47 (.88)
High school math and English grades (%)[a]	
Bottom tertile	32.8
Middle tertile	34.0
Top tertile	33.2
Ever repeated a grade (%)	37.4
Ever expelled (%)	16.6
Ever in special education (%)	47.5
EDUCATION ASPIRATIONS (%)	
High school credential or less	12.1
Some college	14.2
College degree or more	73.8
Number of college prep. activities (mean/SD)	.88 (1.23)
FOSTER CARE CHARACTERISTICS	
Number of foster care placements (mean/SD)	5.8 (5.8)
Ever in congregate care (%)	59.9
Number of school changes (mean/SD)	2.8 (2.0)
Maltreatment instances (%)	
Bottom tertile	26.6
Middle tertile	39.9
Top tertile	33.5
Years in care past age 18 (Mean/SD)	1.5 (1.4)
	(continued)

Table 2.2 (*continued*)

	% / Mean (SD)
RISK AND PROMOTIVE FACTORS	
Parental status (%)	14.1
Social support (mean/SD)	2.93 (.91)
Ever worked for pay (%)	73.6
Delinquency score (mean/SD)	.46 (.46)
Mental health problem (%)	68.7
Alcohol/substance use problem (%)	25.0

picked up on how often youth engaged in ten delinquent behaviors in the past twelve months, such as stealing money and vandalizing property. Scores could range from 0–2, with a 0 indicating that the youth did not engage in any delinquency acts and a 2 indicating that they engaged in all ten behaviors five or more times in the past year. The average delinquency score was about 0.5 (median = 0.30), indicating that on average youth engaged in delinquent behaviors between "never" and "1 or 2 times" in the past twelve months. More than two-thirds of participants had a mental health problem, as indicated by symptoms of depression or PTSD or having received pharmacological, therapeutic, or in-patient care for psychological problems in the past year. About one-quarter of youth had an alcohol or substance use problem, as indicated by symptoms of an alcohol/substance use disorder or receipt of treatment for these problems in the past year.

Chapter Summary

This chapter presented an overview of the Midwest Study, including the main measures investigated in the remainder of this book. It introduced the sample of participants, who displayed some promising and concerning characteristics that may relate to their later postsecondary education outcomes. Notably, at age seventeen, most youth had high hopes of entering college and earning a degree. The next chapter presents the college outcomes for these young people, describes the types of colleges they attended, and explores how well the college that the youth enrolled in aligns with their academic credentials.

––––––––

Appendix A: Strategy to Address NSC Limitations in Identifying College Enrollees

NSC data indicated that 351 of the 732 Midwest Study participants had enrolled in an institution of higher education by May 2015. However, this number is problematic for two main reasons. First, some youth may have enrolled in college but did not appear in NSC records. Second, other youth may have appeared in NSC records but should not be counted as being enrolled. The latter group includes youth who had not completed a secondary school credential before entering college and were likely just taking adult basic education classes that do not count toward college. In this appendix, these two issues are reviewed in more detail, along with steps taken to address them.

After a careful examination of the Midwest Study data on self-reported high school completion dates (collected at Wave 2) and high school status (collected at all waves), 20 of the 351 youths appearing in the NSC data were identified as not having earned a high school diploma, GED, or certificate of completion by the time they entered college. One possibility is that some of these students were taking college-level classes as high school students. If this was the case, these students would likely be academic high flyers. However, data from the Midwest Study suggested that these students were average or below average compared to others in the sample in terms of their high school GPA, reading proficiency score, history of skipping a grade, and history of grade retention. Some of these youths went on to complete a secondary credential, but none enrolled in college after earning the credential. Thus, these 20 youths were counted as having not enrolled in college, decreasing the number of college entrants to 331.

The second issue pertains to under-identification of participants who had enrolled in college but did not appear in NSC data (Dynarski et al., 2013). This could occur two main ways. The first is due to blocked records, which happens when either the student or the institution indicates that the students' enrollment records should not be disclosed. This is an instance of known under-identification, because the NSC report provides the number of blocked records. In total, there were twelve individuals who should have been counted as being enrolled in college but whose records were blocked. Because their identities were not disclosed, it is not possible to identify them.

The second way students could fail to appear in NSC records is if the college they attended did not report to the NSC during the year they were enrolled. This pertains to the issue of undercoverage. A coverage rate is the percent of students enrolled in institutions of higher education (as reported in IPEDS) who appear in NSC records. Although the NSC coverage rates has been very high in recent years (e.g., 97.0% in Fall 2018), the coverage rate was lower in the early 2000s, when most of the Midwest Study students entered college (e.g., 86.5% in fall 2003; NSC, 2019c). Coverage rates were particularly low for two-year colleges during this time, which is the institution type that Midwest Study participants overwhelmingly attended. For example, the fall 2003 coverage rate for two-year colleges was 83.7 percent, compared to 88.2 percent for four-year institutions. What this means is that there is likely a nontrivial number of

Midwest Study participants who were enrolled in college but who did not appear in NSC records due to undercoverage.

Blocked records and undercoverage create a problem that could lead to underestimations of college participation and completion, as well as potentially biased results in the regression analyses. Fortunately, the five waves of the Midwest Study collected information on the college enrollment and completion statuses of the participants, which could be used to identify college students missing from NSC records. Although some youth missing from NSC records will have first enrolled after their last completed Midwest Study interview, which means that their college enrollment would not be detected, this is expected to affect only a small proportion of the sample. For example, of the 331 college entrants identified with NSC data, only 30 (9.1%) first enrolled in college after the median date of the last Midwest Study interview.

The strategy used for recovering missing college students entailed closely inspecting all five waves of the Midwest Study data to identify youth who reported being enrolled in college at some point but who did not appear in the NSC data. Youth were counted as having been enrolled in college if (a) they had completed their secondary credential by the time they reported enrolling in college, and (b) there was no contradictory information about their secondary credential status or their highest completed grade in subsequent interview waves. In total, examination of the Midwest Study data identified seventy-one youths who reported that they had enrolled in college but did not appear in the NSC data. This brings the total number of study participants who had enrolled in college to 401. Since the seventy-one youths did not appear in the NSC data, specific information about the college(s) they attended, their dates of enrollment, and their credential completion date was not available. Therefore, these seventy-one youths were not included in analyses of enrollment trends (chapter 4) and predictors of persistence (chapter 6).

It is possible that the college students identified by the two data sources were different from each other in important ways. To assess the extent to which the 331 college students identified in NSC data differed from the 71 college students identified by Midwest Study data, these two groups were compared along all of the covariates and outcomes analyzed in this book. Only four statistically significant differences ($p < .05$) were found. Compared to youths in the NSC sample, youths identified by self-report were less likely to have experienced pre-entry food insecurity (21.9% vs. 35.2%, $p = .020$), experienced fewer pre-entry economic hardships (0.98 vs. 1.69, $p = .018$), had lower post-entry delinquency scores (0.07 vs. 0.15, $p = .015$), and were less likely to report post-entry alcohol/substance use problems (32.4% vs. 49.7%, $p = .009$). Thus, a few of the measures suggest that the self-reported youth were lower than NSC youth on a few of the risk factors. However, this was not consistent across all measures of risk. For example, the groups differed on rates of post-entry alcohol/substance use problems, but not on pre-entry or baseline measure of alcohol/substance use problems. The same was true for delinquency (only significant for the post-entry measure) and economic hardships and food insecurity (only significant for the pre-entry measures). Moreover, it is important to keep in mind that more than fifty statistical tests were conducted to assess group differences. With this many comparisons, there is a high probability that one or more of these differences were found by sheer chance. Nevertheless, as a precautionary measure, an indicator variable for the source of college identification was included in regression models predicting persistence and degree completion outcomes.

Appendix B: Construction of Pre-entry and Post-entry Factors

To create the pre-entry and post-entry factors, data were used from the five waves of the Midwest Study. Pre-entry measures capture the occurrence of an event (e.g., the participant had a child) or features of youth characteristics (e.g., delinquency score) before enrollment in college. Post-entry measures capture events and characteristics after participants entered college but before they graduated (or were no longer observed).

In an ideal situation, it would be possible to pinpoint when a factor occurred in relation to college entry and completion dates: Did the factor occur (a) before a youth enrolled in college, (b) after she enrolled but before she graduated, or (c) after she graduated? This would generate pre-entry and post-entry measures with precise timing. To do this, exact dates would be needed for the college outcomes and for the factors. Specific dates were available for college students with NSC data. However, precise dates were not available for the one-fifth of college entrants identified by Midwest Study interview data. Their dates of first enrollment and degree completion had to be estimated.[1]

Some factors did have specific date information (e.g., the month and year a youth's child was born). Other factors could be pinned down to having occurred within a specific date range before the interview (e.g., whether the youth experienced food insecurity in the twelve months before the interview or reported having mental health problems since the last interview). A third set of factors were those measured at the time of the interview. For example, the amount of social support that youth perceived having was measured at each interview.

As displayed in Table 2.3, different approaches were used to construct pre-entry and post-entry measures for the factors in light of the measurement issues just described. A first step was to divide the time period between the first Midwest Study interview in 2002 and the date of the 2015 NSC data draw into spring, summer, and fall semesters (41 in total). Information on each factor was then mapped onto each semester based on the approach described in Table 2.3. First, for factors with specific dates (e.g., marriage, birth of a child), information was inputted into each semester. Second, for factors assessed in a time

Table 2.3
Variable Creation Strategies for Pre-entry and Post-entry Predictors

Nature of the Predictor	How the Predictor Was Measured	Approach to Construct Pre- and Post-entry Measures	Predictors
Specific event with start and/or end date	Specific dates (month and year) were collected during the Midwest Study interviews	Can identify the start/end date for the event	Parental status Marital status
Status, experience, or characteristic that endures over time	Factors measured at the time of the interview for a specific time period prior to the interview (i.e., past 12 months, since last interview).	Backlogging: data collected during the current interview were backlogged into semesters since the previous interview	Mental health problem Alcohol/substance use problem Delinquency Economic hardships Food insecurity
Status, experience, or characteristic that endures over time	Factors measured at a point in time (i.e., at the time of the interview).	"Bubble" approach: data collected during the current interview were inputted in a time period halfway to the previous interview and halfway to the next interview	Social support Educational aspirations Employment status

period before the interview (e.g., mental health problem since last interview), all of the semesters between the youths' current interview and previous interview were filled in with the response from the current interview. For example, if at Wave 3 a youth indicated that he had experienced a mental health problem since the last interview wave, all of the semesters between Wave 2 and Wave 3 were marked with a positive screen for mental health. Third, for factors measured at the time of the interview but that endure over time (e.g., amount of social support, educational aspirations), a "bubble" approach was used for filling in semesters surrounding the current interview. The median semester between a youth's current interview and previous interview was identified, as well as the median semester between the youth's current interview and subsequent interview. This identified semesters halfway to the previous interview and halfway to the subsequent interview, essentially creating a "bubble" around the current interview. The data collected during the current interview (e.g., educational aspirations) were inputted into the semesters in the bubble.

In summary, I used the three strategies just described—specific dates, back-logging, and bubble—to fill in data for each of the semesters between fall 2002 and spring 2015. To create pre-entry measures for regression analyses, all of the semesters before youth entered college were identified. For specific events/occurrences that were binary (e.g., becoming a parent, experiencing a mental health problem), indicator variables were created if youth ever experienced the event/phenomenon before entering college. For the continuous measures (e.g., delinquency score, social support score), the average score was calculated across semesters in that period. For the ordered categorical variables (e.g., educational aspirations), the highest level during the pre-entry semesters was identified. Similar procedures were used to create post-entry variables, which covered the time period between the semester of first enrollment to the semester of graduation. This procedure resulted in a single pre-entry measure and a single post-entry measure for each factor in Table 2.3.

Appendix C: Additional Information on Multiple Imputation

Multiple imputation by chained equations was used to address missing data in the analyses (Azur et al., 2011; White et al., 2011). Multiple imputation draws on the distribution of observed data to fill in missing data by estimating a set of plausible values. Plausible values are generated by a series of iterative regression analyses, in which each covariate with missing values is regressed on all of the variables in the analytic model, along with auxiliary covariates used to augment the prediction of plausible values. This process results in the creation of a single dataset that contains both the observed values and imputed values. However, a single imputed dataset is inadequate. The imputed values would be treated with more precision than is truly the case (i.e., as if they had been observed), rather than being treated as estimates drawn from an underlying distribution of the variables. Analysis of a single imputed dataset fails to account for the uncertainty of the estimation of the plausible values, resulting in standard errors that are too small and could result in incorrect conclusions from hypotheses tests (Donders et al., 2006). Thus, the imputation process is repeated, generating multiple imputed datasets with different sets of estimated plausible values. The multiply imputed datasets are analyzed separately, and results are combined into a single set of parameter estimates. The data combination process is automated in Stata.

Multiple imputation is based on the assumption that data are missing at random (MAR), which means that the probability that a value is missing depends on information that is observed, and not on information that is absent from the available data. To the extent that missing data are MAR, multiple imputation far surpasses whole-case analysis and other imputation methods (e.g., mean imputation) in yielding results that are unbiased (Allison, 2009; Donders et al.,

2006). Multiple imputation also preserves statistical power, because cases with missing data are not excluded from analyses. For each regression analysis in the book, forty imputed datasets were generated and analyzed. Checks were performed to ensure both that the imputed values were reasonable (e.g., no extreme outliers) and that the distributions of the imputed values were similar to the distributions of the observed values for each variable (Eddings & Marchenko, 2012; White et al., 2011).

Part II
Findings

3

Exploring College Outcomes

In the previous chapter readers were introduced to the 732 young people who took part in the Midwest Study. This chapter presents findings on their college outcomes. To get a sense of how rates of persistence and degree completion for foster youth compare to other college students, outcomes for Midwest Study participants are compared to those of a nationally representative sample of low-income first-generation students. I then take a more detailed look at the types of colleges in which Midwest Study participants enrolled. Finally, I examine the issue of matching—the extent to which participants enroll in colleges that align with their academic qualifications.

Background: Rates of College Enrollment, Persistence, and Degree Completion Estimates for the U.S. Population

Entering postsecondary education has become common for young people in the United States. About two-thirds (67%) of sixteen- to twenty-four-year-olds enroll in a postsecondary institution within a year of completing high school, and the majority of them enroll in four-year colleges (National Center for Education Statistics [NCES], 2019). Female high school graduates are more likely than male graduates to immediately enroll in college (72% vs. 61%; NCES 2019). When examining differences by race and ethnicity, higher proportions of Asian (87%) students than White (69%), Hispanic (67%), and African American

(58%) students enter college soon after finishing high school (NCES, 2019). There are also differences in immediate college enrollment rates by socioeconomic status. More than four-fifths (83%) of students in the top quintile of family income enroll in college within a year of completing high school compared to about two-thirds (65%) of students whose family income is in the bottom quintile (NCES, 2018).

Persistence is a measure of whether students who enroll in college remain enrolled for a specified period of time.[1] The two most common persistence measures are two consecutive non-summer semesters and three consecutive non-summer semesters (Mortenson, 2012). Making it through two semesters is roughly equivalent to completing a year of college. This is an important measure because the first year is a common time for students to drop out. Persisting for three consecutive semesters means that students not only made it through their first year but also that they returned for a second year to finish their third semester. This is also an important measure because the period between year one and year two is another common drop-off point for college students.

What percentage of first-time college students in the United States persist? National data from the NSC can help answer this question. Among first-time students entering college in fall 2016, just over 70 percent (73.9%) were still enrolled in college in fall 2017 (NSC, 2018). Persistence rates are higher for Asian college students (85.3%) than for White (78.6%), Hispanic (70.7%), and African American (67.0%) students (NSC, 2018). Persistence rates also differ by institution type. Rates are highest in private four-year colleges (85.0%) and public four-year colleges (83.0%), and lower in public two-year colleges (62.2%) and private for-profit four-year colleges (52.9%; NSC, 2018).

In terms of completion of a postsecondary credential, the NSC reports that 58.3 percent of first-time college students beginning in 2012 had earned a certificate, two-year degree, or four-year degree within six years of starting (Shapiro et al., 2018). Six-year completion rates by institution type follow a similar trend as persistence rates, with rates being highest for students in private four-year colleges (76.1%) and public four-year colleges (65.7%), followed by students first attending public two-year colleges (39.2%) and private for-profit four-year colleges (37.3%). The NSC report does not break out completion rates for different types of credentials, but another national study that is a little older does report separate rates. The Beginning Postsecondary Students (BPS:12/17) study was a nationally representative longitudinal study of first-time college students beginning in 2011–2012. Overall, over half of participants (56.2%) attained a college degree or certificate within six years of first enrolling (Chen et al., 2019). About 9 percent (8.5%) of students earned a vocational certificate as their highest credential, 10.9 percent attained an associate's degree as their highest credential, and 36.8 percent attained a bachelor's degree. Completion rates were highest among students beginning at private four-year colleges (77.8%) and public four-year colleges (67.6%), followed by students attending public two-year colleges (39.2%) and private for-profit four-year colleges (35.2%).

Estimates for Youth with Foster Care Histories

To summarize the estimates just presented, most high school graduates enter college, most college entrants make it through the first year of college, and more than half of college entrants earn a postsecondary credential within six years after first enrolling. We do not have reliable national estimates of these outcomes for older youth in foster care, but several smaller studies have pointed to significant disparities. Collectively, these studies indicate that rates of enrollment, persistence, and completion are lower for foster youth than their peers (Gillum et al., 2016). Although nearly 80 percent of older adolescents in care aspire to complete college (Courtney et al., 2014; Courtney et al., 2004; McMillen & Tucker, 1999; Reilly, 2003), it is estimated that only 2 to 10 percent actually earn a two-year or four-year college degree by their mid-twenties (Courtney et al., 2011; Emerson, 2006; Pecora et al., 2006; Wolanin, 2005).

To understand the considerable gap in degree completion between foster youth and their peers, it is important to examine disparities present at lower rungs of the educational ladder. Disparities are evident in rates of high school completion (Frerer et al., 2013). By age nineteen, 60 to 70 percent of foster youth have graduated high school or earned a GED compared to about 90 percent of peers in the general population (Courtney et al., 2005, 2016). Because college entry is related to completion of a secondary credential, high school completion gaps carry over to college entry gaps (JBAY, 2015; Frerer et al., 2013). Only 24 percent of foster youth in the Midwest Study and 32 percent of foster youth in the CalYOUTH Study were enrolled in college at age nineteen, compared to more than 55 percent of youth in a national sample of nineteen-year-olds (Courtney et al., 2016; Courtney et al., 2005). Another factor determining college completion is what happens early in students' college careers. Foster youth are more likely than their peers to require remediation, tend to earn lower GPAs, complete a smaller percentage of attempted courses, persist at lower rates, and progress slower through college (JBAY, 2015, 2017; Day et al., 2013; Day et al., 2011; Frerer et al., 2013; Unrau et al., 2012). Consequently, disparities in rates of high school completion, college entry, and college persistence culminate in the marked disparities in rates of college completion between foster and their peers reported in some studies.

Findings

As we saw in chapter 2, about 88 percent of Midwest Study participants aspired to go to college, and about 74 percent aspired to earn a college degree. As

Table 3.1
Rates of College Enrollment, Persistence, and Degree Completion

Outcome	All Youth (n=732)	Youth Enrolled in College (n=402)	Youth Enrolled in College and Observed for 6+ Years (n=329)
Enrolled in college (%)	54.9	—	—
Persisted first three semesters (%)	N/A	30.2[a]	33.2
Completed any credential (%)	10.9	19.9	24.2
Highest credential completed (%)[b]			
None	89.1	80.1	77.8
Certificate	3.3	6.0	7.3
Two-year degree	3.7	6.7	8.2
Four-year degree	4.0	7.2	8.8

[a] Includes college entrants with NSC records (n = 331).
[b] Highest completed credential as of the date of NSC data draw for youth with NSC data (n = 331) and as of the last Midwest Study interview for youth missing NSC data (n = 71).

displayed in the first column in Table 3.1, we see that about 55 percent had ever enrolled in college. Overall, about 11 percent of participants completed any postsecondary credential (including postsecondary vocational certificates), with 7.7 percent completing a two-year or four-year college degree and 3.3 percent earning a vocational certificate. The second column includes just the Midwest Study participants who enrolled in college. Among all college entrants (n = 402), less than one in three persisted through their first three college semesters. Just about 20 percent of college entrants completed a postsecondary credential: about 14 percent earned a two-year degree or four-year degree and 6 percent earned a vocational certificate. One point to note about the sample in the middle column is that it includes all youth who enrolled in college, regardless of the age at which they first enrolled. However, youth who entered college at a later age may not have had sufficient time to complete a degree by the time NSC data were obtained. Take a youth who first enrolled in college at age twenty-seven. She would have only had two or three years to complete a degree before her NSC record was obtained. To overcome this limitation, the third column restricts the sample to just youths whose degree status could be tracked for at least six years after first enrolling in college (n = 329).[2] Among these youths, the credential completion rate was about 4 percentage points higher than the rate for all college entrants. About one in five (19%) completed either a two-year or four-year college degree.

No statistically significant (p < .05) differences were found in the college outcomes in Table 3.1 by race or ethnicity. However, there were a few statistically significant gender differences, with females faring better than males. Among all participants, females were more likely than males to enroll in college (61.8%

Table 3.2

Credential Completion by First College Type/Selectivity among Youth Enrolled in College Observed for 6+ Years ($n = 329$)

	None %	Certificate %	Associate's Degree %	Bachelor's Degree %
Two-year college ($n = 259$)	81.2	8.5	7.3	2.9
Nonselective/less selective four-year ($n = 32$)	66.0	7.3	12.1	14.6
Selective/highly selective four-year ($n = 38$)	53.9	0.0	9.4	36.7

vs. 47.6%) and to complete a credential (14.6% vs. 7.0%). The credential completion rates were also significantly higher for females than males among all college entrants (23.6% vs. 14.8%) and entrants who could be observed for six or more years (28.7% vs. 18.1%).

Table 3.2 displays rates of highest credential completed, broken down by the type and selectivity of the first college in which the youth enrolled. This table includes youth whose college outcomes could be observed for at least six years. Few students used two-year colleges as an on-ramp to earning a four-year degree; just 3 percent of youth who started in a two-year college later completed a bachelor's degree. Conversely, we see that some students who initially entered four-year institutions wound up completing a certificate or two-year college degree. This was more common among students who first enrolled in minimally selective or nonselective four-year colleges than among those who enrolled in more selective institutions. Indeed, a greater proportion of youth who entered non-selective colleges wound up completing a certificate or two-year degree than a four-year degree. In contrast, students who entered selective and highly selective four-year colleges overwhelmingly completed four-year degrees compared to other credentials. Students who enrolled in selective and highly selective four-year colleges also had the highest graduation rates, with almost half (46.1%) earning a two-year or four-year degree.

To put the persistence and completion rates in context, compare the outcomes of foster youth to those of college students from a nationally representative sample of low-income, first-generation college students. This serves as a meaningful comparison group because many foster youth come from low-income backgrounds and are first-generation college students. The comparison data were obtained from the *Beginning Postsecondary Survey Longitudinal Study* (BPS 04/09), a large, nationally representative study of nearly 16,700 college students who enrolled in college for the first time in the 2003–2004 academic year. These students were followed for six years, and data were available for their two-semester persistence and six-year credential completion. BPS is a fortuitous comparison study because 2003–2004 is the year when most of the Midwest Study college entrants first enrolled in college. The BPS sample was restricted only to students who were the first in their families to attend college and who were classified as low-income (i.e., they either received a federal Pell Grant or had family income at or below the federal poverty level). The analysis of two-semester persistence includes youth who first entered college between ages seventeen and twenty-nine, and the analysis of degree completion includes youth who first enrolled in college between ages seventeen and twenty-five.

As seen in Figures 3.1 and 3.2, the majority of Midwest Study participants and low-income, first-generation students first enrolled in two-year colleges. There were slight differences between the samples in the proportions of students

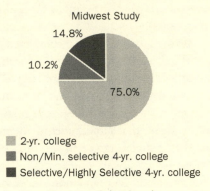

FIG. 3.1 College type/selectivity: Foster youth (Midwest)

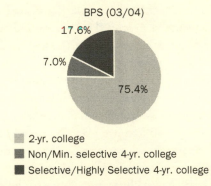

FIG. 3.2 College type/selectivity: Low-income first-generation students (BPS)
NOTES: Differences in college type/selectivity between Midwest Study and BPS were not statistically significant ($p > .05$). BPS (03/04) sample was weighted to represent a population of about 660,430 students.

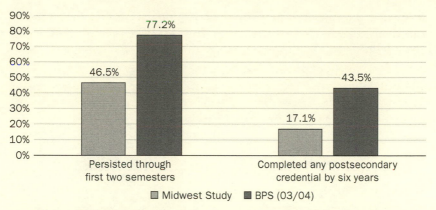

FIG. 3.3 Persistence and credential completion rates: Foster youth (Midwest) vs. low-income first-generation students (BPS)

NOTES: Differences in persistence rates and credential completion rates between Midwest Study and BPS were both statistically significant ($p < .001$). BPS (03/04) sample was weighted to represent a population of about 660,430 students. For the persistence estimate, the Midwest Study sample includes youth with NSC records ($n = 331$). For the credential completed estimate, the Midwest Study sample includes youth enrolled in college (based on self-report and NSC records) who could be observed for at least six years ($n = 329$).

who enrolled in selective versus less selective four-year colleges, but they were not statistically significant. This suggests that differences in the types of colleges students were attending were not a major factor separating the two groups that could explain differences in their later college outcomes.

Although the types of colleges did not significantly differ between the samples, there were substantial differences in persistence and credential completion rates (Figure 3.3). BPS participants were about 66 percent more likely than Midwest Study participants to persist through the first two semesters of college (77% vs. 47%). The difference in college completion rates was even more pronounced. BPS students were about 2.7 times as likely as Midwest Study participants to earn any college credential by six years after first enrolling in college (44% vs. 17%). Foster youth and low-income first-generation students also significantly differed in the types of postsecondary credentials earned (Figure 3.4). When considering just two- and four-year college degrees, BPS students were more than twice as likely as foster youth to complete a degree (28% vs. 12%).

Although not presented in detail here, additional sensitivity analyses were conducted to see if the observed differences in college outcomes were due to other differences between the groups, such as gender, race and ethnicity, and age that students first enrolled in college. To summarize, after adjusting for gender and race/ethnicity,[3] and then for gender and age of entry into college,[4] the estimates changed little: foster youth were still substantially less likely than low-income first generation students to persist and complete a degree.

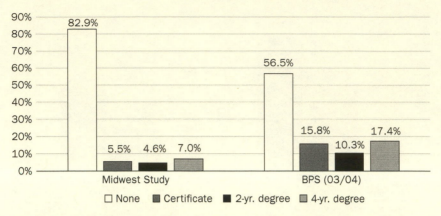

FIG. 3.4 Rates of highest completed credential: Foster youth (Midwest) vs. low-income first-generation students (BPS)
NOTES: Difference between Midwest Study and BPS in highest credential completed was statistically significant ($p < .001$). BPS (03/04) sample was weighted to represent a population of about 660,430 students. The Midwest Study sample includes youth enrolled in college (based on self-report and NSC records) who could be observed for at least six years ($n = 329$).

Types of Colleges in which Midwest Study Participants Enrolled

Table 3.3 presents characteristics of the higher education institutions attended by Midwest Study participants. The middle column pertains to the first college youth attended, and the right column pertains to the college in which youth spent the most amount of time. Because the figures are similar, only characteristics of the first college are described. It is important to note that, beginning with institutional size, data presented in the tables are only available for youth in the NSC records ($n = 331$). Information about the specific college(s) that youth attended were not available for the 71 youths who were identified via self-report in Midwest Study interviews, and thus it is missing in the table. However, multiple imputation estimates were generated, which filled in the missing data for the 71 youths. These estimates are reported in the notes below Table 3.3. The MI estimates were consistently close to the estimates in the table.

According to the NSC records, Midwest Study participants attended 182 different college campuses over the course of their college careers. In terms of the first institution, participants attended 113 different campuses. As displayed in Table 3.3, the majority of youth in the sample first attended a two-year college. Fewer than one in ten youth entered a four-year college that was selective or highly selective. Most youth attended institutions with a large undergraduate student body. The average proportion of part-time students across institutions

Table 3.3

Institutional Characteristics of Colleges Attended ($n = 331$)

	First College % or Mean (SD)	Most Attended College % or Mean (SD)
College type/selectivity (%)		
Two-year college	75.9	73.1
Nonselective/minimally selective four-year college	14.8	15.4
Selective/highly selective four-year college	9.8	11.5
Size of student body (%)		
Less than 2,500	12.4[a]	11.6[i]
2,501–5,000	12.4[a]	11.3[i]
5,001–10,000	31.8[a]	33.5[i]
More than 10,000	43.5[a]	43.6[i]
Percent part-time students (mean/SD)	52.8 (20.9)[b]	53.1 (20.3)[j]
Percent low-income students (mean/SD)	33.2 (21.2)[c]	34.7 (21.0)[k]
In-state tuition cost (mean/SD)	$4740[d] ($4827)	$4817[l] ($4807)
Expenditures on instruction per FTE (mean/SD)	$5147[e] ($3177)	$5526[m] ($3434)
Expenditures on academic services per FTE (mean/SD)	$725[f] ($784)	$821[n] ($1085)
Expenditures on student support services per FTE (mean/SD)	$1124[g] ($767)	$1221[o] ($833)
Retention rate (mean/SD)	55.7 (16.2)[b]	56.2 (15.5)[p]

NOTES: The estimates in the table pertain to the number of youth ($n = 331$), not the number of institutions. For example, if three students attended the same college around the same time, information on this institution was counted three times in calculating the averages reported in the table. Thus, statistics in the table can be thought of as weighted averages, giving more weight to colleges that foster youth frequently attended. This approach was used rather than simply calculating statistics for the institutions (i.e., each of the 113 colleges being counted once), because the latter approach could provide a distorted representation of the colleges that foster youth attend. For example, selective/highly selective institutions attended by one/few youth would be given the same weight as other institutions attended by several youth. Using the weighted average aligns with the student view (rather than institutional view) approach described in chapter 2.

Estimates from multiple imputation (MI) were generated for institutional characteristics missing more than 10%. All 402 youths who had enrolled in college were included in the MI estimates.

[a] MI estimates are less than 2,500 (15.2%), 2,501–5,000 (10.6%), 5,001–10,000 (28.0%), and more than 10,000 (46.2%).

[b] MI estimate: 52.8%.

[c] MI estimate: 32.8%.

[d] MI estimate: $4975.

[e] MI estimate: $5429.

[f] MI estimate: $972.

[g] MI estimate: $1441.

[h] MI estimate: 54.8%.

[i] MI estimates are less than 2,500 (14.1%), 2,501–5,000 (10.0%), 5,001–10,000 (28.9%), and more than 10,000 (47.0%)

[j] MI estimate: 53.2%.

[k] MI estimate: 35.1%.

[l] MI estimate: $5052.

[m] MI estimate: $6,083.

[n] MI estimate: $979.

[o] MI estimate: $1,507.

[p] MI estimate: 55.4%.

attended by foster youth was just over 50 percent, and the average proportion of low-income students was about 33 percent. The average cost of attendance for in-state students was about $4,700. Schools spent most on instruction, followed by student support services and academic support services. Slightly more than half of first-time students attending on a full-time basis re-enrolled at the same institution in the following fall. Although not displayed in Table 3.3, most youth in the NSC sample first attended a public college (81.0%) followed by a private for-profit college (13.9%) and private non-profit college (5.1%). Proportions were similar for the most-attended college (82. 8% vs. 12.4% vs. 4.8%).

College Match

How do students select which colleges to apply to, and ultimately, which college to attend? This can be a complex process, and many factors are typically at play, such as student qualifications, proximity of the college, cost and affordability, size, whether a specific field of study is offered, which colleges students are familiar with, and so forth. One consideration that has gained attention is the extent to which the selectivity of the college a student enrolls in matches the student's qualifications. When students attend colleges that align with their academic credentials, they are said to match. When students attend colleges that are below their qualifications, this is an undermatch. Conversely, when students attend colleges that are above their academic qualifications, this is considered overmatching.

Undermatching is a particular concern for students from low-income backgrounds and first-generation students (Belasco & Trivette, 2015; Bowen et al., 2009; Roderick et al., 2009; Smith et al., 2013). It is easy for even well-qualified low-income and first-generation students to become overwhelmed by the complicated tasks of searching for, applying to, and selecting colleges (Roderick et al., 2009). Compared to students from families and schools where going to college is the norm, low-income and first-generation students are not surrounded by people on standby who are familiar with the technical details of choosing colleges (McDonough, 1997; Perna & Titus, 2005). Unfortunately, students most in need of sound college advising often attend schools where guidance department staff are understaffed, under-resourced, and occupied by other responsibilities; they may be more focused on getting students through high school than into college (Bryan et al., 2011; Plank & Jordan, 2001). This leads students to miss application windows, limit their search to familiar colleges that may not match their qualifications, apply to few schools, miss important financial aid deadlines that affect their chances of receiving state and institutional aid, and focus on the sticker price of college rather than the out-of-pocket cost once aid is factored in (Roderick et al., 2008). Moreover, applying to competitive colleges often means completing applications that are involved and complex and have earlier application deadlines than those of less select colleges—all the while balancing these time-intensive tasks with their school, home, and work responsibilities (Roderick et al., 2009). Consequently, some highly qualified low-income students forgo applying to or enrolling in college altogether, while many others land in colleges that are well below their academic qualifications (Smith et al., 2013).

What are the potential consequences of undermatching? Low-income students who enroll in colleges that match or overmatch their qualifications fare better than students with similar qualifications and background characteristics who start in undermatched colleges (Alon & Tienda, 2005; Cohodes & Goodman, 2012; Melguizo, 2008; Shamsuddin, 2016). More selective colleges tend to retain students at higher rates. The selectivity of an institution correlates with factors that promote student success: how much is invested in academics and services to support students and the proportion of students who attend full-time versus attend college as a side endeavor. In short, the college that students enroll in matters to their chances of finishing.

To assess the degree of match between a student and a college, measures of the student's academic credentials are considered against the admissions criteria of different tiers of colleges. Unfortunately, commonly used measures of student credentials (e.g., cumulative high school GPA, standardized test scores, and advanced coursework) were not available in the current study. However, reading proficiency was assessed during the baseline interview of the Midwest Study and was used as a substitute for academic credentials. Midwest participants completed the Wide Range Achievement Test: Third Edition (WRAT3; Wilkinson, 1993), which is a brief standardized assessment requiring participants to read aloud a list of words that increase in difficulty. Raw scores are converted to an age-based standardized scale similar to the IQ scale (mean = 100, $SD = 15$). Youth were then classified into one of four quartiles based on the percentile of their reading score: 0–24 percentile, 25–49 percentile, 50–74 percentile, and 75–100 percentile.

As displayed in Figure 3.5, nearly half of Midwest Study participants who enrolled in college were well below the average reading level for their age (bottom quartile), and another one-fifth were below the average reading level (bottom middle quartile). Only one-third of participants were at or above the average reading level for their age (top two quartiles). If Midwest Study youth matched youth their age in reading level, each of the four groups would have about 25 percent of Midwest participants.

Figure 3.6 maps the reading quartiles onto the type of college in which a student first enrolled. Among youth in the bottom quartile, about 90 percent attended a two-year college or less selective four-year college, which was comparable to the proportion of youth in the bottom middle quartile who attended these institutions. Two-year and less selective four-year colleges may be an

FIG. 3.5 Age-normed reading percentiles among college entrants, divided into quartiles (*n* = 402)

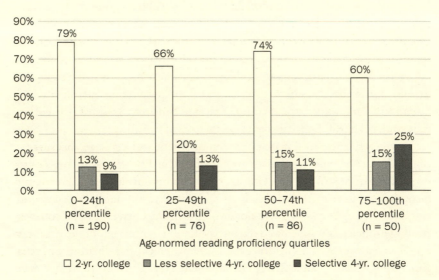

FIG. 3.6 College type/selectivity of first college, by age-normed reading proficiency quartile (n = 402)

appropriate match for these students, given that these institutions generally have open enrollment policies or admit 85 percent or more of applicants. What is interesting is that a small percentage of college entrants who were in the bottom two reading quartiles gained admission to colleges in the selective category.

Among youth reading at or above the average reading level for their age (top middle quartile and top quartile), most attended two-year colleges. Only one-quarter of youth in the top reading quartile attended selective four-year colleges. As a rough estimation of undermatching, let us assume that youth in the third and fourth quartiles could have gained admission to selective four-year colleges, and therefore those in these quartiles who entered colleges below these levels were undermatched. This is reasonable, because the lowest level of colleges included in the "selective/highly selective" category were four-year colleges that admitted freshmen in the top 50 to 65 percent of their class who earned mostly B- grades in high school (with some Cs). Using these criteria, about

32 percent of all college entrants in the Midwest Study were undermatched. When interpreting this finding, it is important to remember that a brief assessment of youths' reading proficiency is the only measure of their academic credentials. Thus, these estimates of college match are best interpreted as rough estimates.

Chapter Summary

This chapter examined rates of college enrollment, persistence, and degree completion for Midwest Study participants. Although almost 90 percent of youth at age seventeen aspired to complete at least some college, only 55 percent enrolled, and slightly less than 8 percent earned a two- or four-year degree. No statistically significant differences were found by race or ethnicity, although females were more likely than males to enroll in college and earn a credential. In terms of the types of colleges in which foster youth enrolled, two-year institutions were the most common path into higher education, with about three-quarters of college entrants attending these institutions. Compared to four-year colleges, these institutions tend to have higher rates of part-time students, lower retention rates, and smaller average expenditures on instruction, academic services, and student support services. The other quarter of college entrants tended to enroll in noncompetitive or minimally competitive four-year colleges; fewer than one in ten Midwest Study youth enrolled in a selective or highly selective four-year college. The final analysis showed that the majority of foster youth were reading below their grade level. Although the analysis of college match should be interpreted cautiously, the results suggest that a sizable proportion of foster youth who were reading at or above their grade level still attended two-year colleges, even though they may have been able to gain admission to a four-year school.

Now that we have a good picture of the colleges in which foster youth enroll, we turn to identifying common patterns of enrollment.

4

College Enrollment Patterns

In the previous chapter we saw that about 47 percent of Midwest Study participants who enrolled in college persisted through their first two semesters and 30 percent persisted through three semesters. These persistence rates are important milestones but only give a glimpse into students' journeys through college. These journeys can span many years and institutions, and they can take many different paths. However, noticeable trends may be discernible. Like dirt trails through a grass field, enrollment pathways capture the well-trodden routes through college. This chapter examines the enrollment histories of the Midwest Study participants to identify common pathways.

Shifting Trends in College Enrollment

In the last few decades, the timing and pattern of enrollment have increasingly deviated from what was once considered the "traditional" route: entering college immediately after high school, remaining at one institution, and continuously attending until graduation (Adelman, 2006; Borden, 2004; Peter & Cataldi, 2005). Students today may transfer to different institutions and most take longer than four years to complete a bachelor's degree (or two years for an associate's). For example, a recent analysis of 2.8 million college students who first enrolled in fall 2011 found that 38 percent transferred at least once within their first six years (Shapiro et al., 2018). Some students have breaks in enrollment where they stop attending school for a period of time but then return later (known as a *stopout*; Ramist, 1981).[1] Other students go back and forth between multiple institutions (called *swirling*), whereas still others enroll in two or more institutions at the same time (called *double dipping*; Borden, 2004; de los Santos & Wright, 1990; McCormick, 2003). Students' enrollment through college is not always a straight arrow from start to finish.

One of the reasons it is important to study the different paths that students take through college is because of the implications those journeys have for chances of finishing college. In general, time off from college and movement between colleges are associated with lower odds of finishing. Students who swirl, stopout, transfer vertically, and transfer horizontally are less likely to earn college degrees than are students who remain consistently enrolled at the same institution (for a review, see Mayhew et al., 2016). Low-income students and two-year college students are particularly likely to have interrupted enrollment patterns, contributing to lower rates of degree attainment (Adelman, 2006; Cabrera et al., 2012; Crosta, 2014; Goldrick-Rab, 2006; Hearn, 1992; Terriquez et al., 2013).

Classifying Students Based on Their Enrollment Pathway

How have education researchers sought to classify students in terms of enrollment? Some studies identify groups based on students' reasons for attending, their academic goals, level of engagement with faculty, and other characteristics (e.g., Ammon et al., 2008; Hagedorn & Prather, 2005; VanDerLinden, 2002). However, a growing number of studies classify students based on their pathways through college (Adelman, 2005; Bailey et al, 2004; Goldrick-Rab, 2006). As Crosta (2014) explains, enrollment pathways are "the time-ordered series of courses that students complete as they advance toward their education goals" (p. 118). Pathways can be characterized by their features, such as continuity (i.e., consecutiveness of attendance) and intensity (e.g., full-time versus part-time). Distinguishing common pathways, and then determining the percentage of students who follow each pathway, is useful information for colleges. It helps identify important points when students break off from college and can inform service planning that meets the distinct needs of students who follow different pathways.

Studies on enrollment pathways fall into two baskets. The first basket includes studies that use relatively simple analytic methods to identify pathways. These studies can yield interesting findings, but a critique is that a fair amount of subjective judgment is used to create the different pathways. Another researcher analyzing the same data may wind up identifying different pathways. The second basket includes studies that use sophisticated statistical methods to identify pathways. Some of the common analytic techniques are cluster analysis and latent trajectory analysis. In essence, these analyses take information about students' enrollment that is observable (i.e., in the data) to identify underlying (called *latent*) groups or trajectories. A strength of this approach is that the sheer amount of information the analyses can process far surpasses the amount that can be assessed by mere human brainpower. Although there are still many analytic decisions that must be made when using those techniques, overall, the process is less subjective than creating groups based on a researcher's inspection of the data.[2] A main downside of these sophisticated analyses is that they typically require very large sample sizes to produce reliable results. Additionally, sometimes the analyses generate results that fit the data well statistically but make little practical sense. With these strengths and limitations in mind, a summary of studies that fall into the two baskets follows.

Identifying Enrollment Pathways Based on Descriptive Data

An early study that falls in the first basket is Adelman's (2005) analysis of the National Education Longitudinal Study of 1988 (NELS: 88/2000) data. NELS included a sample of about 8,900 students enrolled in community colleges representing 2.2 million students nationally. This analysis included only "traditional age" students; that is, students between the ages of eighteen and twenty-four who had first enrolled in college before their twenty-first birthday. Adelman's report is divided into three parts, which he calls portraits, that draw attention to different phases of the college journey. He also created a typology of three enrollment groups based on two criteria: whether students (a) completed at least thirty community college credits and (b) earned 60 percent or more of all undergraduate credits (including credits from four-year colleges) at community colleges. He called the members of the first enrollment group "homeowners" (37%): they were students who made a substantial investment in community college, earning more than thirty community college credits and completing more than 60 percent of their credits in community colleges. The second group, "tenants with longer-term contracts" (18%), also earned thirty or more community college credits, but less than 60 percent of all their undergraduate credits were earned in community colleges. This group was particularly oriented to transferring to four-year colleges. Finally, "visitors" (45%) are students who earned more than one but less than thirty credits, and when they left community college, they tended never to return. Adelman's analyses produced interesting findings, but the two criteria used to differentiate groups is somewhat arbitrary. For example, there is nothing magical about a 60 percent cutoff. Had he used a different threshold, the compositions of the groups would have likely been different.

Identifying Enrollment Pathways Based on Advanced Statistical Analyses

The second basket of studies uses sophisticated statistical methods designed to identify distinct groups or distinct enrollment trajectories. Although identification of latent groups and trajectories is a relatively new area in education research, recent statistical advances are facilitating its more widespread use (Barban & Billari, 2012; Beath & Heller, 2009; Lanza & Collins, 2006; Verbeke et al., 2014).

Two studies used cluster analysis to identify groups of students based on their enrollment characteristics. First, Bahr (2010) analyzed data on more than 165,000 students in California community colleges. Thirteen continuous variables were used to identify groups: eight measures related to students' credit-bearing courses (e.g., total number of units, number of math units, number of English units) and five other measures (e.g., number of noncredit courses attempted, average number of credits attempted each semester, number of semesters enrolled). Bahr found that a six-group solution best fit the data, and he named the six groups based on each group's enrollment and credit accumulation profile. Nearly one-third (32%) of students were classified in the Drop-in group, which included students who typically attempted few nontransferrable vocational units for an average of two semesters. Another third of students (30%) fell in the Experimental group; they were enrolled for a very short period of time and completed few courses. These two short-stay groups captured about three-fifths of all community college students. Two other groups were small and included students who enrolled in college over the course of several semesters but attempted mostly noncredit courses (Noncredit students, 3%) and students who enrolled in many nontransferrable vocational courses (Vocational group, 3%). The remaining one-third of students fell into either the Transfer group (13%), who attempted the most courses each semester including transferable credit-bearing courses, or the Exploratory group (19%), who enrolled in a hodge-podge of transferrable and nontransferrable courses for fewer semesters than the Transfer group. There were important differences in college outcomes between the groups. Fewer than 10 percent of students in the Drop-in, Experimental, and Noncredit groups completed a credential or transferred to another college. In contrast, about one-third of the Vocational group (35%) and Exploratory group (31%) and about two-thirds of the Transfer group (67%) either finished a credential or transferred.

Crosta (2014) used cluster analysis to identify enrollment pathways among 14,400 students attending one of five community colleges in a single state. His analyses were limited to degree- and transfer-seeking students and thus did not include students enrolled in vocational programs, noncredit programs, and adult basic skills programs. Whereas Bahr's (2010) study created groups based on credit attempts and completions, Crosta's analysis was based solely on the attributes of student enrollment, such as the total number of terms enrolled, percentage of full-time terms, number of transitions between full-time and part-time terms, and the first semester they did not enroll. The study identified six distinct groups. As with Bahr's analysis (2010), the largest group consisted of students who enrolled for a few terms (usually just one) and then dropped out or stopped out, which Crosta named the Early Leavers (35%). On the other end of the spectrum were two groups who had the highest average numbers of completed semesters. Early Attachers (5%) and Later Attachers (10%) each completed an average of nine or more terms, but the former group displayed a period of prolonged, uninterrupted enrollment early on, whereas the latter group had a disruption in their enrollment within the first few semesters followed by an on-again, off-again period of enrollment. Full-time Persisters (20%) enrolled primarily full-time, had few changes in enrollment intensity, and completed an average of 4.5 semesters. Early Persistent Switchers (14%) enrolled for an average of four terms, about half of which were full-time and half were part-time. Finally, Mostly Part-Timers (16%) enrolled predominantly on a part-time basis, usually for only the first two terms. The six groups identified by Crosta had markedly different credential completion rates. The highest rates belonged to the Early Attachers (43%), Late Attachers (37%), and Full-time Persisters (18%), whereas the Early Persistent Switchers (6%), Most Part-Timers (5%), and early Leavers (1%) had very low completion rates.

A third study using advanced statistical analyses was conducted by Marti (2008), who used latent trajectory analysis to identify underlying sequences in the number of credit hours completed per semester over the course of students' first three years (fall and spring terms only). He conducted this analysis on three different datasets of community college students: a sample of nearly 3,500 students in twenty-seven Florida colleges, about 750 students in eleven Hispanic-serving institutions, and more than 78,000 students in twenty-three colleges in the Achieving the Dream (atD) initiative.[3] Five enrollment trajectories were identified across the samples. In the sample with the largest number of students (atD), the most common enrollment trajectory was the One-Term-and-Out group (30%), who completed less than five credits the first term and then dropped out. The Two-Years-and-Out group (13%) completed ten or more credits in the first three semesters; credit accumulation declined precipitously after that. The Long-Term Decliners (27%) completed less than nine credits their first term and displayed a gradual trend of declining credits over the remaining semesters. The last two groups displayed more consistent credit completion patterns. The Part-Time, Long-Term group (13%) completed about four to five credits each term throughout the two years. The Full-Time, Long-Term group (18%) completed an average of nine to ten credits each semester over the course of the six semesters and were on the best track for completing a credential or transferring.

Although these three studies differed in analytic approach, variables used to create enrollment groups, and samples, there are some commonalities in the findings. All three identified a large group, hovering around one-third of students, who enrolled for a very short period of time and then dropped out. On the other end of the spectrum, relatively few students were on a pathway that followed a "traditional route" of consistent, intensive enrollment. Less than one-fifth of students in each of the studies were on this path (Transfers in Bahr's study, Early Attachers and Late Attachers in Crosta's study, and Full-Time Long-Term in Marti's study). The remaining large middle of students displayed various intermittent and inconsistent patterns of enrollment, characterized by changing enrollment intensities, stopping out and then returning, and a (typically) decreased credit load.

Enrollment Pathways for Foster Care Youth

The findings from the four studies summarized above provide relevant context for the analyses of Midwest Study data. It is important to keep in mind that these studies were conducted with students attending two-year colleges, and enrollment patterns probably look different for students in four-year colleges. Nevertheless, these studies are relevant to youth with foster care histories given that most enroll in two-year colleges. What do enrollment pathways look like for college students with care histories? We turn to this question now by identifying pathways of college students in the Midwest Study.

The analyses in this chapter are based on the 331 Midwest Study participants with NSC data. The available sample ($n = 331$) was not large enough to use advanced statistical analyses, and so the data analysis is more in line with Adelman's (2005) study than the other studies summarized earlier. My analysis considered semesters that spanned more than a dozen years, beginning with fall 2001 and ending with spring 2015: I examined a total of 41 fall, spring, and summer semesters during that time span.

Classifying the 331 college students into enrollment groups involved an iterative process that took place over several weeks. First, I created a master Excel spreadsheet that documented each student's enrollment status for every semester between 2002 and 2015. For each semester, it included information about the student's enrollment intensity (not enrolled, part-time, and full-time), school type (two-year or four-year), a numeric code for the specific institution, and credential attained (none, certificate, two-year degree, or four-year degree).

Once I had that information, the next step was to select criteria that could be used to create enrollment groups. Unlike some of the earlier studies, information was not available on the specific types of courses students enrolled in or the number of credits they completed. Thus, I created groups based on three features of their enrollment over time: sustained persistence, stopouts, and multi-institution attendance. These three measures are commonly used descriptors of college students' enrollment patterns (Seidman, 2012).

Sustained persistence captures whether a student ever had a period of continuous enrollment for a sustained period of time. It was operationalized as ever having enrolled continuously for at least two full years of college (i.e., four consecutive non-summer semesters). I selected four semesters because by this point in college students have typically moved past remedial and introductory courses, have selected an area of study, and are taking more intermediate/advanced courses. Thus, the two-year point represents a deepening engagement and immersion in college.

Stopout is the second criterion used to create enrollment groups. Youth were classified as having stopped out if they enrolled in college, dropped out for at least one year, and then reenrolled. Some scholars designate a stopout as a lapse of just one semester (e.g., Schulte, 2015). I decided to use one year because one-semester lapses in enrollment were common in this sample and was thus not a meaningful distinction.

Finally, multi-institution attendance captures information on the number of different colleges a student attended during their college career. In this analysis, I distinguished between students who had attended three or more institutions versus those who had attended just one or two institutions. I chose three institutions as the cutoff point rather than two institutions for two reasons. First, attending two or more schools was fairly common in the sample (48%). Second, I wanted to avoid counting enrollments that were short in duration and strategic (e.g., a student in a four-year college enrolling in a two-year college to complete extra credits).

Taken together, the three indicators capture whether students had a sustained period of enrollment, had a break from college lasting a year or more, and had attended several different institutions. Based on these criteria, four mutually exclusive enrollment groups were created. Table 4.1 maps the four enrollment groups onto the three criteria. Each student's enrollment history

Table 4.1
Decision Rules Used to Create the Four Enrollment Groups

Attendance Characteristic	Enrollment Group			
	Toe in the water	Consistently enrolled	Boomerang	Buffet
Completed two consecutive years of college	No	Yes	No	No
Stopped out of college for a year or more	No	Yes or no	Yes	Yes or no
Enrolled in three or more different colleges	No	Yes or no	No	Yes

was individually examined, and the student was classified into one of four groups based on its characteristics. Students enrollment histories and classifications were then individually rechecked to ensure there were no misclassification errors.

Four Enrollment Groups

The first and largest group was named the "Toe-in-the-water" group. These students enrolled for three or fewer semesters, dropped out, and never returned to college. One- or two-semester enrollment was the norm; only 7 of the 163 youths in this group had enrolled for a total of three semesters. About half of the sample fell into the Toe-in-the-water group ($n = 163$, 49.2%). The hallmark of this group is that students had barely put their toe in the water before leaving college for good. This group is similar to groups identified in earlier studies, including Adelman's (2005) Visitors (45% of sample), Bahr's (2010) Drop-in (32%) and Experimental (30%) groups, Crosta's (2014) Early Leavers (35%), and Marti's (2008) One-Term-and-Out group (30%).

The second group was named the "Consistently enrolled" group. Youth in this group had enrolled in four consecutive non-summer semesters with no withdrawals from any of these semesters.[4] These students displayed a pattern of sustained engagement in college over the course of two full years. The four semesters could have been completed at the same institution or at different institutions. They could have occurred at the very beginning of their college career or later on. Only about one-quarter ($n = 89$, 26.9%) of students met the criteria for this group.

The last two enrollment groups displayed intermittent patterns of college attendance. The hallmark of the "Boomerang" group is that students came in and out of the same institution for short enrollment spells. That is, youth attended an institution for three or fewer semesters, stopped college for at least a year, and reenrolled in the same institution later. Some students had multiple enrollment spells, in which they were in and out of the same college over the course of several years. Some Boomerang youth did attend a second institution (but no more than two). Less than one-fifth of students were classified in the Boomerang group ($n = 57$, 17.2%).

The last group displayed a different pattern of intermittent enrollment. Students in the "Buffet" group attended three or more different institutions, and never for more than three consecutive semesters in any given enrollment spell (one or two semesters was the norm). Thus, rather than going in and out of the same college, students in the Buffet group sampled several different colleges for short spurts of time. This was the smallest group, containing fewer than one in ten youth ($n = 22$, 6.7%).

Enrollment Group Differences in Colleges Attended and Credential Completion

To summarize, Consistently enrolled students completed at least two consecutive years of college, Toe-in-the-water students had a brief trial run with college, Boomerang youth went in and out of the same college, and Buffet youth sampled several different colleges. Table 4.2 shows that these four groups differ in terms of the colleges they attended and whether they ultimately completed a certificate or degree. The far-right columns display whether there were statistically significant differences ($p < .05$) between the groups.

In terms of the number of different colleges attended, students in the Buffet group attended the most: 3.5 colleges on average (median = 3). Youth in the Consistently enrolled group attended an average of just over two colleges (median = 2), and students in the Boomerang group and Toe-in-the-water group attended about 1.5 and 1.3 colleges, respectively (median = 1 for both).

Enrollment in four-year colleges was highest for the Consistently enrolled youth (38%) and Buffet youth (36%). Only about one-quarter of Boomerang youth and Toe-in-the-water youth first entered four-year colleges. A finding that jumps out is that students in the Consistently enrolled group were more than twice as likely as students in the other groups to have enrolled in a selective/highly selective four-year college. A relatively large proportion of Buffet youth got their start in nonselective or less selective four-year institutions.

We can see stark differences in credential completion rates between the groups (Table 4.2). By definition, none of the youth in the Toe-in-the-water group completed college; they all dropped out after a short stint in higher education. However, the majority of youth in the Consistently enrolled group did earn a credential, and their rate of completion was substantially higher than for the two groups that displayed intermittent enrollment patterns. Although Boomerang youth were nearly twice as likely as Buffet youth to have earned a credential, the difference was not statistically significant ($p = .259$). It is important to keep in mind that the Buffet group had very few students, and there may have been insufficient statistical power to detect differences between the groups. In terms of the types of the credentials that were earned, roughly similar proportions of Consistently enrolled youth earned certificates, two-year degrees, and four-year degrees. Although not shown in the table, most of the four-year degrees earned by Consistently enrolled students came from those who first entered selective/highly selective four-year colleges. Nearly two-thirds of Consistently enrolled student who first attended these institutions earned a bachelor's degree (63.2%), compared to just one-fifth of Consistently enrolled students who first entered nonselective/less selective four-year colleges (20.0%) and less than one-tenth of Consistently enrolled students who first entered two-year colleges (7.3%).

Table 4.2

College Type/Selectivity and Credential Completion, by College Enrollment Group ($n = 331$)

	Enrollment Group				
	Consistently enrolled	Toe in the water	Buffet	Boomerang	Sig.
Percent of enrollees (%)	26.9	49.2	6.7	17.2	N/A
Number of different colleges attended (Mean/SD)	2.2 (1.0)	1.3 (.5)	3.5 (1.0)	1.5 (.8)	***
First college type/selectivity (%)					*
Two-year	61.8	76.4	63.6	73.7	
Non-/minimally selective four-year	16.9	16.8	27.3	15.8	
Selective/highly selective four-year	21.4	6.8	9.1	10.5	
Earned a credential (%)	64.0	0.0	9.1	17.5	***
Type of credential (%)					***
None	36.0	100.0	90.9	82.5	
Certificate	23.6	0.0	4.6	3.5	
Two-year degree	19.1	0.0	4.6	8.8	
Four-year degree	21.4	0.0	0.0	5.3	

NOTE: $*p < .05$ $***p < .001$.

Differences in the Characteristics of the Enrollment Groups

Given the differences in the types of colleges attended and completion percentages, we may wonder whether students in the four groups had different backgrounds and experiences before and after entering college. As we shall see, most of the differences existed between the Toe-in-the-water group and one or more of the other enrollment groups.

As seen in Table 4.3, the Consistently enrolled group had a significantly greater proportion of females than did the Toe-in-the-water group ($p = .001$) and the Boomerang group ($p = .032$). The groups did not significantly differ in terms of race/ethnicity or state in which they were in foster care. However, there were several poignant differences in the youths' academic histories. The Toe-in-the-water group had significantly lower reading scores than the Consistently enrolled group ($p = .031$) and the Buffet group ($p = .036$). The Toe-in-the water group was also academically behind in terms of the highest grade completed at baseline and had higher rates of grade repetition, school expulsion, and special education involvement.[5] In terms of foster care history, the Toe-in-the-water students were more likely than Consistently enrolled students ($p = .014$) and Boomerang students ($p = .004$) to have ever been in congregate care. Youth

Table 4.3

Baseline Characteristics, by College Enrollment Groups ($n = 331$)

Characteristic	Consistently enrolled	Toe in the water	Buffet	Boomerang	Sig.
DEMOGRAPHIC CHARACTERISTICS					
Gender (%)					***
Male	28.1	49.7	45.5	45.6	
Female	71.9	50.3	54.5	54.4	
Race/ethnicity (%)					n.s.
White	33.7	30.7	18.2	28.1	
African American	58.4	51.5	68.8	42.1	
Hispanic	2.3	9.2	13.6	17.5	
Other race	5.6	8.6	0.0	12.3	
State (%)					n.s.
Illinois	67.4	63.8	77.3	71.9	
Wisconsin	25.8	25.8	18.2	17.5	
Iowa	6.7	10.4	4.5	10.5	
ACADEMIC HISTORY					
Highest completed grade (%)					*
10th grade or lower	23.6	34.6	4.5	24.6	
11th grade	61.8	53.1	68.2	59.6	
12th grade	14.6	12.3	27.3	15.8	
Reading level, standardized (Mean)	−.38	−.67	−.18	−.45	*
High school grades (%)					n.s.
Bottom tertile	33.1	39.0	27.3	24.6	
Middle tertile	24.8	27.5	27.3	36.8	
Top tertile	42.2	33.4	45.5	38.6	
Ever repeated a grade (%)	25.8	40.5	13.6	19.3	**
Ever expelled (%)	6.7	20.2	9.1	7.0	**
Ever in special education (%)	25.8	47.2	27.3	47.4	***
Education aspirations (%)					n.s.
Some college	15.8	20.9	18.5	12.9	
College degree	49.9	55.8	43.4	49.3	
More than college degree	34.4	23.3	38.1	37.8	
FOSTER CARE HISTORY					
Number of foster care placements (mean)	5.2	6.4	5.6	4.9	n.s.
Number of school changes (mean)	2.7	2.8	2.8	2.8	n.s.
Ever in congregate care (%)	48.3	64.4	59.1	42.1	*
Years in care past age 18 (mean)	1.8	1.5	2.2	2.0	*
AGES					
Age completed high school (mean)	18.7	19.2	18.4	18.6	*
Age first enrolled in college (mean)	20.0	21.8	19.0	19.6	*

NOTE: $*p < .05$ $**p < .01$ $***p < .001$. Since some of the covariates had nontrivial proportions of missing data, group differences were tested using multiple imputation.

in these types of settings typically have higher rates of behavioral health problems than youth in family-like placements. There were also differences in the ages at which youth completed educational milestones. Toe-in-the-water students finished their secondary credential at least a half-year later than students in the other three groups (all $p < .05$). A particularly pronounced difference was in the age at which youth first entered college. Toe-in-the-water youth were about two to three years older than youth in the other three groups when they first enrolled (all $p < .001$). Finally, the Toe-in-the-water group spent about a half-year less in extended care than did the Buffet group and Boomerang group (both $p < .05$).

Nearly all of the group differences in baseline characteristics were found between the Toe-in-the-water group and the other groups. However, a handful of statistically significant differences were found between the other three groups. Buffet youth were more likely to have finished twelfth grade than tenth grade than Consistently enrolled youth ($p = .046$) and Boomerang youth ($p = .054$). Consistently enrolled youth were less likely than Boomerang youth to have been in special education ($p = .008$). Overall, there were no statistically significant differences between these three groups in educational aspirations, high school grade tertiles, maltreatment history, number of foster care moves, or school changes.

Group differences were also found in the life events and characteristics of youth groups in the years before entering college (pre-entry measures; see Table 4.4). Similar to the findings just discussed, most group differences were

Table 4.4
Pre-entry Characteristics, by College Enrollment Groups ($n = 331$)

Characteristic	Enrollment Group				
Pre-entry risk and promotive factors	Consistently enrolled	Toe in the water	Buffet	Boomerang	Sig.
Parental status (%)	24.7	32.3	22.7	15.8	*
Marital status (%)	3.4	5.0	4.5	1.8	n.s.
Employment (%)					*
Not employed	36.0	39.1	54.5	31.6	
Employed < 35 hrs/week	39.3	21.1	27.3	38.6	
Employed 35+ hrs/week	24.7	39.8	18.2	29.8	
Social support (mean)	3.98	3.89	3.78	3.97	n.s.
Delinquency score (mean)	0.31	0.37	0.36	0.27	n.s.
Mental health problem (%)	75.2	82.0	72.3	75.4	n.s.
Alcohol/substance use problem (%)	22.4	46.6	27.3	12.3	***
Economic hardship (mean)	1.03	1.73	0.09	0.60	***
Food insecurity (%)	19.1	37.9	0.0	19.3	***

NOTE: $*p < .05$ $**p < .01$ $***p < .001$.

present between Toe-in-the-water youth and the other groups. Although parenthood rates were higher in the Toe-in-the-water group than in the other groups, the only statistically significant difference was with the Boomerang group ($p = .020$). The Toe-in-the-water youth were also more likely to have had alcohol/substance use problems than Consistently enrolled youth and Boomerang youth (both $p < .001$), to have experienced more economic hardships than all three groups (all $p < .01$), and to be food insecure than the other three groups (all $p < .05$). In terms of pre-entry employment, the Toe-in-the-water group had a distinct bimodal distribution: most youth fell in the extremes of not working (39%) and working full-time (40%), while just 19% fell in the middle and worked part-time. Most of the significant group differences were present between the Toe-in-the-water youth and youth in the other groups and were related to this bimodal distribution.[6]

Recall that Toe-in-the-water youth were older than youth in the other three groups when they first entered college. It may be that some of the group differences in pre-entry characteristics are due to the age differences or differences in the amount of time in which these problems could have occurred. Youth in the Toe-in-the-water group had an extra two to three years before enrolling in college in which they could have gotten pregnant, experienced financial hardships, and so on. The pre-entry differences were therefore reexamined after statistically controlling for age differences. After doing so, differences in parental status, economic hardships, and food insecurity became smaller and were no longer statistically significant (all $p > .20$). However, the employment status and alcohol/substance use differences remained. Thus, some, but not all, of the differences in pre-entry characteristics are explained by the fact that the Toe-in-the-water group entered college at a significantly later age than the other groups.

Just as with their baseline characteristics, the Consistently enrolled, Boomerang, and Buffet groups did not significantly differ on most pre-entry characteristics. The only difference was that the Buffet group experienced fewer economic hardships than youth in the Consistently enrolled group ($p = .033$); this difference became nonsignificant after controlling for high school completion age and college entry age ($p = .120$).

Table 4.5 examines group differences in life circumstances and events after youth first enrolled in college (post-entry measures). Statistically significant differences were not found in most of the measures, although Consistently enrolled youth reported fewer financially trying experiences. The Consistently enrolled group experienced fewer economic hardships than did the Toe-in-the-water group ($p = .002$) and the Buffet group ($p = .027$), and a marginally significant difference was found with the Boomerang group ($p = .076$). Consistently enrolled youth were significantly less likely to have been food insecure than Toe-in-the-water youth ($p = .046$) and marginally significantly

Table 4.5
Post-entry Characteristics, by College Enrollment Groups ($n = 331$)

Characteristic	Enrollment Group				
Pre-entry risk and promotive factors	Consistently enrolled	Toe in the water	Buffet	Boomerang	Sig.
Parental status (%)	58.2	62.9	61.4	52.9	n.s.
Marital status (%)	16.4	24.2	23.4	18.6	n.s.
Employment (%)					*
Not employed	15.3	17.1	4.5	3.6	
Employed less than 35 hrs/week	23.5	16.4	22.7	9.0	
Employed 35+ hrs/week	61.2	66.4	72.7	87.3	
Social support (mean)	3.72	3.82	3.88	3.85	n.s.
Delinquency score (mean)	0.14	0.17	0.15	0.12	n.s.
Mental health problem (%)	67.1	76.4	77.3	74.5	n.s.
Alcohol/substance use problem (%)	41.2	52.9	63.6	49.1	n.s.
Economic hardship (mean)	2.48	3.38	3.59	3.13	**
Food insecurity (%)	47.1	60.7	63.6	61.8	*

NOTE: *$p < .05$ **$p < .01$.

less likely to have been food insecure than Boomerang youth ($p = .089$). The other post-entry differences pertained to employment status between Boomerang youth and other youth. Boomerang youth had the highest rate of full-time employment. More specifically, these young people were significantly more likely than Consistently enrolled youth to be employed full-time than to be unemployed or employed part-time (both $p < .05$). Boomerang youth were more likely than Toe-in-the-water youth to have been employed full-time than unemployed ($p = .016$).

Chapter Summary

This chapter examined enrollment trends in Midwest Study participants who enrolled in college. One key finding is that more than half dropped out after their first or second semester of college, so the first year is a critical point of intervention. The analysis of enrollment pathways identified four groups that differed in their engagement with postsecondary education, the types of colleges they attended, their completion rates, and a number of characteristics. The Toe-in-the-water group, in particular, faced considerable challenges and would likely need intensive support to promote their postsecondary success. This group had more academic difficulties (i.e., lower reading scores and was more likely to have repeated a grade and more likely to have been in special education) and more behavioral problems (i.e., more likely to have been expelled from school and to have ever been placed in congregate care) at age seventeen than did the other groups. Importantly, the Toe-in-the-water group entered college about two to three years later than the other groups. Consequently, these young people were more likely to be parents, to experience an alcohol or substance use problem, to be working full-time, and to encounter economic hardships and food insecurity when they first enrolled. Entering college at an older age can also be a disadvantage because supports designated specifically for foster care youth that are age-limited (e.g., extended care) are cut short or missed altogether. Indeed, about 48% of Toe-in-the-water youth first enrolled in college after they turned twenty-one. They were overwhelmingly enrolled in two-year colleges. This is also of concern because, to date, many of the campus support programs with robust services are housed in four-year colleges.

The remaining 51 percent of college entrants were split between the Consistently enrolled group (27%), the Boomerang group (17%), and the Buffet group (7%). Few statistically significant differences were found between these three groups. The Consistently enrolled group had more females, and there were a few group differences in post-entry characteristics. Consistently enrolled youth had fewer problems than the other groups with economic hardships and food insecurities, and a larger proportion of Boomerang group worked full-time than the other groups. The types of institutions that youth in these groups attended may also help explain some of the group differences. Overall, Consistently enrolled youth (21%) were twice as likely as Boomerang and Buffet youth (about 10% each) to have enrolled in selective institutions. However, these differences do not appear to be caused only by differences in the academic qualifications of the two groups. For example, if we parcel out youth in these groups who were at or above age level in reading proficiency (third and fourth reading proficiency quartiles), Consistently enrolled youth were still about twice as likely as Boomerang and Buffet youth to have attended selective colleges (32% vs. 17%). Attending schools with higher graduation rates and more resources, and that better match foster youths' academic qualifications, may partly explain why Consistently enrolled youth were able to spend more uninterrupted time in college and ultimately graduate compared to youth with interrupted enrollment patterns.

What is clear is that Consistently enrolled youth started college early and clocked a long stint of uninterrupted time. In contrast, youth in the other two groups either boomeranged in and out of the same college or skipped among several different colleges. The Boomerang group may be capturing the experiences of youth making dogged attempts to chip away at a college credential, interrupted by life circumstances such as the need to work. The Buffet group may include youth who try different schools after having a poor fit with a previous institution, who have unstable housing situations and relocate often, or who change their minds about their postsecondary goals. These are speculations, and more information is needed to get the full story. However, one may wonder whether supports could have been put in place that would have reduced some of the enrollment instability among Boomerang and Buffet youth, so that they could have made more progress toward earning a credential.

This chapter provided an in-depth look at enrollment characteristics of foster youth in college. The next three chapters take a closer look at factors that influence foster youths' likelihood of enrolling in college, persisting in college, and completing a degree.

5

Predictors of
College Enrollment

This chapter explores a wide range of factors related to the odds of enrollment. Of the three college outcomes evaluated in this book, college enrollment has been researched the most by empirical studies. Some studies are regional and focus on foster youth in a particular state or college (e.g., Barnow et al., 2015; Courtney & Hook, 2017; Okpych & Courtney, 2017; Okpych et al., 2017; White et al., 2018). Their strengths are their well-defined samples of foster youth and their investigation of a wide range of potential contributors, but their findings may not be representative of foster youth nationally.

Other studies are national in scope, analyzing data collected by NYTD or other education studies (e.g., Gross et al., 2019; Kim et al., 2019; Rosenberg & Kim, 2018; Watt et al., 2018). Although the National Youth in Transition Database (NYTD) includes a clearly defined population of foster youth, it collects information on relatively few potential predictors. This means that the many factors suspected to predict foster youths' odds of enrollment cannot be investigated because there are not measures of them in NYTD. In addition, most NYTD questions are simple yes–no questions that miss important nuance and details, and outcomes are only tracked up to age twenty-one. The response rates for NYTD have also been low, especially for the first cohort, which can provide inaccurate estimates of outcomes and predictors (National Data Archive on Child Abuse and Neglect, 2014, 2019).[1]

Other researchers have analyzed data from large postsecondary education studies that have some way to identify students with prior foster care involvement. Gross and colleagues (2019) analyzed data from two national education datasets: the National Postsecondary Student Aid Study 2016 (NPSAS:16), which is a nationally representative study of students attending postsecondary institutions in the United States, and the Freshman Survey (TFS), which is a nationally representative sample of first-time full-time freshmen enrolled in four-year colleges. A key limitation of the NPSAS:16 is that the FAFSA question used to identify foster youth also captures students who were never in foster care (e.g., students whose parents became deceased after age thirteen and those who are emancipated minors). There were also issues with how the researchers created the foster youth sample from the NPSAS:16 data, which likely resulted in an overrepresentation of academically successful foster youth.[2] The question used to identify former foster youth in the TFS (i.e., "At any time since you turned 13, were you in foster care or were you a dependent of the court?") is more precise than the one used in NPSAS:16. However, as the authors acknowledge, the study is limited to just the subset of former foster youth enrolled in four-year institutions on a full-time basis (Gross et al., 2019). Therefore, the TFS data do not capture the majority of foster youth who enroll in two-year colleges, as well as foster youth who enroll part-time or less than part-time in four-year colleges.

The existing literature on youth with care histories has identified several factors that contribute to the likelihood that foster youth will enroll in college. A fairly consistent finding is that females are more likely than males to enroll (Courtney & Hook, 2017; Gross et al., 2019; Kim et al., 2019; Watt et al., 2018; White et al., 2018)—although some studies did not find statistically significant gender differences (Okpych & Courtney, 2017; Okpych et al., 2017). Findings on the impact of race and ethnicity are also mixed. Some studies find that African American youth and Hispanic youth (Courtney & Hook, 2017; Kim et al., 2019; Watt et al., 2018) are more likely than White youth to enroll in college, whereas other studies report no statistically significant differences (Barnow et al., 2015; Okpych & Courtney, 2017; Okpych et al., 2017; White et al., 2018).

Perhaps the strongest and most consistent predictors of college enrollment are measures of foster youths' academic background and performance. Students who repeated a grade are less likely to enroll than their peers (Courtney & Hook, 2017; Okpych & Courtney, 2017; Okpych et al., 2017). Conversely, studies that assessed youths' reading level at age seventeen found that higher proficiency was predictive of increased odds of enrollment (Courtney & Hook, 2017; Okpych & Courtney, 2017; Okpych et al., 2017). One study also found that self-reported high school grades increased the odds of college enrollment, whereas ever being in a special education classroom decreased the odds of enrollment (Okpych & Courtney, 2017). Another consistent predictor is educational aspirations. Foster youth who aspire to earn a college degree are more likely than their peers with lower aspirations to go to college (Courtney & Hook, 2017; Okpych & Courtney, 2017; Okpych et al., 2017).

Some factors that have been suspected of hindering foster youths' chances of college enrollment have not been found to have a significant effect in empirical studies. Previous experiences with physical abuse, sexual abuse, and neglect were not significantly related to college enrollment (Kim et al., 2019; Okpych & Courtney, 2017; Okpych et al., 2017). That this relationship did not attain significance may be because most participants in studies of foster youth have experienced maltreatment, and the small amount of variation hides its impact. Mental health and alcohol and substance use problems have also not been found to be significantly related to college enrollment in studies of foster youth (Okpych & Courtney, 2017; Okpych et al., 2017; Rosenberg & Kim, 2018).

Findings on the roles of placement changes and school mobility on college enrollment for foster youth have been mixed. Some studies have found that greater placement instability decreases the odds of college enrollment (Okpych et al., 2017; Rosenberg & Kim, 2018), whereas other studies report no statistically significant association (Okpych & Courtney, 2017; White et al., 2018). School mobility has been found to hurt foster youths' chances of finishing high school (e.g., Clemens et al., 2016; Okpych et al.,, 2017), but its effects on college enrollment are less conclusive (Okpych & Courtney, 2017; Okpych et al., 2017; White et al., 2018).

Other various risk factors have been found to decrease foster youths' chances of enrolling. A fairly consistent finding is that becoming a parent at a young age lowers the probability of going to college (Courtney & Hook, 2017; Okpych & Courtney, 2017; Okpych et al., 2017). What is not clear from these studies is whether early parenthood affects males and females similarly or whether the impact is more deleterious for one gender. One study also found that youth with a history of incarceration were less likely to enroll in college than their peers (Rosenberg & Kim, 2018), although this factor was not significantly associated in other studies that controlled more extensively for academic background (Okpych & Courtney, 2017; Okpych et al., 2017). A few studies investigated the effect of youths' placement type on college enrollment. Two studies found that youth who resided in group homes were less likely than their peers in foster homes to enroll in college (Courtney & Hook, 2017; Rosenberg & Kim, 2018). A third study did not find a statistically significant difference between youth in group homes and foster homes, but it did find that youth in relative foster homes were more likely than youth in nonrelative foster homes to enroll (Okpych & Courtney, 2017). Findings about placement types must be interpreted with caution because they are correlated with other youth characteristics. For example, congregate care settings such as group homes tend to be reserved for youth with more severe behavioral health problems, and it may be these other characteristics that are causing the enrollment differences rather than the placement itself (Whittaker et al., 2014).

Several studies have also identified factors that promote college enrollment. One study using NYTD data found that receipt of education- and employment-related independent living services increased the odds of postsecondary enrollment, although this study did not control for background academic factors that could have confounded this association (Kim et al., 2019). Certain types of social support have also been found to promote college entry. An analysis of CalYOUTH Study participants found that the greater number of adults with college degrees whom youth nominated as people they could turn to for advice and guidance significantly increased youths' odds of enrollment by age twenty (Okpych & Courtney, 2017). The same study found that receiving encouragement from school personnel to pursue education beyond high school also increased the chances of enrolling in college.

My analyses that are presented next build on this body of work by examining predictors of enrollment by age twenty-one and by age twenty-nine/thirty. My study also advances the field by investigating enrollment in two-year and four-year colleges separately, as well as identifying factors that correlate with the timing of when youth enroll.

Description of the Sample, Measures, and Analyses

Sample

The analyses in this chapter include all 732 Midwest Study participants. The outcome of interest is whether participants enrolled in college. College enrollment is assessed at two ages: by age twenty-one and by age twenty-nine/thirty. Enrollment by age twenty-one is an important benchmark, both because students who enroll younger tend to have better chances of finishing college and age twenty-one was the foster care age limit in Illinois. Enrollment by the NSC data draw (age twenty-nine or thirty) is important because it captures enrollment of youth who got a late start in college. Of the 402 Midwest Study participants who enrolled in college, 287 (71.4%) had first enrolled by their twenty-first birthday, and the other 115 youths (28.6%) first enrolled after they turned twenty-one.

Measures of the Outcome and Predictors

The main outcome of interest is a binary measure of whether participants enrolled in a two- or four-year college (1 = yes, 0 = no). Additionally, a three-category version of enrollment is analyzed: no college, enrolled in a two-year college, and enrolled in a four-year college. This outcome is important because the same factors may play different roles in contributing to the chances of enrolling in two-year colleges versus four-year colleges. Finally, the last analysis of this chapter focuses on timing of enrollment. The binary measure and the three-category measure of enrollment do not distinguish between youth who first enrolled at age eighteen and a half and youth who first enrolled at age twenty. Thus, the final analysis evaluates how factors affect the rate at which foster youth enroll in college after age seventeen and a half.

The literature review in the first part of the chapter presented many sets of factors as potential contributors of enrollment: demographic characteristics of the youth, aspects of their academic background, foster care and maltreatment history characteristics, behavioral health, social support, and parental status, among others. All of these factors were measured at the baseline interview when youth were seventeen or eighteen years old.

Statistical Analyses

Three types of analyses are used in this chapter. The potential contributors are called "predictors" in regression analyses. *Logistic regression analysis*, which is used for binary outcomes, assesses the relationship between each predictor and the odds that youth enrolled in college. Although not shown, the first step was to examine each predictor one at a time (using what are called *bivariate* regression models) before running more complex regression models that include multiple predictors (*multivariable* regression models). This is an important first step, because if a factor is found to be predictive of college enrollment by itself, it is a good candidate to include in multivariable models. Multivariable logistic regression models examine several predictors at once, which is a huge strength of regression analysis. Including multiple predictors in the same regression model allows our estimates of the effect that each predictor has on the outcome to be adjusted to account for the influence of the other predictors in the model. Ultimately, the multivariable models increase the accuracy of our estimates of the associations between the predictors and the outcome. For a plain-spoken explanation of what multiple regression models do and why they are needed, see Appendix A at the end of the book.

The second type of analysis in this chapter is called *multinomial logistic regression*, which is designed to handle a three-category outcome like (1) not enrolled, (2) enrolled in two-year college, and (3) enrolled in four-year college. *Survival analysis* is the third type of analysis, which is used to analyze the timing of events. In this case, we are interested in seeing whether each predictor affects the *rate* at which youth enroll in college. For example, does having a child at an early age delay college enrollment? More information about multinomial logistic regression and survival analysis is presented later in the chapter.

Findings

Predictors of the Odds of College Enrollment

Results from the bivariate regression models pointed to several factors that were statistically significant predictors of the expected odds of enrollment. There were also multiple factors that did not significantly predict enrollment.[3] Because of space limitations, results of the bivariate models are not presented in this chapter.

One of the main decisions when building a multivariable regression model is which predictors to include. On the one hand, it is imperative to include factors that are important predictors of enrollment: those that were found to significantly predict enrollment in the bivariate models and factors that are substantively important, regardless of their statistical significance (e.g., youth demographic characteristics). It is also important, on the other hand, to avoid overloading the regression model with unnecessary predictors. Having too many predictors can compromise the model's ability to detect statistically significant findings (i.e., inadequate statistical power) and can also lead to quirky results that are based on peculiarities of the sample (i.e., overfitting). Thus, a good regression model is a parsimonious model—one that includes relevant predictors without overdoing it. Factors that had marginally statistically significant ($p < .10$) associations with the odds of enrollment either at age twenty-one or twenty-nine/thirty in the bivariate models were included in the multivariable regression model. The factors that were not significantly associated ($p \geq .10$) with the outcome were omitted from the multivariable model.[4] A few exceptions were made for youth demographic characteristics, which were substantively important to include in the regression models.

Another statistical consideration when selecting predictors has to do with *multicollinearity*. When two or more predictors are strongly correlated with one other, including both in a multivariable model can lead to surprising, counterintuitive, and even misleading results. Thus, in the multivariable regression models, care was taken to avoid the pitfalls of multicollinearity. Specifically, variables with moderate or strong correlations were examined in separate multivariable regression models. This was the case for a few sets of predictors. First, highest grade completed at the time of the baseline interview was correlated with a history of grade repetition (corr = -.41). Grade repetition was included in the model in Table 5.1, but results from a supplemental regression analysis that swapped the variable, highest completed grade, for grade repetition are summarized in text. Second, a few variables tapped underlying behavioral problems: school expulsion, placement in group care, delinquency score, and alcohol/substance use problems. In the final model, delinquency and alcohol/substance were included in the multivariable regression model in Table 5.1, and school expulsion and congregate care were omitted.[5] Results of supplemental

Table 5.1

Multivariable Logistic Regression Results: Baseline Predictors of College Entry by Age 21 and by Age 29/30 (n = 732)

	Enrollment by Age 21		Enrollment by Age 29/30	
	OR	p	OR	p
DEMOGRAPHIC CHARACTERISTICS				
Male (ref: female)	0.70*	.049	0.65**	.012
Race/ethnicity (ref: White)				
African American	0.80	.337	1.08	.741
Hispanic	0.92	.798	1.13	.702
Other race	1.04	.905	1.36	.382
Age at baseline interview	0.55*	.035	0.74	.277
State (ref: Illinois)				
Wisconsin	0.38***	<.001	0.83	.427
Iowa	.031**	.001	0.80	.508
ACADEMIC HISTORY				
Reading level, standardized	1.47***	<.001	1.60***	<.001
High school math and English GPA from most recent marking period	1.28**	.020	1.16	.149
Aspirations (ref: H.S. or less)				
Some college	2.23*	.033	1.47	.241
College degree or more	2.53**	.004	2.65***	<.001
Ever repeated a grade	0.53***	<.001	0.64*	.010
Ever in special education	0.99	.979	1.03	.896
Number of college prep. activities (0–4)	1.09	.242	1.14^	.070
FOSTER CARE HISTORY				
Number of foster care placements (0–40)	0.98	.319	1.01	.573
RISK AND PROMOTIVE FACTORS				
Ever worked for pay	1.82**	.004	1.66**	.008
Delinquency score (0–3)	0.75^	.086	0.76^	.082
Alcohol/substance use problem	0.56**	.009	0.55**	.004

NOTE: $^p < .10$ $^*p < .05$ $^{**}p < .01$ $^{***}p < .001$.

regression analyses are summarized in the text of this chapter, but the full results do not appear in a table.

Table 5.1 displays results of the multivariable regression models investigating enrollment by age twenty-one (middle column) and enrollment by age twenty-nine/thirty (right column). As a reminder, if you are not familiar with ORs, please go Appendix B for a plainspoken guide to interpreting ORs. The results are presented as odds ratios (OR).[6] Here is a brief explanation for reading odds ratios: 1.0 is the center point, ORs greater than 1.0 mean that the predictor *increases* the odds of enrollment, and ORs that are less than 1.0 means that the predictor *decreases* the odds of enrollment. It is important to consider whether each predictor's OR is statistically significant. The level of statistical significance is indicated by the presence of asterisks next to the OR. For a user-friendly explanation of interpreting statistical significance, see Appendix A at the end of the book.

After adjusting for the other predictors in the model, males are significantly less likely than females to enroll in college. The odds of college enrollment are about 31 percent less for males than females after controlling for differences in race/ethnicity, state where the youth was in foster care, reading level, and the other predictors. Differences between states in the odds of enrollment are also present, with youth in Wisconsin and Iowa being less likely than youth in Illinois to enroll in college by age twenty-one. No statistically significant state differences were found for enrollment by age twenty-nine/thirty. Some of the academic history measures are also predictive of enrollment in the multivariable model. Youths' reading level and college aspirations both increased the odds of enrollment by age twenty-one. There was a marginally statistically significant association between GPA and enrollment by age twenty-one (top tertile vs. bottom tertile), but this was not significant for enrollment by age twenty-nine/thirty. The high school grades measure may not have been a strong predictor because it only included information from youths' English and math grades in their most recent high school marking period, rather than their cumulative high school GPA. Additionally, self-reported grades are less reliable then grades taken from administrative records (Kuncel et al., 2005).

Youth who had ever repeated a grade were less likely to go to college than their peers. Although special education was strongly and negatively associated with college entry by age twenty-one in the bivariate model ($OR = .55, p < .001$), it was not significant after controlling for demographic characteristics and other academic history characteristics ($p = .983$). This is due largely to the fact that youth in special education had markedly lower reading scores than youth who had never been in special education (-1.16 vs. -.48). After controlling for these differences, special education was not a significant contributor. Finally, there was a marginally significant association between participation in college preparatory activities and the likelihood of going to college by age twenty-nine/thirty ($p = .052$): taking part in more types of activities increased the predicted odds of entering college.

In terms of youths' foster care history, the number of foster care placements was not significantly associated with enrollment after accounting for other characteristics of the youth. Ever working for pay increased the odds of enrollment by age twenty-one and age twenty-nine/thirty, whereas having an alcohol or substance use problem decreased the odds of enrollment at both ages. The score that captured youths' engagement in delinquent behavior was not significantly associated with the odds of enrollment.

The predictors omitted from the regression models due to collinearity were examined in separate regression models (not shown in the table). After removing grade repetition, the highest grade that youth completed by Wave 1 was significantly associated with college enrollment. Relative to youth who had completed tenth grade or lower at baseline, youth who had completed eleventh grade ($OR = 2.16$, $p < .001$) and youth who had completed twelfth grade ($OR = 2.18$, $p = .012$) were significantly more likely to enter college by age twenty-one. When examining enrollment by age twenty-nine/thirty, completing eleventh grade ($OR = 2.00$, $p < .001$) and completing twelfth grade ($OR = 2.29$, $p = .008$) were also significant predictors. Taken together with the results of grade repetition, foster youth who were academically behind in late adolescence were less likely to go to college than youth who were not behind.

After removing the delinquency score and alcohol/substance use problems from the model, youth who had ever been placed in congregate care had significantly lower expected odds of enrolling in college by age twenty-one ($OR = .56$, $p = .002$) and by age twenty-nine/thirty ($OR = 0.68$, $p = .042$). History of school expulsion was another statistically significant predictor of enrollment by age twenty-one ($OR = 0.56$, $p = .020$) after omitting delinquency and alcohol/substance use problems; it was marginally statistically significant when predicting enrollment by age twenty-nine/thirty ($OR = 0.67$, $p = .084$). Taken together, these variables suggest that foster youth with behavioral issues and substance use problems were less likely than their peers to go to college.

Examining Predictors of Two-Year and Four-Year Enrollment

Multinomial logistic regression is used for outcomes with three or more categories. In the model in Table 5.2, "enrollment in two-year college" and "enrollment in four-year college" are each compared to the reference outcome of "no college." The coefficients in multinomial logistic regression models are called relative risk ratios (RRRs). Similar to ORs, a $RRR > 1.0$ means that a predictor increases the likelihood of the outcome occurring and a $RRR < 1.0$ means that a predictor decreases the likelihood of the outcome occurring.

Table 5.2 displays the results of the multinomial logistic regression model, which contains the same predictors as in Table 5.1. The far-left column lists the predictors, followed by results from a multinomial regression model that predicts enrollment by age twenty-one and then by results from a second multinomial model that predicts enrollment by age twenty-nine/thirty. Note that each regression model has two outcomes: enrollment in a two-year college (vs. no college) and enrollment in a four-year college (vs. no college).

One helpful way to analyze these results is to compare enrollment into two-year versus enrollment into four-year colleges (within each enrollment age). One interesting finding is that the gender difference observed in the earlier models is only present for two-year enrollment. Females are significantly more

Table 5.2

Multinomial Logistic Regression Results: Baseline Predictors of Entry into Different Types of College ($n = 732$)

	Enrollment by Age 21				Enrollment by Age 29/30			
	Two-year college enrollment		Four-year college enrollment		Two-year college enrollment		Four-year college enrollment	
	RRR	p	RRR	p	RRR	p	RRR	p
DEMOGRAPHIC CHARACTERISTICS								
Male (ref: female)	0.61*	.010	1.27	.433	0.58**	.003	1.01	.971
Race/ethnicity (ref: White)								
African American	0.81	.388	0.77	.512	1.00	.985	1.47	.278
Hispanic	0.85	.663	1.28	.672	0.91	.800	2.40^	.067
Other race	0.99	.994	1.32	.667	1.18	.648	2.31	.115
Age at baseline interview	0.50*	.019	0.87	.786	0.62	.095	1.46	.374
State (ref: Illinois)								
Wisconsin	0.35***	<.001	0.55	.196	0.68	.125	1.67	.149
Iowa	0.33**	.003	0.20*	.029	0.84	.601	0.49	.269
ACADEMIC HISTORY								
Reading level, standardized	1.40***	<.001	1.78**	.001	1.50***	<.001	1.98***	<.001
H.S. math and English GPA, most recent marking period	1.20^	.095	1.64*	.010	1.09	.442	1.49*	.013

(continued)

Table 5.2 (continued)

| | Enrollment by Age 21 | | | | Enrollment by Age 29/30 | | | |
| | Two-year college enrollment | | Four-year college enrollment | | Two-year college enrollment | | Four-year college enrollment | |
	RRR	p	RRR	p	RRR	p	RRR	p
Aspirations (ref: H.S. or less)								
Some college	2.32*	.031	1.53	.644	1.53	.217	1.11	.884
College degree or more	2.31*	.012	3.46	.105	2.41**	.002	3.65*	.020
Ever repeated a grade	0.64*	.021	0.18***	<.001	0.70*	.047	0.46**	.009
Ever in special education	1.22	.336	0.38*	.017	1.22	.332	0.53*	.048
Number of college prep. activities (0–4)	1.10	.209	1.04	.756	1.13^	.097	1.17	.130
FOSTER CARE HISTORY								
Number of foster care placements (0–40)	0.98	.402	0.98	.555	1.01	.569	1.01	.714
RISK AND PROMOTIVE FACTORS								
Ever worked for pay	1.77**	.009	2.18^	.071	1.70**	.008	1.55	.172
Delinquency score (0–3)	0.81	.215	0.62	.132	0.81	.188	0.65^	.094
Alcohol/substance use problem	0.58*	.020	0.50	.112	0.61*	.021	0.39*	.010

NOTE: $^\wedge p < .10$ $^* p < .05$ $^{**} p < .01$ $^{***} p < .001$.

likely than males to enroll in two-year colleges, but no significant difference exists for enrollment into four-year colleges. This is true both by age twenty-one and by age twenty-nine/thirty. Another interesting finding pertains to measures of academic proficiency/performance. Although reading scores are predictive of enrollment into two-year colleges, the associations are stronger when predicting entry into four-year colleges. For instance, for enrollment by age twenty-one, each standard deviation increase in reading score increases the relative risk of enrollment by 40 percent for two-year colleges. The relative risk increases by nearly 80 percent for four-year colleges. Youth in the top third of GPA are significantly more likely than youth in the bottom third of GPA to enroll in four-year colleges than not to enroll, but no significant association is found between GPA tertiles and enrollment into two-year colleges.

Two indicators of academic difficulty also appear to have stronger effects when predicting enrollment into four-year colleges than for two-year colleges. Although grade repetition decreases the chances that youth enroll in two-year colleges (vs. no college), the associations are stronger when predicting four-year enrollment (vs. no enrollment). Ever being in a special education classroom is associated with a decrease in the risk of enrolling in a four-year college but not a two-year college.

Finally, in terms of educational aspirations, desiring to earn a four-year degree (vs. no college) is the only distinction that significantly predicts enrollment into four-year colleges. Youth who aspire to complete some college are not significantly more likely than youth who aspire to just finish high school to enroll in a four-year college. In contrast, for enrollment by age twenty-one, youth who aspire to complete some college or earn a college degree are both more likely to enroll in a two-year college than youth who aspire to complete high school or less. Thus, young people who are not dead-set on finishing a degree (i.e., just interested in "some college") may use a two-year school to explore their options and sort out their educational and career plans.

Survival Analysis: Predicting the Rate of College Enrollment

The analysis in this section examines rate of college enrollment; that is, whether predictors are associated with how soon youth enroll in college after age seventeen and a half years. Thus, these analyses put the element of time front and center. A Cox proportional hazard model is used to assess the role that predictors have on the rate of college entry (Rothman et al., 2008). The Cox model is a type of regression analysis designed to assess the association between predictors and the rate at which an outcome occurs.

Midwest Study participants are "at risk" of enrolling if they have not yet enrolled at a given time. In this analysis, the clock starts on the day each youth turned 17.5 years old, and the days are counted until they either enroll in college or reach the last day that their enrollment is tracked.[7] This information is then used to create a rate of college enrollment (i.e., how fast youth enrolled after age 17.5) and to assess the influence that predictors have on the rate.[8] Some factors may delay college enrollment, other factors may speed it up, and still others may be unrelated to the rate of enrollment.

The specific measure of time estimated in Cox models is called the *hazard rate*, which is the instantaneous likelihood of entering college at a given time among youth who have not yet enrolled. To ease the interpretation of the Cox model results, the coefficients for the predictors are expressed as *hazard ratios* (HRs). This is the ratio hazards of two groups (e.g., males vs. females) or of a one-unit change in a predictor (e.g., receipt of one college preparatory activity vs. no activities). As with ORs, when interpreting HRs, 1.0 is the middle point, HRs above 1.0 indicate that the predictor increases the rate of college enrollment, and HRs below 1.0 and approaching zero indicate that the predictor decreases the rate of enrollment. Thus, an HR of 1.5 indicates that the predictor speeds up enrollment, whereas an HR of 0.7 indicates that the predictor delays enrollment. As before, we consider HRs in conjunction with their level of statistical significance.

In the analyses in the previous section, we assessed the odds of enrolling in college by age twenty-one and by age twenty-nine/thirty. Ideally, we would do the same here and look at the rate of enrollment at both of these ages. However, one of the key assumptions of the Cox model is violated in models that assessed enrollment up to age twenty-nine/thirty.[9] Therefore, the Cox analysis only assesses factors that influence the rate of college enrollment by age twenty-one.[10] As stated earlier, age twenty-one is a meaningful outcome, both because enrollment at an earlier age is associated with better chances of finishing college and because key foster care supports end at age twenty-one in many states.

Table 5.3 presents results from the survival model. Similar to the steps taken in the logistic regression models, bivariate associations were first examined to identify significant predictors ($p < .10$), which informed creation of the multi-variable model. Predictors examined in the survival models include those measured during the first Midwest Study interview, as well as factors assessed at multiple interview waves. These latter predictors could change over time. For example, a youth could be not working at age seventeen but be working full-time at age nineteen and twenty-one. These time-varying predictors are shown at the bottom of Table 5.3.

After controlling for the other predictors in the model, males were found to enroll in college at a slower rate than females. The rate of college enrollment was also slower for youth in Wisconsin and Iowa than in Illinois. In terms of academic background, reading at a higher level, having higher grades, and aspiring to go to college were each associated with an increased rate of college enrollment. Conversely, youth who were in more foster care placements enrolled in college at a significantly slower rate than did youth in fewer placements. The

Table 5.3

Multivariable Cox Proportional Hazard Model Results: Baseline and Time-Varying Predictors of Rate of College Enrollment by Age 21 ($n = 732$)

	Enrollment by Age 21	
	HR	p
DEMOGRAPHIC CHARACTERISTICS (AGE 17)		
Male (ref: female)	0.65**	.001
Race/ethnicity (ref: White)		
African American	0.96	.818
Hispanic	1.09	.724
Other race	0.96	.879
Age at baseline interview	0.68^	.063
State (ref: Illinois)		
Wisconsin	0.49***	<.001
Iowa	0.40**	.001
ACADEMIC HISTORY (AGE 17)		
Reading level, standardized	1.38***	<.001
H.S. math and English GPA, most recent marking period	1.34***	<.001
Aspirations (ref: H.S. or less)		
Some college	2.13*	.015
College degree or more	2.30**	.002
Number of college prep. activities (0–4)	1.05	.315
FOSTER CARE HISTORY (AGE 17)		
Number of foster care placements (0–40)	.097*	.022
RISK AND PROMOTIVE FACTORS (CHANGE OVER TIME)		
Parental status	0.46***	<.001
Number of hours employed (ref: not employed)		
1–19 hrs./week	0.96	.868
20–34 hrs./week	1.26	.168
35+ hrs./week	1.07	.734
Delinquency score (0–3)	0.76	.131
Alcohol/substance use problem	0.81	.318

NOTE: $^{\wedge}p < .10$ $^*p < .05$ $^{**}p < .01$ $^{***}p < .001$.

only risk or promotive factor that was significantly associated with enrollment rate is youth's parental status. Youth who had a child were significantly delayed in enrolling in college compared to their peers without a child. Gender differences were not found in the association between parental status and rate of enrollment.[11] The parental status variable in Table 5.3 includes students with children, whether or not the student was living with their children. Although not displayed in the table, results were similar for a parental status variable that only counted students who lived with all of their children ($HR = 0.46, p < .001$).

Two predictors were assessed in separate survival models after excluding variables due to collinearity. After omitting youths' delinquency score, school expulsion was found to significantly decrease the rate of enrollment by age twenty-one ($HR = 0.52$, $p = .001$). Similarly, after the delinquency score was removed, youth who had been in a congregate care setting enrolled at a slower rate than did youth who had never been in one of these placements ($HR = 0.62$, $p = .001$).

Chapter Summary

This chapter explored predictors of college enrollment from two angles. First, logistic regression models explored the odds that youth enrolled in college by age twenty-one and by age twenty-nine/thirty. Each of these analyses were indifferent to the age at which youth enrolled. Second, survival analysis explored how different predictors affect the rate of college enrollment by age twenty-one. In these analyses, timing of enrollment was of central importance.

One of the most consistent findings across analyses is the role of youths' academic standing and background. For example, youth with higher reading scores and higher grades were more likely than other youth to enroll in college, and they enrolled at a faster rate. Conversely, signs of academic difficulty or trouble (e.g., grade repetition) decreased the odds of enrollment and the rate of enrollment. The amount of education that youth aspired to complete also predicted their odds and rate of enrollment. The associations with academic factors held after taking into account youths' behavioral health problems, aspects of their foster care history, and other risk and promotive factors. These are not earth-shattering findings; youth who have been doing well in school tend to advance to college. However, what these findings underscore is the primacy of academic achievement in secondary school. We need to make sure that youth who are doing well in school continue to do well (e.g., they do not experience unneeded disruptions while in care) and to intervene as best as possible with youth who show signs of struggle. The channel carved in secondary schools becomes the pipeline to higher education.

The results about parenting youth told an interesting story. The logistic regression analyses did not find that youth who were parents at the time of their first Midwest Study interview (age seventeen) had lower odds of attending college than their peers who were not parents. By age twenty-one, 35.3 percent of the young parents had enrolled in college, which was not significantly lower than the percentage of those who were not young parents (39.8%). Similarly, the enrollment percentages at age twenty-nine/thirty did not significantly differ for participants who had a child by age seventeen and their peers (52.0% vs. 55.4%). However, results from the survival analysis shed a different light. Recall that this analysis took a moving picture of youths' parental status. If youth became a parent after their first Midwest Study interview, these births counted in assessing the outcome. These results found that being or becoming a parent significantly decreased the rate of college enrollment. Putting the findings together, youth who became parents at an early age eventually enrolled in college at percentages similar to other foster youth, but becoming a parent delayed going to college. This is important because timing matters. Starting college at age eighteen versus age twenty can make a world of difference for foster youth, particularly if they are in a state with extended foster care.

Survival analysis also allowed us to make sense of temporal processes pertaining to the state in which the foster youth was placed. We found that youth in Wisconsin and Iowa were less likely than youth in Illinois to enroll in college by age twenty-one, but state differences were not present by age twenty-nine/thirty. This is because youth in Illinois entered college at significantly higher rates in their late teens and early twenties than did youth in the other states. This was evident in the results of the survival analyses. However, in the long run, youth in Iowa and Wisconsin eventually caught up to Illinois youth. We come back to this point in the chapter on extended foster care.

Gender differences also emerged, with males having lower chances and lower rates of college entry than females. Results from the multinomial logistic regression analyses added important nuance to these findings. The gender differences in the odds of enrollment were only present for two-year colleges; males and females did not significantly differ in their odds of enrolling in four-year colleges. However, because two-year colleges are the most common entryway into higher education for foster youth, the importance of the gender differences should not be overlooked. Results of the multinomial models also found that several significant predictors identified earlier predicted entry into both two-year and four-year colleges (vs. no college), but the associations tended to be stronger for enrollment into four-year colleges.

This chapter points to strong contributions of gender, academic factors, and other youth characteristics in the likelihood of going to college. Do these predictors continue to exert influence after youth enter college? In the next chapter we examine factors associated with the odds of persisting through the first few semesters.

6

Predictors of College Persistence

Although getting into college is the first step to the dream of graduating, it is only the beginning. This chapter investigates factors that contribute to foster youths' chances of making it through the first year and into the second year.

Previous Research on Predictors of College Persistence for Foster Youth

Compared to college enrollment, fewer studies examine college persistence for foster youth. A few studies in California report persistence rates of foster youth in two-year colleges. One study reported that about 54 percent of youth made it to their second term versus 67 percent of other two-year students (John Burton Advocates for Youth, 2017), and another study found that about 41 percent of students persisted into their second year of college versus 62 percent of other two-year students (Frerer et al., 2013). A third study in California included a sample of foster youth who were enrolled in both two- and four-year colleges and reported that about half (49.6%) made it through their first two semesters (Courtney, Okpych, & Park, 2018). A study by Day and colleagues (2011) included foster youth enrolled in a single public four-year university in the Midwest. Foster youth were found to persist through the first year at a lower rate than low-income first-generation students at the same school (79% vs. 87%; Day et al., 2011).

Persistence rates reported earlier in this book are consistent with those reported in the three California studies: about 47 percent of Midwest Study college entrants persisted through the first two semesters in college. Taken together, the results of these studies suggest that less than half of foster youth who enroll in college make it through their first year, although this rate is likely higher if we consider just foster youth in four-year institutions. Substantially less research has investigated factors that influence the likelihood of persistence for college students with care histories.[1] This chapter presents my analyses that identify those factors that increase or decrease the expected odds of persistence.

Description of the Sample, Measures, and Analyses

Sample, Outcome, and Predictors

The sample for this chapter includes 331 youths who appeared in NSC records. The NSC data provide semester-by-semester enrollment information needed to create a measure of persistence. Persistence is operationalized as remaining enrolled either full-time or part-time for the first three consecutive semesters after enrolling in college (not counting summer semesters); in other words, a student made it through the first year of college and the first semester of the second year.

The predictors examined in this chapter include some of the background characteristics examined in the previous chapter, as well as a set of "pre-entry" factors that were created from the interview waves conducted before a youth first enrolled in college. The pre-entry factors include educational aspirations, job status, mental health problems, social support, and parental status. Another set of predictors capture information on the types of colleges in which youth first enrolled. The institutional characteristics provide information on the college itself, characteristics of the student body, and the college's expenditures in various areas.

Statistical Analyses

Binary logistic regression analyses were first used to investigate potential predictors of persistence. These findings informed the selection of variables for the multivariable logistic regression model, which examines the associations between each factors and persistence after statistically controlling for the other predictors in the model. Finally, as a robustness check, a probit model with sample selection was run to assess whether findings remained consistent after addressing a potential problem with the multivariable logistic model. Findings from the robustness check are summarized in the Technical Appendix at the end of this chapter.

Findings

Examining Potential Predictors of Persistence

Recall that just under one-third (30.2%) of foster youth completed their first three consecutive, non-summer semesters of college. The bivariate analyses identified several characteristics of the youth, their situation before enrolling in college, and the institution they attended that were significantly associated with their odds of persisting through three consecutive semesters. Predictors that were not marginally significantly related ($p \geq .10$) to persistence in in the bivariate models were excluded from the multivariable model.[2] The remaining predictors were measures of participants' gender, age at baseline, and state where the youth was in foster care.

As discussed in the previous chapter, a critical limitation of the bivariate analyses is that other predictors can influence the estimated relationship between a predictor and persistence. Failing to adjust for these related predictors can yield an inaccurate estimate of their relationship to persistence. For example, attending four-year selective colleges was found to increase the odds of persistence in a bivariate model. However, youth who are admitted to these colleges probably also have stronger academic backgrounds. To get a more accurate measure of the association between college selectivity and the odds of enrollment, it would therefore be important to statistically control for aspects of youths' academic backgrounds. As with the previous chapter, care was taken to avoid collinearity among predictors, which could lead to distorted results if highly correlated predictors were included in the model all at once. Consequently, the multivariable regression model in Table 6.1 included grade repetition (and omitted the highest completed grade), pre-entry delinquency and pre-entry alcohol/substance use problems (and omitted school expulsion and congregate care placement), pre-entry economic hardships (and omitted pre-entry food insecurity), and college selectivity (and omitted % part-time students and expenditures on academic support services). The predictors omitted from the model in Table 6.1 were investigated in separate models, which are summarized in this chapter.

Results of the multivariable logistic regression analyses are displayed in Table 6.1. The estimated ORs and significance levels (indicated by asterisks) are displayed in the middle column, and the p-values are displayed in the right column. After controlling for the other predictors in the model, a statistically significant difference was found by ethnicity. The odds of persistence for Hispanic youth is about 77 percent lower than the odds of persistence for White youth. Although not shown in this model, Hispanic youth were also significantly less likely than African American youth to persist ($OR = 0.26, p = .040$). There was also a marginally significant ($p < .10$) association between youth in the other race category versus White youth, with the odds of persistence being

Table 6.1

Multivariable Logistic Regression Results: Predictors of Persistence ($n = 331$)

	OR	p
DEMOGRAPHIC CHARACTERISTICS		
Male (ref: female)	0.85	.607
Race/ethnicity (ref: White)		
African American	0.86	.687
Hispanic	0.23*	.024
Other race	0.26^	.075
Age at baseline interview	2.25^	.087
State (ref: Illinois)		
Wisconsin	1.19	.685
Iowa	1.52	.472
Age first enrolled in college (ref: under age 19)		
19 to 20	0.65	.247
21 or older	0.35^	.069
ACADEMIC AND FOSTER CARE HISTORY		
Reading level, standardized	1.35^	.061
High school math and English GPA from most recent marking period	1.16	.402
Ever repeated a grade	0.77	.452
Ever in special education	0.70	.291
Number foster care placements (1–40)	0.97	.434
Ever in congregate care	0.63	.145
PRE-ENTRY FACTORS		
Employment (ref: did not work)		
1–19 hrs./week	10.1***	<.001
20–34 hrs./week	2.23*	.039
35+ hrs./week	2.59*	.043
Delinquency score (0–3)	0.81	.551
Alcohol/substance use problem	0.70	.370
Economic hardships (0–6)	1.01	.979
INSTITUTIONAL CHARACTERISTICS		
Type/selectivity(ref: 2-year college)		
Non-/minimally selective four-year	0.54	.163
Selective/highly selective four-year	1.74	.167

NOTE: ^$p < .10$ *$p < .05$ ***$p < .001$.

lower for the former group. We also see that foster youth who first enrolled in college after the age of 21 were marginally significantly less likely to persist than youth who first enrolled in college before the age of 19. Youth who enter college at later ages tended to have lower baseline reading scores and higher prevalence rates of grade repetition and special education. However, even after controlling for these differences, the persistence gap by age of first enrollment still remained.

In terms of academic background, reading proficiency was the only predictor associated with the expected odds of persistence, and the relationship was marginally significant. Each standard deviation increase in reading proficiency is expected to increase the odds of persisting by about 35 percent.

The only pre-entry factor that was significantly related to persistence was youths' employment. Overall, having employment experience before enrolling in college increased youths' expected odds of persisting in college. The associations were strongest for youth who had worked less than 20 hours per week, with the odds of persistence for these youth being about 10 times the odds of persistence for youth with no work experience. Although pre-entry delinquency scores, alcohol/substance use problems, and economic hardships were significant predictors of persistence in the bivariate regression models, they were not found to be significantly associated with persistence after accounting for other predictors. Higher pre-entry delinquency scores were positively correlated with alcohol/substance use problems and the number of foster care placements, and accounting for these two factors reduced the magnitude of delinquency. The reduction in the OR for alcohol/substance use problems is attributable largely to enrollment age and economic hardships. Older youth and youth who had experienced more economic hardships were more likely to have had an alcohol or substance use problem before entering college, and because all these factors were negatively correlated with persistence, including all three in the model weakened the predictive relationship between alcohol/substance use problems and persistence. Relatedly, the weakening of the relationship between economic hardships and persistence is accounted for by the age of first enrollment and alcohol/substance use problems.

The type and selectivity of the college youth attended were also found to be associated with youths' odds of persistence. A statistically significant difference was not found between youth in selective four-year colleges and two-year colleges. However, the expected odds of persistence was significantly greater for students who enrolled in selective four-year colleges than for students in less selective four-year colleges (OR = 3.25, p = .029). Relative to the bivariate estimate, the OR for college type/selectivity was reduced due to associations with several covariates that were controlled for in the model. Youth who entered selective and highly selective institutions were typically younger, fared better academically (i.e., had higher reading scores and lower rates of repetition and special education), engaged in fewer delinquent behaviors before entering college, and were less likely to have had an alcohol or substance use problems before college. After accounting for these differences the odds ratios for college type/selectivity became smaller and nonsignificant.

Supplemental analyses were conducted to investigate each of the predictors omitted from Table 6.1 due to collinearity: highest completed grade, school expulsion, pre-entry food insecurity, percent part-time students, and expenditures on academic support services. Each of these predictors were assessed by rerunning the logistic regression model in Table 6.1 and omitting the collinear predictor that was originally included in the model. No statistically significant ($p < .05$) results were found for any of the omitted predictors.

As an additional supplemental analysis, an interaction term of gender and pre-entry parental status was added to the model in Table 6.1. Recall that pre-entry parental status was not significantly associated with the expected odds of persistence in the bivariate model; this was also the case when pre-entry parental status was added to the model in Table 6.1 (OR = 1.26, $p = .588$). However, when pre-entry parental status and the interaction term (male × pre-entry parental status) were added to the model, there was a statistically significant interaction between gender and pre-entry parental status (OR = .06, $p = .021$).[3] These findings suggest that being a parent before entering college had a significantly worse effect on the odds of persistence for males than for females. In fact, the OR for pre-entry parental status, which reports the estimated odds ratio for just females when the interaction term is present, is positive but nonsignificant.[4]

From an analytic standpoint, one concern about the findings reported in Table 6.1 is that the results may be biased if a selection effect were at play. For interested readers, the Technical Appendix explains selection and summarizes the analytic steps taken to check whether selection influenced the findings. The results of these supplemental analyses did not suggest that a selection effect unduly influenced the results in Table 6.1.

Chapter Summary

This chapter investigated predictors of persistence among the 331 Midwest Study participants who enrolled in college and for whom there was NSC data. There were some demographic differences in the expected odds of persistence. After adjusting for a wide range of youth characteristics, pre-entry factors, and the selectivity of the college in which youth enrolled, Hispanic youth had lower odds of persistence than White youth and African American youth. Other earlier studies examining college persistence and completion among foster youth did not report differences by race and ethnicity (Day et al. 2013; Day et al., 2011; Salazar, 2012), although in the broader student population, Hispanic college students persist at lower rates than do White youth (for review, see Crisp et al., 2015). Research points to several factors that may be driving this difference, such as sociocultural characteristics, racial/ethnic beliefs and coping styles, perceptions of campus climate, and interactions with supportive individuals

(Crisp et al., 2015). These and other factors may be at play among Hispanic youth in this sample, but a degree of caution is in order because of the small number of Hispanic youth in the sample analyzed in this chapter ($n = 30$).

Youth who were reading at a higher level were more likely to persist (a marginally significant difference). Although youth who entered college after age twenty-one were more likely than youth who entered college before age nineteen to have had early educational difficulties (e.g., grade repetition, special education, lower reading scores), even after controlling for these and other factors, youth who entered college later still faced a disadvantage in persistence. It is important to keep in mind, however, that although youth who entered college early fared better than their peers who entered later, the persistence rates of even the most favorable age group are still quite low. Among youth who entered college before turning nineteen years old, less than half made it through their first three semesters in college (43.9%).

Most of the pre-entry characteristics did not predict youths' likelihood of persisting after adjusting for other factors. The exception was pre-college employment, with youth who had work experience being significantly more likely to persist than youth who had never worked. Work may be capturing unmeasured skills and attributes that are also associated with persistence (e.g., ability to budget time, balance work and other responsibilities, and complete tasks even when one does not feel like it), it may have given youth an opportunity to develop these skills and attributes, or both may be at work. There may also be other benefits of pre-entry employment. Practically, work may have allowed youth to save money for college expenses or set them up with a job that they could continue after enrolling in college. Early employment may also give youth a dose of reality. For example, working long hours at low pay can give youth perspective about the value of a college degree.

Overall, pre-entry parental status was not significantly associated with the expected odds of persistence. However, a statistically significant interaction effect was found between gender and pre-entry parental status: entering college as a parent was significantly worse for males than for females in terms of their expected odds of persistence. In the Midwest Study, males were far less likely than females to reside with their children. Male parents may have had to pay child support (either formally or informally), which could have been a barrier to remaining in school. Having a child to provide for may have also created greater incentives for leaving college to go to work, which meets more immediate needs than does remaining in school with the promise of a long-term payoff from completing a degree.

Few institutional characteristics were significantly related to persistence. After controlling for other background and pre-entry characteristics, youth who attended a selective four-year institution were more likely to persist than youth attending a nonselective or less selective four-year institution.

Overall, few predictors of persistence remained statistically significant after adjusting for other predictors. In the next chapter we look beyond an early marker of college progress to the long-term outcome of whether youth ultimately completed a college degree.

Technical Appendix

As a robustness check to the results of the logistic regression model in Table 6.1, I conducted a probit model with sample selection. One potential problem with the logistic regression model is that the sample is limited to foster youth who enrolled in college. Failing to account for unmeasured factors influencing both events—enrollment and persistence—could yield biased estimates of predictors of persistence (Angrist & Pischke, 2009). A selection process may be at play, in that college entrants are a nonrandom subset of the general population of foster youth. Enrolling in college and persisting in college would be correlated if they are influenced by a shared set of observed and unobserved youth characteristics. Failing to account for influential unmeasured factors could yield biased estimates of predictors of persistence (Angrist & Pischke, 2009). For example, some unmeasured student characteristics (e.g., motivation to study long hours) may have helped youth gain admission to highly competitive colleges, and inadequately controlling for student characteristics could have led to an overstatement of the positive effects of college selectivity on persistence.

Probit models with sample selection address endogeneity due to unmeasured confounding by simultaneously modeling the selection equation and the regression equation (Angrist & Pischke, 2009; Bhattacharya et al., 2006; Heckman, 1977). These models investigate whether the results reported in the logistic regression models are robust after accounting for possible selection effects. For the outcome of college persistence, the selection equation models the odds of entering college among all 732 participants, and the regression equation models the odds of persisting among the 331 college entrants.

Two-stage models require a covariate that can serve as an exogenous predictor of the main outcome (Holm & Jaeger, 2011). This entails selecting a variable that is substantively and statistically related to the first-stage outcome (i.e., enrolling in college) and satisfies the exclusion restriction. The exclusion restriction states that the error term in the second-stage equation is not correlated with the error term in the first-stage equation. Put another way, it is assumed that the exogenous covariate is not related to the likelihood that students persist, other than though its influence on the odds that students enter college. The inclusion of exogenous predictors in the selection equation breaks the correlation between the error terms in the selection and regression equations.

The expected probabilities for college enrollment obtained from the selection equation are modeled as predictors in the regression equation. Modeling enrollment and persistence jointly accounts for potential sample bias into college that could arise if enrollment and persistence are modeled separately.

The variable selected as the exogenous covariate is the number of types of college preparation activities in which youth took part. During the Wave 1 interview, participants were asked whether they participated in each of the following types of activities: SAT preparation, assistance with college applications, assistance with financial aid/loan applications, and participation in college fairs. A count variable of the number of types of activities ranged from 0 to 4 and had good internal reliability (Cronbach's alpha = .73). Substantively, partaking in these types of activities is expected to increase students' odds of enrolling in college. This was empirically supported, as participation in more activities increased the odds of college enrollment (OR = 1.25, $p < .001$). This lends support to the first assumption of two-stage models.

Unlike the first assumption, the exclusion restriction cannot be tested empirically. However, it is doubtful that partaking in college preparatory activities would have a long-lasting impact on the odds of persisting. For example, attending college fairs and completing college applications may help students gain admission to college but are unlikely to have an impact on doing well in college and persisting. Similarly, other than expensive, private SAT preparation that has been shown to have modest impacts even on SAT scores (Montgomery & Lilly, 2012) and that foster youth are unlikely to have received, it is doubtful that SAT preparation affects college persistence for foster youth. Empirically, the number of college preparatory services that students received is not significantly related to the expected odds of persisting (OR = 1.04, $p = .625$). However, it is plausible that there are attributes of students that could be associated with partaking in college preparatory activities and persisting in college. For example, students with higher academic skills may be more likely to participate in activities that help them gain admission to college and also are more likely to remain enrolled in college. This concern appears to be warranted; higher reading proficiency scores were positively associated with partaking in more education activities ($p < .05$). Although this particular covariate can be statistically controlled, it raises the question of whether other unmeasured characteristics that influence persistence are also correlated with participation in education services. This is a limitation of the following analysis, and the results should be interpreted with the caveat that the exclusion restriction assumption may not be completely satisfied. Several other candidates for exogenous predictors were considered, but these alternatives were either unrelated to college entry or statistically related to college persistence.

To examine whether the findings reported in Table 6.1 were robust after accounting for possible selection on unobservable variables, a more

Table 6.2

Comparison of Probit and Bivariate Probit Results: Predictors of Persistence

	Persistence in College			
	Probit (n =331)		Bivariate probit (n = 331)	
	B	p	B	p
DEMOGRAPHIC CHARACTERISTICS				
Male (ref: female)	−0.26	.123	−0.26	.249
Race/ethnicity (ref: White)				
African American	−0.04	.846	−0.04	.847
Hispanic	−0.93*	.011	−0.93*	.012
Other race	−0.74^	.057	−0.74^	.060
Age at baseline interview	0.44	.104	0.44	.133
State (ref: Illinois)				
Wisconsin	0.07	.768	0.07	.780
Iowa	0.20	.547	0.20	.562
Age first enrolled in college (ref: under age 19)				
19 to 20	−0.39^	.056	−0.39^	.058
21 or older	−0.88**	.001	−0.88**	.001
ACADEMIC AND FOSTER CARE HISTORY				
Reading level, standardized	0.21*	.015	0.20	.247
Number foster care placements (1–40)	−0.04*	.017	−0.04*	.018
PRE-ENTRY FACTORS				
Employment (ref: did not work)				
1–19 hrs./week	1.43***	<.001	1.43***	<.001
20–34 hrs./week	0.51*	.023	0.51*	.023
35+ hrs./week	0.69**	.007	0.69**	.007
INSTITUTIONAL CHARACTERISTICS				
Type/selectivity (ref: two-year college)				
Non-/minimally selective four-year	−0.14	.534	−0.14	.544
Selective/highly selective four-year	0.54*	.033	0.54*	.033
DEMOGRAPHIC CHARACTERISTICS				
Male (ref: female)			−0.26**	.007
Race/ethnicity (ref: White)				
African American			−0.04	.690
Hispanic			0.08	.687
Other race			0.08	.688
Age at baseline interview			−0.24	.123
State (ref: Illinois)				
Wisconsin			−0.20	.131
Iowa			−0.23	.236
ACADEMIC AND FOSTER CARE HISTORY				
Reading level, standardized			0.28***	<.001
Number foster care placements (1–40)			0.00	.910
Number of college prep. activities (0–4)			0.08*	.034
ρ			−.02	.982

NOTE: ^p < .10 *p < .05 **p < .01 ***p < .001.

parsimonious version of the multivariable regression model was run: it used a probit model with sample selection using Stata's heckprobit command. Because two-stage models are taxing on statistical power, a small subset of predictors from the final logistic regression models was used in the probit models with sample selection. The following predictors were included in the model: gender, race/ethnicity, state, age at Wave 1, age at first enrollment, and reading proficiency. Five variables that were not significantly associated with persistence in Table 6.1 were omitted: special education, grade repetition, pre-entry delinquency, pre-entry alcohol/substance use problems, and pre-entry economic hardships.

Table 6.2 presents the results of a probit regression model predicting the likelihood of persistence among college entrants (left panel) and the two-stage selection model (right panel). A probit model was run instead of a logistic regression model so that the results from these two models could be directly compared. Note that the second-stage model included some covariates specific to college persistence (i.e., institution type/selectivity pre-entry covariates) that are not included in the first-stage model. The coefficients are in the unit of z-scores.

In the first stage of the selection model (bottom-right panel), the number of educational activities that youth partook in remained a significant predictor of college entry, although the association is not very strong. Rho (ρ) is a measure of the correlation between the error terms of the two stages, and it is used to test the presence of unobservable variables (Holm & Jaeger, 2011). Large and statistically significant values of ρ indicate that the unexplained variance in both models is influenced by the presence of unmeasured variables, whereas small and nonsignificant ρ values do not support this hypothesis. When ρ is statistically different from zero, this suggests that not accounting for unobserved characteristics introduces bias in the regression coefficients in the second-stage equation.

The value of ρ in the bivariate probit model in Table 6.2 is .02 ($p = .98$). As seen later, covariates in the two-stage selection model are virtually the same as coefficients in the probit model. The one exception is the coefficient for reading scores, which decreased from 1.21 to 1.20 and fell below the .05 alpha level. This may be due in part to the bivariate probit model, which increases standard errors and decreases statistical power to detect true differences. Overall, the results do not support the presence of a strong selection process that is introducing bias into the results in the probit model.

7

Predictors of Degree Completion

This chapter explores factors that affect what is perhaps the most important outcome in the book: completing a college degree. Only 8 percent of Midwest Study participants earned a two- or four-year degree. The findings presented in this chapter make an important contribution to the very limited research that has investigated factors that influence foster youths' chances of earning a degree.

Description of the Sample, Measures, and Analyses

Sample

The sample for the degree completion analyses includes Midwest Study youth who enrolled in college and had a reasonable amount of time to earn a degree. Most youth first enrolled in college in their late teenage years and early twenties (average age was twenty-one), which would give them several years to earn a degree before they were last observed when NSC data were pulled at age twenty-nine/thirty. However, some youth first enrolled in college in their mid- to late twenties, and they would have only had a few years to complete a degree before NSC data were acquired. Thus, the sample includes just youth whose degree status could be observed for six or more years after they first enrolled in college ($n = 329$). The six-year cutoff was chosen because this is a common time frame within which four-year college degree completion is assessed (150% of the expected time to earn a bachelor's degree). The sample of 329 youths include 276 who were identified by NSC records and 53 who were identified by survey data from the Midwest Study. The two groups of youth identified by different data sources (NSC vs. Midwest Study) were compared on the outcomes and all of the predictors in the analyses. This was done to assess whether these groups differed in important ways from one another. The results of these analyses suggested that the groups were largely comparable, and only a couple of differences were found.[1] As a statistical precaution, the multivariable regression model included a binary variable (labeled "NSC indicator" in Table 7.1) to indicate whether a youth was identified by NSC data or Midwest Study self-report.

Measures of the Outcome and Predictors

The main outcome is a binary variable that indicates whether a youth earned a college degree (two-year degree or four-year degree) or not. Because of the small number of youths who completed each type of degree, it was not possible to evaluate two-year and four-year degree completion separately.

The Midwest Study offers a wide range of potential predictors of degree completion, including youth background characteristics, pre-entry and post-entry factors, and institutional characteristics. Findings from bivariate regression analyses informed the variables included in the multivariable logistic regression model. Results of bivariate models found few background factors that were marginally significantly ($p < .10$) associated with the odds of completing a degree.[2] Enrolling at an older age, ever repeating a grade, ever being expelled, and the number of foster care placements each decreased the odds of degree completion. Conversely, a higher math and English GPA increased the odds of degree completion at a marginally significant level ($p < .10$). In the final multivariable regression analyses, additional youth characteristics were included in the model, because they served as substantively important controls for other predictors. These youth characteristics include demographic characteristics (gender, race/ethnicity, age at baseline, state), academic history (educational aspirations, reading level, ever in special education), and a foster care history characteristic (ever in congregate care).

The next set of predictors are pre-entry and post-entry measures. If either the pre-entry measure or post-entry measure of a factor significantly predicted degree completion in the bivariate regression model, then both the pre- and post-entry measures were included.[3] Youths' parental status, marital status, employment status, social support, and economic hardships were all included in the multivariable model based on statistically significant bivariate regression results. Additionally, pre- and post-entry measure were included for mental health problems and alcohol/substance use problems. These are substantively important controls, and there is considerable interest in the field in these factors. The post-entry food insecurity measure was also marginally statistically significant in the bivariate regression model but was omitted from the multivariable model because of its collinearity with post-entry economic hardships. Food

Table 7.1

Multivariable Logistic Regression: Predictors of Degree Completion ($n = 329$)

Predictor	OR	p
DEMOGRAPHIC CHARACTERISTICS		
Male (ref: female)	0.31*	.018
Race/ethnicity (ref: White)		
African American	0.86	.788
Hispanic	0.33	.158
Other race	0.56	.490
Age at baseline interview	4.53*	.028
State (ref: Illinois)		
Wisconsin	2.33	.177
Iowa	1.25	.787
Age first attended in college (ref: 18 or under)		
19 to 20 years	0.30*	.028
21 to 24 years	0.16*	.048
NSC indicator	0.82	.743
ACADEMIC AND FOSTER CARE HISTORY		
Reading level, standardized	1.24	.334
High school math and English GPA from most recent semester	0.78	.350
Ever repeated a grade	0.43	.147
Ever in special education	1.66	.308
Educational aspirations (ref: some college)		
College degree	0.80	.734
More than a college degree	1.67	.440
Number foster care placements	0.92	.162
Ever in congregate care placement	1.83	.177
PRE-AND POST-ENTRY CHARACTERISTICS		
Pre-entry parent	1.02	.973
Post-entry parent	0.40^	.058
Pre-entry married	2.09	.631
Post-entry married	0.47	.264
Pre-entry employment (ref: did not work)		
1–19 hours/week	1.53	.542
20–34 hours/week	1.41	.524
35+ hours/week	1.71	.419
Post-entry employment (ref: did not work)		
1–19 hours/week	2.29	.463
20–34 hours/week	0.52	.358
35+ hrs./week	0.22*	.014
Pre-entry social support	1.69^	.067
Post-entry social support	0.73	.314
Pre-entry mental health problem	1.19	.735
Post-entry mental health problem	1.03	.949

Table 7.1 (*continued*)

Predictor	OR	*p*
Pre-entry alcohol/substance use problem	1.18	.782
Post-entry alcohol/substance use problem	0.93	.873
Pre-entry economic hardships	1.31	.151
Post-entry economic hardships	0.67**	.002
INSTITUTIONAL CHARACTERISTICS		
Type/selectivity (ref: two-year college)		
Non-/minimally selective four-year college	3.86*	.023
Selective/highly selective four-year college	14.1***	<.001

NOTE: ^*p* < .10 **p* < .05 ***p* < .01 ****p* < .001.

insecurity was assessed in a separate multivariable model, and the results are summarized later.

Most of the institutional characteristics of the school a youth first enrolled in were significantly associated with degree completion in bivariate models. These factors included college type/selectivity, percentage of part-time students, in-state tuition cost, expenditures on academic services, and expenditures on student support. A few institution-level characteristics were not significantly related to degree completion, but were examined in separate multivariable models.[4] Because of strong correlations between the institutional predictors, college type/selectivity was included in the multivariable regression model in Table 7.1, and the other predictors were examined separately in multivariable models. The results are presented in later in the chapter.

Statistical Analyses

Multivariable logistic regression was used to examine predictors of degree completion. As a robustness check, a probit model with sample selection was run to assess whether the findings from the multivariate logistic regression model remained consistent after addressing a possible selection effect. These findings are summarized in the Technical Appendix at the end of the chapter.

Findings

Background Characteristics

Overall, less than one in five of the 329 youths in the sample completed a two- or four-year college degree (17.0%). The findings from the multivariable regression analysis in this chapter that examines predictors of degree completion are presented in Table 7.1. Three pieces of statistical information are presented: the odds ratio (OR), significance level indicated by asterisks, and the *p*-value. The results show that males were significantly less likely than females to earn a college degree. Indeed, the odds of completing a degree was about 69 percent lower for males than for females after controlling for the other predictors in the model. No significant differences were found by race/ethnicity, state, or age at baseline interview. Another finding from the regression analysis in Table 7.1 is that youth who started college at an older age were less likely to earn a degree than were youth who enrolled before age nineteen. Studies of nontraditional-age college students also find that older students are less likely to graduate than students who start earlier, in part because they have more life demands that impede their ability remain in college (e.g., Davidson & Wilson, 2016).

An unexpected finding is that none of the measures of youths' academic background significantly predicted their odds of completing a degree. Another unexpected finding is that aspects of youths' foster care histories did not predict the odds of graduating from college. The number of foster care placements that youth resided in did have a marginally significant ($p < .10$) relationship with the odds of degree completion in a regression model that did not control for other youth characteristics. However, after accounting for other aspects of youths' background that were correlated with the number of foster placements they were in (e.g., ever repeated a grade, being in a special education classroom), the number of placements was no longer significant.

Pre-entry and Post-entry Factors

Several factors measured in the time frame before youth enrolled in college and in the time frame after youth enrolled in college were also examined as predictors of degree completion. In the multivariable model, the only pre-entry factor found to be associated with degree completion was social support, which was marginally statistically significant. Having a pre-entry social support score that was 1 point higher (on a scale that ranged from 0 to 4) increases the odds of degree attainment by about 69 percent. Interestingly, the amount of social support that youth perceived having after they enrolled in college did not significantly predict their chances of finishing college.

The pre-entry and post-entry measures of marital status, mental health problems, and alcohol/substance use problems were not significantly associated with degree completion after accounting for other characteristics. This sample had relatively high rates of behavioral health problems, and this lack of variability may have led to the nonsignificant findings for having mental health and alcohol/substance use problems. Had the sample included non-foster youth, there would have been more variability in behavioral health statuses, which may have led to a significant relationship for these factors. It is also possible that the behavioral health factors were not measured with enough acuity. For example, the mental health measure was not able to distinguish between youth with temporary PTSD symptoms from those with more chronic and severe mental health problems.

There were three post-entry factors that each decreased the odds of degree completion, even after accounting for a wide range of youth characteristics. First, youth who worked full-time after entering college were significantly less likely to finish college than were youth who did not work. Second, youth who were or became parents after starting college were marginally significantly less likely than youth without children to complete their degree.[5] Third, the number of economic hardships that youth experienced after enrolling in college significantly decreased their chances of finishing. Each additional type of hardship that they faced (e.g., not being able to pay utility bills) decreased their expected odds of completing college by about 33 percent.

The implicit assumption about these three post-entry factors is that each was a hindrance to earning a degree. In other words, it is assumed that each factor led participants to drop out of college or was a barrier to returning to college. However, other explanations are conceivable. Regarding employment, youth may have chosen to forgo finishing college because better work opportunities arose. In this case, full-time employment would be something participants *intentionally pursued* rather than something that deterred them from finishing college. Similarly, the decision to have a child may have taken precedence over finishing a degree for some youth. In terms of encountering economic hardships, participants may have exited college without a degree, which in turn increased their economic hardships. In this case, hardships would be a *consequence* of not finishing college, rather than a hindrance to completing college.

These competing explanations challenge the assumption that full-time work, parenthood, and economic hardships were each hindrances to degree completion. Fortunately, data were collected during the Midwest Study interviews that allow us to put these assumptions to the test. In the third, fourth, and fifth interview waves, participants who had dropped out of college were asked about the reasons they left and the barriers to returning to school that they encountered. Both of these questions assessed the need to work, parental responsibilities, and not being able to afford tuition as possible hindrances, which align with the three post-entry predictors. The responses that youth gave to these questions during the interviews allow us to check the assumptions about the three post-entry factors. For example, we would expect that participants who encountered greater numbers of post-entry economic hardships would be more likely to report that an inability to afford tuition was a hindrance to completing college (a reason for dropping out or a barrier to returning). The same goes for parenthood and employment. To test the assumptions, two regression models were run for each post-entry factor—one for the dropout reason and one for the barrier to continuing college. If youth reported that college affordability was a dropout reason, they were assigned a 1, and if youth did not report affordability as a dropout reason (or they did not drop out) they were assigned a 0. Similar binary measures were created for the other two dropout reasons

Table 7.2

Results of Six Logistic Regression Models: Post-entry Factor Predicting Its Corresponding Reason for Dropout/Barrier to Reenrollment (*n* = 329)

Regression Model	OR	*p*
1. Post-entry economic hardships predicting tuition cost as a reason for dropout	1.57***	<.001
2. Post-entry economic hardships predicting tuition cost as a barrier to returning	1.54***	<.001
3. Post-entry employment predicting needing to work as a reason for dropout (ref: not employed)		
1–19 hrs./week	0.42	.264
20–34 hrs./week	1.39	.510
35+ hrs./week	3.54**	.002
4. Post-entry employment predicting needing to work as a barrier to returning (ref: did not work)		
1–19 hrs./week	1.12	.874
20–34 hrs./week	1.82	.236
35+ hrs./week	4.18**	.001
5. Post-entry parental status predicting parental responsibilities as a reason for dropout	4.32***	<.001
6. Post-entry parental status predicting parental responsibilities as a barrier to returning	4.36***	<.001

NOTES: **$p < .01$ ***$p < .001$. Control variables (not shown) include the pre-entry counterpart of the post-entry measure, the age youth first entered college, the NSC indicator variable, and educational aspirations.

(parental responsibilities and needing to work). The same procedure was used to create binary measures for barriers to continuing college.

Table 7.2 presents abbreviated results from six logistic regression models. Each model controls for a small number of relevant covariates (not shown in the table): the pre-entry counterpart of the post-entry measure, the age youth first entered college, the NSC indicator, and educational aspirations. The results of the first model in Table 7.2 show that each additional economic hardship youth encountered in the post-entry period significantly increased (by about 57%) the odds that they reported that tuition cost was a reason to drop out. A similar relationship was found between the number of economic hardships and the likelihood that youth reported college affordability as a barrier to returning to college. The third and fourth regression models in the table examine post-entry employment status. Youth who worked full-time were significantly more likely than youth who did not work to report that needing to work was a dropout reason and a barrier. Youth who were employed full-time were also more likely than youth who worked fewer hours per week to report work as a hindrance.[6] Finally, youth who were or became parents after starting college were significantly more likely than nonparents to report childcare responsibilities as a reason for dropping out and a barrier to returning (fifth and six regression models in Table 7.2).

In sum, the findings from these supplemental analyses support the interpretation about the three post-entry factors acting as hindrances to degree completion. Each factor was not merely a desirable alternative or a consequence of leaving college.

College-Level Predictors of Degree Completion

After the brief detour where we more closely examined the three post-entry factors, we now return to the results in the main regression analysis in Table 7.1. The final set of predictors included characteristics of the colleges in which youth first enrolled. An important finding is that youth attending four-year colleges, especially selective/highly selective four-year colleges, were significantly more likely to complete a degree than were youth attending two-year colleges. This finding remained after adjusting for aspects of their background (e.g., academic credentials) and college life circumstances (e.g., having a child, working) that could explain the association between college type and the odds of degree completion.

A discerning reader may point out that one of the reasons foster youth in four-year colleges are more likely than youth in two-year colleges to earn a degree is that may not have been the goal of youth in two-year schools. Perhaps they wanted to earn a postsecondary certificate, and not a degree. This is a good point. Although not displayed here, another multivariable regression analysis was conducted with the same predictors as in Table 7.1 but examined credential completion (i.e., certificate, two-year degree, or four-year degree) as the outcome. In this model, the role of college type/selectivity was still present but not as strong. The OR for nonselective/minimally selective four-year college (vs. two-year college) decreased to 2.54 and was marginally significant ($p = .066$). The OR for selective/highly selective four-year college decreased to 4.85 and remained statistically significant ($p = .002$). Thus, institution type was still important even after considering the full range of postsecondary credentials that youth may have been pursuing.

Supplemental multivariable regression models examined the other college-level predictors individually, controlling for the background, pre-entry, and post-entry factors that appear in Table 7.1. Several college-level factors were found to significantly increase the odds that youth completed a degree. The proportion of part-time students and the proportion of students receiving a Pell Grant are expressed as 10-percentage point changes, and in-state tuition and the three expenditure variables are expressed in $1,000 changes. In these models, each institutional factor was significantly associated with degree completion. Every 10-percentage point increase in the proportion of part-time students is expected to decrease the odds of completion by about 37 percent ($OR = 0.63, p = < .001$).

The cost of tuition and expenses ($OR = 1.25$, $p = < .001$), expenditures on academic support ($OR = 3.95$, $p < .001$), expenditures on student services ($OR = 3.48, p < .001$), and expenditures on instruction ($OR = 1.25, p = .011$) were found to increase the expected odds of degree completion. An unexpected finding is that the proportion of students receiving need-based grants *increased* foster youths' chances of completing a degree. Colleges with greater proportions of students receiving Pell Grants means that there are more students at the college from low-income backgrounds, and these students may face more or greater barriers to finishing a degree. However, in this analysis, every 10-percentage point increase in the proportion of Pell grant recipients increased the estimated odds of completion by about 61 percent ($OR = 1.61, p = .005$).

The regression analyses showed that youth who were similar in academic and other background characteristics had different chances of succeeding in college depending on the type of school they entered and the resources available within those colleges. It is important to think about this finding in conjunction with the findings on undermatching; notably, a nontrivial proportion of youth "undermatch" (i.e., enroll in colleges lower in selectivity that they could likely have been admitted to). Putting these two findings together underscores the importance of college guidance. To ensure that foster youth enroll in colleges that match their qualifications, needs, and preferences, these young people will need to be provided with high-quality hands-on guidance with the college search, application, and selection process.

Supplemental Analyses to Check for a Selection Effect

From an analytic standpoint, one concern about the findings reported in Table 7.1 is that the results may be biased if a selection process was at play. For interested readers, the Technical Appendix to this chapter explains the potential selection process and summarizes analytic steps taken to check whether selection influence the findings. The results of these supplemental analyses did not suggest that a selection effect unduly influenced the results in Table 7.1.

Chapter Summary

This chapter identified several background characteristics, life events and circumstances after youth start college, and characteristics of the colleges they attend that influenced foster care youths' expected chances to complete a degree. Males fared worse than females in their odds of completing a degree. A finding that ran contrary to expectations is that none of the academic history characteristics predicted the expected likelihood that youth would graduate from college. This may be due in part to the fact that, with each passing year, the academic measures (e.g., reading proficiency) become a less reliable assessment of the youths' current level of academic skill and ability. Moreover, events and life circumstances that occurred after youth enrolled in college appear to play a more prominent role in predicting college completion than do factors measured at an earlier time. In addition, some of the academic measures may have not adequately captured what they were intended to capture. For example, the high school grades were self-reported, based on youths' English and math grades in their most recent high school marking period before the Wave 1 interview. A stronger measure would have been their cumulative high school GPA from their transcripts.

Events and life circumstances that occurred after youth enrolled in college were found to play a pronounced role in predicting college completion. Being or becoming a parent, encountering economic hardships, and needing to work full-time lowered the expected odds of earning a degree. The age at which youth first entered college was an important predictor of whether college entrants earned a degree. This is consistent with findings from studies of nontraditional-age college students, which report that older students have more life demands than younger students that impede their ability remain in college (e.g., Davidson & Wilson, 2016).

It was found that youth who entered college with more social support at the outset were significantly more likely to have completed college than were those who entered with less support. Earlier research with foster youth reports that access to certain types of social support (e.g., tangible support and advice from adults with a college education) increases youths' likelihood of entering college (Okpych & Courtney, 2017). Youth high in social support may have more dense networks of individuals that can be accessed later in college. It is important to recognize that there are different reasons why youth vary in their perceptions of the availability of social support. For example, higher social support scores could result from (a) youth actually having more available social support, (b) youths' proclivity to forming relationships with others who can be relied on for support, or (c) youths' likelihood of perceiving and acknowledging the support that is available to them. The regression analyses controlled for the amount of social support youth had after entering in college, which suggests that the amount of support with which youth enter college has an independent relationship with completing a degree. Another point to recognize is that the social support scale used in this study is a composite measure that captures four different types of support. It may be that the sum total of youths' perception of available support drives their success in college. Alternatively, certain types of support may serve different functions in promoting college completion. For example, emotional support may help alter youths' appraisals of threats (e.g., providing reassurance after failing an exam that leads youth to question whether they are cut out for college). Instrumental support may help with solving practical problems (e.g., giving them emergency money for unexpected expenses). Informational support may give youth access to information needed to solve problems, complete tasks, and access resources (e.g., assisting youth with completing the FAFSA; Cohen et al., 2000). Disentangling the specific roles that different types of social support play is an important next step for research with college students with care histories.

Several characteristics of the colleges that participants attended were related to the odds of earning a degree. As expected, youth who attended four-year colleges (especially selective colleges) were more likely to earn a degree than were youth who entered two-year colleges. Attending institutions that spent more on academic support, on student services, and on instruction were each found to increase the odds that foster youth completed college. Conversely, enrolling in those colleges with higher proportions of part-time students decreased the estimated odd of degree completion for foster youth. Not only does having a large part-time student body make it difficult to establish a cohesive, palpable, supportive college culture but it also reflects a student body that has commitments outside of school. In contrast to findings from other studies, higher proportions of Pell Grant recipients at a college increased foster youths' chances of completing a credential. It is suspected that this finding resulted from characteristics of the sample. Transition-age foster youth are a subgroup of students with few material resources who are generally living on the verge of economic hardship. Among this group, enrolling in colleges in which aid is adequately distributed may be particularly critical to their college success. There may also be a psychosocial component. When the culture of the college and its study body is consistent with the students' own background, that can create a sense of belongingness and comfortability that is not present when there is mismatch between the youths' sociocultural upbringing and the college culture (e.g., working-class students attending elite colleges) (Stephens et al., 2012). Overall, the results suggest that the type and nature of institutions are a powerful influence on the success of their students after accounting for individual characteristics of the students.

The current chapter, along with the two previous chapters, examined broad sets of predictors of enrollment, persistence, and completion. In the next two chapters, we drill down on two factors that deserve special attention: avoidant attachment and extended foster care.

Technical Appendix

As a robustness check to the results of the logistic regression model in Table 7.1, I ran a probit model with sample selection. See the Technical Appendix at the end of chapter 6 for an explanation of selection effects and how probit models with sample selection are designed as a check for the influence of those selection effects. The selection effect of concern in this chapter is that college entrants are a nonrandom subset of the general population of foster youth, so analyzing only these college entrants could lead to biased estimates of predictors of degree completion. The variable selected as the exogenous covariate is the number of types of college preparation activities in which youth participated. Participation in these activities is significantly associated with enrollment ($p < .001$), but it is doubtful that partaking in college preparatory activities would have a long-lasting impact on the odds of degree completion. Empirically, the number of college preparatory services that students received was unrelated to the expected odds of completing a degree (OR = 1.05, $p = .620$).

To examine whether the findings reported in Table 7.1 were robust after accounting for possible selection on unobserved confounding, I ran a more parsimonious version of its regression model using a probit model with sample selection. The following predictors were included in the first-stage model, which predicted college enrollment among all Midwest Study participants: gender, race/ethnicity, state, age at Wave 1, age at first enrollment, and reading proficiency. The second-stage model, which predicted degree completion among college entrants, included the predictors in the first-stage model, as well as pre- and post-entry measures of parental status, employment, economic hardships, and social support. The second-stage model also included a measure of institutional type/selectivity.

Rho (ρ), a measure of the correlation between the error terms of the two stages used to test the influence of unobserved factors (Holm & Jaeger, 2011), was small and nonsignificant in the supplemental two-stage model ($\rho = -.08$, $p = .923$). The finding supports the contention that unmeasured variables did not exert undue influence on the model estimating college completion. Although not displayed because of space constraints, the estimates of the probit model and the two-stage probit model were similar. For example, estimates between models were comparable for the post-entry measures for parental status (probit model: beta = -0.52, $p = .036$; two-stage model: beta = -0.51, $p = .036$), full-time employment (probit model: beta = -0.79, $p = .012$; two-stage model: beta = -0.78, $p = .014$), and economic hardships (probit model: beta = -0.20, $p = .001$; two-stage model: beta = -0.19, $p = .002$).

8

The Role of Avoidant Attachment on College Persistence and Degree Completion

> Because of foster care, you don't know
> who to trust. You have been hurt, taken
> away from your family. Something is
> done wrong and now you . . . don't want
> to put your trust in anyone.
> —Foster care alumnus, quoted from a
> study by Batsche and colleagues (2014)

This quote is from a foster care alumnus who is reflecting candidly on his past experiences of trauma and loss and how they have influenced the way he sees and approaches future relationships. It speaks volumes about how broken relationships have compromised his capacity to trust. Maltreatment, school and placement mobility, and relationship ruptures can disrupt learning and cause academic setbacks. But they also take a toll on foster youth in less visible but still gripping ways. Repeated and profound experiences of loss and trauma lead some young people to adopt a self-protective stance toward relationships (Kools, 1999; Morton, 2018; Samuels & Pryce, 2008). In developmental psychology, a durable pattern of avoidance of intimacy, minimization of dependence on others, and denial of emotional needs is called *avoidant attachment* (Mikulincer &

Shaver, 2003). Although this guarded stance to relationships offers some protection from future loss and trauma, it may also cut foster youth off from needed social support. Put succinctly, many foster youth will need help from resourceful individuals to make it through college, but if past trauma has made them reluctant to seek and accept help, this can hurt their chances of graduating. Although this may seem like a plausible explanation, it has not yet been tested empirically. The main focus of this chapter is to examine whether increased levels of avoidant attachment does in fact hinder foster youths' odds of persisting in college and earning a degree.

As discussed in chapter 1, a major limitation of several qualitative studies of foster youth in college is they typically involve students who are academically successful—individuals who are still enrolled in or graduated from college (Day et al., 2012; Morton, 2015; Rios & Rocco, 2014). Youth high in avoidant attachment may be missing from these studies, particularly if they are more likely to drop out or are reluctant to talk to researchers about their experiences, difficulties, and feelings. Findings from a study by Hines and colleagues (2005) exemplify this possibility. In their interviews with twelve foster youths enrolled in a four-year college, they found, "In spite of their fierce self-sufficiency, most (10 [participants]) were also able to accept help from others and realized that this was integral to their ability to survive" (p. 388). The majority of youth in this study sought help as a survival strategy, whereas youth high in avoidant attachment deflect relationships as a survival strategy. Many qualitative studies miss or underrepresent foster youth who are high in avoidant attachment. If these youth are at heightened risk of dropping out, we need to hear from them the most to begin strategizing interventions.

What Is Avoidant Attachment?

An individual's attachment style is a durable pattern of expectations, emotions, and behaviors that the person has about relationships. Through the accumulation of experiences in relationships, starting from infancy, individuals develop internal blueprints about relationships. These blueprints affect what we expect relationships to be like, how we expect others to respond to us, and how we interact with others (Ainsworth, 1979; Bowlby, 1973). Our customary expectations and comportment in relationships form our attachment style. An "avoidant attachment" style, which is characterized by a tendency to avoid intimacy and emotional closeness, minimize dependence on others by being highly self-reliant, downplay threats, and suppress acknowledging personal faults and shortcomings (Mikulincer & Shaver, 2003). Individuals high in avoidant attachment view relationships with distrust and are reluctant to acknowledge needing others. When faced with an obstacle, their modus operandi is DIY. An individual's level of avoidant attachment falls on a continuum with low, medium, and high levels; it is not a hard-and-fast binary as if either you have it or you don't.

How does an avoidant attachment style develop? Attachment theory views experiences with caregivers in infancy and early childhood as especially formative (Bowlby, 1973). When caregivers are consistently unresponsive to or unavailable to meet the needs of the child, the child learns to stop expecting and seeking help from them. These repeated experiences over time form the child's blueprint for their expectations about relationships (Ainsworth, 1979; Bowlby, 1973). Importantly, traumatic experiences later in life can also influence a person's attachment style, particularly when the experiences are long-lasting and there is an absence of effective resources needed to restore psychological functioning (e.g., Mikulincer et al., 1999; Murphy et al., 2016). Mikulincer and colleagues (2015) emphasize that, even though attachment styles are generally stable over time, "they can be altered by powerful experiences that affect a person's beliefs about the value of seeking help from attachment figures and the feasibility of attaining safety, protection, and comfort" (p. 85). Thus, even if a child has developed a reasonably secure attachment style, trauma later in life can change it.

Avoidant Attachment in Youth with Foster Care Histories

Severe maltreatment and relational instability in foster care, such as frequent and abrupt placement changes, exemplify "powerful experiences" that can shake one's sense of safety, stability, and basic trust in relationships. As a result of these experiences, foster youth may adopt avoidant attachment strategies or increase their use of avoidant strategies that are already part of their attachment repertoire. By not allowing themselves to become emotionally attached to and reliant on others, foster youth protect themselves from reexperiencing the psychological distress that accompanied past disappointment, loss, and injury in relationships (Boss, 2006).

Not all youth with care histories, however, will have an avoidant attachment style. Some youth experienced less maltreatment and fewer relationship ruptures (e.g., changes in caregivers, placements, and schools) in foster care than others. Additionally, youth also vary in how much support was available to them at key times to process the trauma and loss, which can help stave off avoidant attachment and restore psychological functioning. As explored later in this chapter, it is expected that more severe maltreatment and more relationship ruptures will increase a youth's level of avoidant attachment.

Although they did not explicitly name the phenomenon of avoidant attachment, several studies of interviews with foster youth and alumni did document their self-protective response to trauma (Kools, 1999; Lee & Whiting, 2007; Morton, 2018; Perry, 2006; Riebschleger et al., 2015; Samuels, 2009; Unrau et al., 2008). Abrupt changes in caregivers, home, school, and community can have a long-lasting effect on the relationships foster youth form with others. For example, Samuels and Pryce (2008) described participants in their study as developing "survivalist self-reliance," which involved a disavowal of dependence on others and survivors' pride. Kools (1999) summarized the experience of the participants in her study in the following way: "The repeated transitions in caregiving that the adolescents experienced seemed to recapitulate losses and rejections in their preplacement histories. The adolescents talked about their difficulties in continuing to invest in relationships with adults that might have little future. The willingness to trust or get close to new caregivers seemed to subside with this instability" (p. 145). As a foster youth in a study by Samuels (2009, p. 56) put it, foster care

> affects my ability to wanna latch on to somebody, because every time it seems like I've latched on to someone, I lose them. And not in a sense of latching on to 'em, but just getting close to 'em, like. . . . Through the years of latching on to people, from adult figures, to even friends . . . it's affected my ability to want to, for the fact that, every time I do, somethin' bad happens. And it really tears me apart every time it happens. I take it harder than I should. So, it really affects me, so it jus' feels like I haven't really been tryin' to latch close to people as much as, you know, one would. Jus' because of everyone that I've lost. I don't know how to deal with it. It's hard.

How Is Avoidant Attachment Expected to Influence College Outcomes?

Although avoidant attachment protects foster youth by keeping others at a distance, it may also lead to negative consequences. Addressing the academic, financial, logistical, and psychological challenges that arise in college will require most foster youth to acknowledge their own needs, identify resourceful individuals who could assist them, and be willing to rely on others for support. By definition, young people who are high in avoidant attachment resist acknowledging vulnerability and relying on the assistance of others. Thus, foster youth high in avoidant attachment will likely build fewer relationships to resourceful individuals in college (i.e., would have smaller social networks), and they would be less likely to turn to others in their networks when faced with challenges beyond their own capacities to meet (Morton, 2018; Samuels & Pryce, 2008). For these reasons, it is expected that attachment avoidance will hurt foster youths' success in college. My research presented in this chapter tests both this hypothesis and one that holds that less social support among youth high in avoidant attachment helps explain decreased chances of persisting and graduating.

Findings

Measure of Avoidant Attachment

The measure of avoidant attachment comes from a widely used adult attachment scale called the Experiences in Close Relationships-Revised (ECR-R; Fraley et al., 2000). Typically, to gauge an adult's attachment style, researchers either conduct an in-depth interview with the person about their perceptions of relationships or administer a battery of survey questions that are designed to measure adult attachment (Mikulincer & Shaver, 2007). The ECR-R does the latter. The original ECR-R instrument has thirty-six items, including eighteen items for avoidant attachment. However, because of time constraints, only eleven of the eighteen items were administered in the Midwest Study. In addition, the ECR-R was designed to ask about respondents' perceptions of their relationship with a romantic partner; in the Midwest Study, the questions were modified to ask about respondents' relationships generally. The ECR-R was only administered during Wave 1 when participants were seventeen/eighteen years old. All eleven questions had seven Likert-style response choices, ranging from 1 ("disagree strongly") to 7 ("agree strongly").

Table 8.1 displays the eleven ECR-R items asked in the Midwest Study. The far-right columns report the average score and standard deviation (SDs) for each item. Notice that the questions asked in the opposite direction (boldfaced) have been reverse-coded, so that for all items, a higher average indicates higher avoidant attachment. Following the ECR-R instructions, an avoidant attachment

Table 8.1
Descriptive Statistics of Items Used to Create Avoidant Attachment Scale (*n* = 726)

Item	Mean (SD)
(1) I usually discuss my problems and concerns with others	3.30 (1.87)
(2) I feel comfortable sharing my private thoughts and feelings with others	3.76 (1.91)
(3) I don't feel comfortable opening up to others	3.86 (1.94)
(4) I prefer not to show others how I feel deep down	4.02 (2.04)
(5) Others really understand me and my needs	3.41 (1.76)
(6) I find it difficult to allow myself to depend on others	4.29 (1.94)
(7) I feel comfortable depending on others	4.44 (1.99)
(8) It helps to turn to others in times of need	2.71 (1.55)
(9) I get uncomfortable when others want to be very close	2.99 (1.75)
(10) I am very comfortable being close to others	3.01 (1.67)
(11) It's easy for me to be affectionate with others	3.43 (1.83)

NOTE: Boldfaced items are reverse coded when calculating the means in this column so that a higher score indicates greater avoidant attachment for all items. The mean of each item ranges from 1–7.

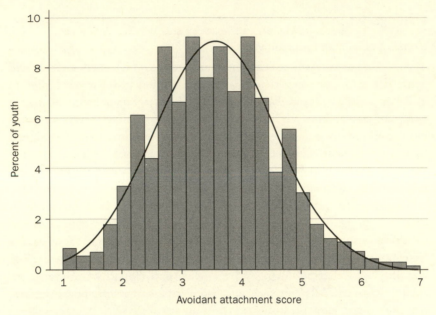

FIG. 8.1 Distribution of avoidant attachment scores ($n = 726$)

score was created for each participant by taking the average of the eleven items. The average score ranged from 1 to 7, with higher scores indicating greater attachment avoidance. As seen in Figure 8.1, the average score was about right in the middle (*mean* = 3.58); this figure also gives us a sense of how spread out the scores are across the range of 1–7. Most scores fell close to the mean, and extreme scores—very low avoidant attachment and very high avoidant attachment—were relatively rare. A standard deviation was equal to about one point on the avoidant attachment scale (*SD* = 1.02).

An important feature of scales like the ECR-R is internal reliability: the extent to which the questions adhere as a single measure of a characteristic. Cronbach's alpha was used to assess internal reliability, which can range from 0–1.0, with higher scores indicating greater internal reliability. A score of 0.70 or higher is typically deemed an indication of good internal reliability. In this study, the Cronbach's alpha for the avoidant attachment measure is 0.77, which suggests good internal reliability. Avoidant attachment scores did not differ significantly by gender or race/ethnicity (both $p > .10$) and followed a roughly normal distribution in the full Midwest Study sample (see Figure 8.1). Although not displayed, avoidant attachment scores and distributions were similar in the persistence sample ($n = 331$; *mean* = 3.54; *SD* = 1.04) and degree completion sample ($n = 329$; *mean* = 3.53; *SD* = 1.07).

Associations between Avoidant Attachment and Wave 1 Variables

Bivariate regression analyses were run to investigate whether youths' avoidant attachment scores were correlated with other youth characteristics measured at age seventeen/eighteen.[1] These associations tell us whether youth high in avoidant attachment differ from youth low in avoidant attachment, which can point to variables that are important to statistically control for when evaluating the role of avoidant attachment on college outcomes. The analyses were run on both the persistence sample ($n = 331$) and the degree completion sample ($n = 329$). Associations that were statistically significant ($p < .05$) are summarized.

Most youth characteristics were not significantly associated with avoidant attachment scores, with a few exceptions. First, mental health problems and alcohol/substance use problems were associated with higher avoidant attachment. The avoidant attachment scores were nearly 0.4 points higher for youth who had mental health problems ($p < .01$) and more than 0.3 points higher for youth who had alcohol/substance use problems ($p < .05$). Second, some measures indicative of behavior problems were correlated with higher avoidant attachment scores. Compared to their peers, avoidant attachment scores were higher for youth who were ever in congregate care ($0.3, p < .01$) and youth who were ever expelled ($0.4, p < .05$). Additionally, higher delinquency was also related to the avoidant attachment score (a 1-point increase in delinquency was associated with a 0.3-point increase in avoidant attachment, $p < .05$). Third, social support and participation in college preparation activities had negative associations with avoidant attachment. The association between avoidant attachment and pre-entry social support was particularly strong. Youth higher in avoidant attachment reported that they perceived having less social support around the time they entered college than did youth who were lower on avoidant attachment (differences of -0.7 points, $p < .001$). This is consistent with previous research that suggests that adults with insecure attachment styles, including avoidant attachment, tend to perceive that they have less social support than individuals with secure attachment styles (Collins & Feeney, 2004). Youth higher in avoidant attachment also reported participating in fewer college preparatory activities. Each increase of 1 point in avoidant attachment correlated with about 0.2 fewer activities ($p < .001$). This is also consistent with a DIY approach to taking on challenges that is characteristic of individuals high in avoidant attachment. These statistically significant associations suggest that foster youth with higher avoidant attachment may be more likely than youth lower in avoidant attachment to be grappling with issues that can disrupt college success.

Associations between Past Maltreatment/Relational Instability and Avoidant Attachment

Figures 8.2–8.4 show the associations between avoidant attachment and youths' history of maltreatment and of relational instability. Figure 8.2 examines three types of maltreatment: physical abuse, neglect, and sexual abuse. Maltreatment history was assessed by the Lifetime Experiences Questionnaire (Rose et al., 2000), which captured neglect (nine items), physical abuse (seven items), and sexual abuse (two items). Cronbach's alphas for the neglect and physical abuse items were .77 and .84, respectively. Sexual abuse was coded as a binary variable indicating whether youth had ever been sexually assaulted or molested. To show this history graphically, Figure 8.2 divides youth into groups based on the number of instances of maltreatment they experienced. The average avoidant attachment score for youth in each group is reported at the top of each bar. A clear pattern emerges for physical abuse and neglect: the more instances of each, the higher the avoidant attachment score ($p < .05$). The jump in scores is particularly large when comparing youth who experienced three to four types of physical abuse to youth who experienced five or more types of physical abuse. We see a similar jump that is slightly less pronounced for instances of neglect ($p < .05$). Additionally, youth who were sexually abused had a higher average avoidant attachment score than did youth who had not been sexually abused ($p < .05$).

The next two figures examine different aspects of relational instability: the number of school changes youth experienced due to a foster care change or a family move (Figure 8.3) and the number of foster care homes youth were in

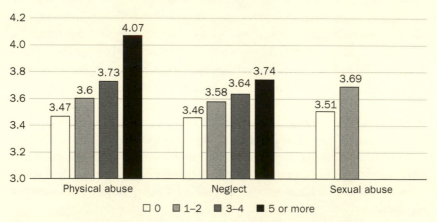

FIG. 8.2 Average avoidant attachment scores for different amounts of maltreatment, by maltreatment type ($n = 732$)

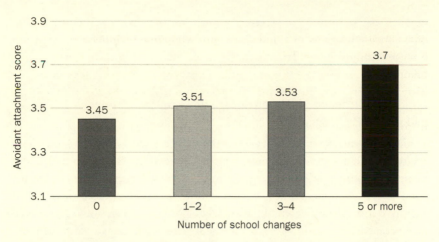

FIG. 8.3 Average avoidant attachment score, by number of school changes ($n = 732$)

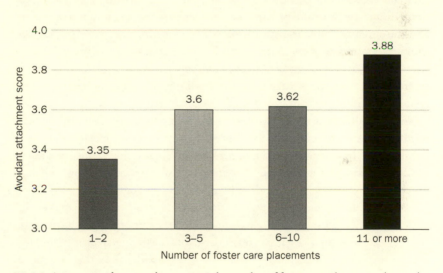

FIG. 8.4 Average avoidant attachment score, by number of foster care placements ($n = 732$)

(Figure 8.4). Changes in foster homes and schools disrupt relationships that foster youth have with people and places. Similar to the findings on maltreatment, more relational instability is associated with an increase in youths' avoidant attachment (both $p < .05$). This is particularly true for youth with the highest numbers of foster care placement changes and school mobility.

These figures show that foster youth who had experienced more maltreatment and relational instability had higher scores on the avoidant attachment measure. These findings are consistent with findings from qualitative studies of foster care youth, which find that youth who are emotionally guarded and wary of relationships tend to report past experiences with painful and disrupted relationships.

Avoidant Attachment Predicting College Persistence and Degree Completion

Table 8.2 presents findings that answer the main question of the chapter: Does avoidant attachment decrease foster youths' chances of persisting in college and completing a degree? Several regression models were run for each outcome. Model 0 is the simplest model, which does not statistically control for any other factors. Models 1–6 become increasingly rigorous as each adds new sets of factors that are statistically controlled. The specific covariates added at each step are listed in the far-right column of Table 8.2. These sets of control variables were included because they were theorized or observed to be associated with avoidant attachment and the college outcomes. Statistically controlling for them allows us to examine the relationship between avoidant attachment and the outcomes after statistically parsing out the influence of these factors. Only the estimates of the relationship between youths' avoidant attachment score and outcome are included in the table (presented as odds ratios [ORs]).

In Model 0 (no statistical controls), a 1-point increase on the 7-point avoidant attachment scale is associated with a 29 percent decrease in the odds of persisting through the first three semesters and a 31 percent decrease in the odds of earning a two-year or four-year degree. The estimated association between avoidant attachment and the odds of persistence remains fairly consistent across Models 1–6, ranging between an OR of 0.70–0.76.[2] After controlling for behavior problems in Model 3, we see a reduction in the strength of the association between avoidant attachment and persistence. Controlling for mental health and substance use problems slightly increases the strength of the association (Model 4), while adjusting for characteristics of youths' maltreatment and foster care history minimally changes the estimates (Model 5). In the final model that included all control variables including college type/selectivity (Model 6), a statistically significant relationship is found between avoidant attachment and persistence. Each point higher in avoidant attachment predicts a 27 percent decrease in the odds of persistence. The degree completion regression models also showed a fairly consistent relationship between avoidant attachment and graduation. In the final regression model with all of the controls (Model 6), each 1-point increase in avoidant attachment significantly decreased the expected odds of earning a degree by about 37 percent.

The very last models in the table (Model 6M) explore whether youths' amount of perceived social support explains the relationships between avoidant attachment and the two college outcomes. Earlier in the chapter we saw

Table 8.2

Multivariable Logistic Regression Results: Avoidant Attachment Predicting College Persistence and Completion (controls not shown)

	Persistence ($n = 331$)		Degree Completion ($n = 329$)		
	OR	p	OR	p	Controls Added[a]
Model 0	0.71**	.006	0.69*	.012	None
Model 1	0.70**	.006	0.66*	.010	**Demographics:** Gender, Race/ethnicity, Age, State, Age first enrolled, Parental status
Model 2	0.71*	.013	0.66*	.016	**Educational history:** Highest completed grade, Reading score, Grade repetition, Special Education, Expulsion, Number of college prep activities, College aspirations
Model 3	0.76*	.048	0.65*	.011	**Behavioral problems:** Delinquency score, Ever in congregate care
Model 4	0.73*	.035	0.64*	.012	**Behavioral health:** Mental health problems, Alcohol/substance use problems
Model 5	0.73*	.039	0.61*	0.10	**Foster care history:** Years in care past age 18, Number of foster care placements, Number of school changes, Maltreatment tertiles
Model 6	0.73*	.047	0.63*	.021	**Institutional factor:** College type/selectivity
Model 6M[b]	0.73^	.073	0.67^	.075	**Mediator:** Pre-entry and post-entry social support[b]

NOTES: $^p < .10$ $^*p < .05$ $^{**}p < .01$. Avoidant attachment scores are presented as standard deviations in this table. A 1-unit change represents a 1 standard deviation change in avoidant attachment. This is roughly equivalent to a 1-point change in the attachment score.

[a] The sets of controls in a given model include all of the controls from the previous models. For example, Model 3 controls for the covariates in Model 2 and Model 1.

[b] Only pre-entry social support was included as a mediator for college persistence, whereas both pre-entry and post-entry social support were included as mediators of degree completion.

that youth high in avoidant attachment reported having significantly less social support than did youth lower in avoidant attachment. If social support explains some of the association between avoidant attachment and the college outcomes, we should see the ORs move closer to 1.0 after the social support measure is added to the model. We should also see the p-value increase above .05. There is some support for mediation, particularly in the degree completion analysis. For both persistence and degree completion, the ORs are no longer statistically significant ($p < .05$), and in the degree completion analysis the OR increases from 0.63 to 0.67.

One limitation of Model 6M is that the measure of social support used in the Midwest Study does not fully capture how avoidant attachment is theorized to influence youths' social networks and help seeking. The Midwest Study collected information on a youth's *perceived* social support, which is an individual's subjective appraisal about the assistance that is available in times of need (Haber et al., 2007). This measure may not have sufficiently captured what we are really interested in. Ideally, measures would be collected of (a) youths' social *network size* in college (i.e., how many people they can turn to for support), and (b) and how often youth used others in their social network (i.e., *received support*), especially in times of need. It would be expected that youth higher in avoidant attachment would have smaller network sizes and would use people in their network less often, and this would help explain their decreased chances of persisting in and graduating from college. Future research should collect more detailed information of youths' social networks and their received social support to determine whether, in fact, there are differences by youths' level of avoidant attachment.

Supplemental Analyses to Check for a Selection Effect

Although not presented in detail here, supplemental analyses were conducted to assess whether the findings from the regression models in Table 8.2 were biased due to a selection effect. Readers interested in these supplemental analyses can refer to the Technical Appendix at the end of this chapter. The results did not find that a selection effect was at play.

Chapter Summary

This chapter examined whether avoidant attachment decreased the expected odds that foster youth persist in college and complete a degree. Results from our descriptive analyses found that youth who experienced more maltreatment and relational instability had higher levels of avoidant attachment, which provides quantitative support for qualitative studies based on in-depth interviews of foster youth. Moreover, higher avoidant attachment decreased the likelihood of persisting in college and earning a degree. To put the magnitude of the relationships in perspective, consider two hypothetical groups of foster youth. The two groups are identical in terms of all of the control variables included in Model 6 in Table 8.2, except that the second group is 1 *SD* higher in avoidant attachment. This is about a 1-point difference on the 7-point scale used in this study. Let us assume that the expected probability of persisting for the first group is 33.0 percent. Being 1 *SD* higher in avoidant attachment drops the second group's expected probability of persisting by about six percentage points to 26.4 percent. The difference is slightly greater when we consider two hypothetical groups in the degree completion analysis. If the first group's expected probability of earning a degree is 24.0 percent, the group higher in avoidant attachment is expected to have a graduation rate of about 16.6 percent. Thus, the results suggest that avoidant attachment is expected to play a considerable role in foster youths' chances of persisting and earning a degree.

The findings also suggested that youth higher in avoidant attachment in adolescence were more likely to display signs of mental health problems, alcohol/substance use problems, and behavior problems. One implication is that foster youth higher in avoidant attachment may present with a constellation of behavioral health difficulties that could interfere with their college success. A second implication has to do with the interplay of trauma, behavioral health problems, and avoidant attachment. This study cannot disentangle the developmental sequence of these three factors. For example, information on youths' attachment styles in early childhood was not available, so it cannot be determined whether high avoidant attachment observed in late adolescence is a continuation of insecure attachment from early childhood.

In this book, an individual's attachment style is viewed more as an evolving organization of behaviors and expectations about relationships than as a fixed trait (Sroufe, 2005). Early attachment experiences are formative in that they establish a working model of relationships that children bring with them to future relationships. However, working models can be thought of more as thick clay than as granite: they shape and are shaped by future relationships throughout periods of life (Caspi et al.,1989; Mikulincer et al., 2015). As Mikulincer and colleagues (2015) observe, "The constant mental reactivation of a trauma, particularly man-made trauma that shatters one's trust in others' goodwill and one's sense of personal value and lovability, can gradually increase the strength of negative working models of self and other, thereby heightening attachment insecurities and reducing the likelihood of attaining a calmer, more secure mental state" (p. 86). Thus, for youth who entered early childhood/adolescence with attachment styles in the securely attached range, later experiences of maltreatment and relational instability could bring about attachment difficulties. However, for those who already had attachment difficulties as they entered early childhood/adolescence, later experiences of maltreatment and relational instability would likely amplify and reinforce the difficulties.

It is important to underscore that avoidant attachment is adaptive; it is a response that originally protected foster youth when they were in the line of fire. However, if a highly avoidant attachment style is maintained even in the absence of threat, then this could backfire on youth in situations when they need others' help. In college, youth who try it to do it all on their own raise the risk of being overrun by problems they encounter.

Avoidant attachment was measured at age seventeen/eighteen, which was two to three years before most participants started college. This suggests that youths' attachment insecurities measured in late adolescence may be a fairly durable characteristic. If it is the case that avoidant attachment is durable over time and deleteriously affects college outcomes, a critical question is whether it is responsive to intervention. Can youth high in avoidant attachment become less emotionally guarded and self-reliant, and what interventions may facilitate this change?

These are complex questions that elude simple answers, and we return to them in the final chapter of the book. The next chapter investigates the role that extended foster care has on youths' chances of enrolling in, persisting in, and completing college.

Technical Appendix

As a robustness check to the findings in Table 8.2, I ran additional regression analyses to account for selection into college (see Technical Appendix, chapter 6). Probit models with sample selection were conducted on each outcome to examine whether results for avoidant attachment were robust after accounting for possible selection effects. The selection equation models college entry among all 732 participants, whereas the regression equation models the college outcome among college entrants. More parsimonious versions of Model 6 in Table 8.2 were run as biprobit selection models for each of the two outcomes. The first- and second-stage models each controlled for demographic characteristics, reading proficiency, grade repetition, educational aspirations, delinquency, mental health problems, maltreatment tertiles, number of school changes, number of foster care placement changes, age of college entry, and college type/selectivity. The first-stage selection equation also included the number of college preparatory activities as the exogenous predictor. Probit models that did not account for selection were also run for the two outcomes to compare with the results from the model that accounted for selection. Coefficients for avoidant attachment in the probit model and the probit model with selection were similar for persistence ($B = -.16$, $p = .059$ vs. $B = -.13$, $p = .055$) and degree completion ($B = -.21$, $p = .039$ vs. $-.21$, $p = .035$). The similar estimates were reflected in the small *rho* values in both the persistence model and degree completion model, which suggest that the correlation between of the error terms of the two stages was small and regression estimates were not unduly influenced by the presence of unmeasured variables (Holm & Jaeger, 2011). Thus, the robustness checks did not find evidence of selection that could have biased the avoidant attachment estimates.

9

Impact of Extended Foster Care on College Outcomes

This chapter presents findings on the impact of one of the watershed laws for transition-age foster youth. Beginning with its implementation in 2010, the Fostering Connections law fundamentally changed federal child welfare policy by giving states the option to extend the foster care age limit up to age twenty-one. Previously, the foster care age limit was eighteen in all but a few states. To participate in extended foster care (EFC), a youth must be in care on their eighteenth birthday and must either be working toward a secondary or postsecondary education credential, employed at least eighteen hours per month, participating in training that addresses employment barriers, or qualify for a medical exemption (Geen, 2009).

As reflected in the eligibility criteria, an ostensible objective of EFC is to promote the acquisition of human capital by not only finishing high school and gaining work experience but also by pursuing a postsecondary credential. To date, few studies have evaluated the impact of EFC on college outcomes. This chapter presents results from my analysis of the Midwest Study on the impact of EFC on three college outcomes: enrollment, persistence, and degree completion.

Ways That EFC May Affect College Outcomes

EFC provides a foundation of support during an age when young people typically make the transition from secondary to postsecondary education. It may have an impact on college outcomes in several ways. One of the most basic mechanisms is through the direct financial benefits that come with remaining in care. Housing is a formidable cost that is paid for or subsidized by EFC, and existing research finds that remaining in care past age eighteen diminishes the likelihood that foster youth become homeless or couch-surf in the late teenage years and early twenties (Courtney et al., 2005; Courtney & Okpych, 2017; Courtney, Okpych, & Park, 2018). When EFC covers the cost of housing, food, utilities, and other daily living expenses, foster youth may be less encumbered by full-time employment and economic hardships and can pursue a college education.

Another important way that EFC may improve college outcomes is by increasing foster youths' connections to resourceful individuals. Child welfare workers and other professionals with whom youth come in contact in EFC, such as CASA volunteers (Court Appointed Special Advocates), can serve as cultural guides, motivators, resource bridges, and brokers of information (Stanton-Salazar, 2011). These adults can help foster care youth navigate time-sensitive tasks, connect them to resources (e.g., tutoring, mental health services, college grants earmarked for foster youth), assist them with setting realistic goals, and advocate on their behalf.

Review of Studies That Evaluated the Impact of EFC on College Outcomes

Although it is thought that the material support and social capital made available through EFC will improve college outcomes, whether that is actually the case is an empirical question. A few studies, however, provided early evidence on the positive impact of EFC on college enrollment and persistence. One previous analysis of Midwest Study data found a positive impact of EFC (Courtney & Hook, 2017). As the outcome, the authors considered the highest education level attained by the last interview wave at age twenty-five: no high school credential, high school diploma or GED, or completion of one or more years of college. Results from ordinal logistic regression found that each additional year in care predicted a 46 percent increase in the odds of attaining higher categories of attainment (OR = 1.46, $p < .001$). The benefit of EFC held in a more rigorous instrumental variable analysis. Some limitations of the study are that educational attainment was based on self-report, about 20 percent of the Midwest Study sample was missing because they did not participate in Wave 3, and the outcome measure pooled secondary and postsecondary attainment. Thus, the results apply to educational attainment generally, not just postsecondary outcomes.

Recent analyses conducted by data from the CalYOUTH Study provide additional evidence on the impact of EFC on early postsecondary outcomes.

The first analysis involved more than 600 youths participating in the California longitudinal study similar to the Midwest Study; data on their college enrollment around age twenty were obtained from NSC (Courtney & Okpych, 2017). Results from logistic regression analyses found that each additional year in care increased the expected odds of college enrollment by a factor of 1.8 ($p < .001$). Two subsequent CalYOUTH Study analyses used a more rigorous analytic approach (instrumental variable). One drew on California administrative data of about 13,500 young people who had been in foster care for at least six months on or after their sixteenth birthday between 2006 and 2015 (Courtney, Okpych, & Park, 2018). Importantly, this sample included youth in care before and after California had implemented its EFC law in 2012. Using NSC data, each year in EFC increased the expected probability of enrolling in college by age twenty-one by about 8.5 percentage points. EFC was not found to have an impact on two-semester persistence or the number of semesters completed by age twenty-one among youth who enrolled in college. A third analysis from CalYOUTH using a different sample of about 22,000 youths reached similar conclusions: EFC significantly increased the probability that youth enrolled in college by age twenty-one by about four percentage points per year in EFC, but time in EFC was not significantly associated with persistence or semesters completed by age twenty-one among college entrants (Okpych et al., 2019). Although these two latter studies are the most rigorous analyses of EFC to date, they had several limitations: about 10 percent of youth had blocked NSC records, the range of available control variables was limited, and early college outcomes were only assessed up to age twenty-one.

The evidence thus far suggests that EFC increases college enrollment, but no statistically significant relationships have been found for persistence or the number of semesters completed. This chapter builds on these findings by examining the impact of EFC on college enrollment, persistence, and the yet-to-be-studied outcome of degree completion.

Description of the Samples, Measures, and Analyses

Outcomes

There were three primary outcomes in this chapter. First, college enrollment by age twenty-one is a binary outcome indicating whether youth had enrolled in a two-year or four-year college by their twenty-first birthday. Enrollment by age twenty-nine/thirty was analyzed as a supplemental analysis. Second, college persistence is a binary outcome indicating whether college entrants had completed two consecutive semesters before reaching their twenty-first birthday. As a supplemental analysis, we also examined persistence through three consecutive semesters (reported later in the chapter). The analyses that examine enrollment and persistence by age twenty-one focus on the time frame during which youth could have directly benefited from being in EFC. Third, degree completion is a binary measure indicating whether college entrants had completed a two-year or four-year college degree by age twenty-nine/thirty.[1]

Samples

Each outcome has a distinct sample. The college enrollment sample included all 732 Midwest Study participants, the persistence sample was limited to just youth who had enrolled in college before age twenty-one and who appeared in NSC records ($n = 232$), and the degree completion sample included Midwest Study participants who had enrolled in college and who could be observed for six or more years ($n = 329$).

Measure of EFC

The main variable of interest was the number of years a Midwest Study participant remained in foster care past their eighteenth birthday, which was calculated from child welfare discharge data. The amount of time in EFC ranged from 0 years (if a youth exited care on or before their eighteenth birthday) to 3 years (if a youth exited care on their twenty-first birthday).

Control Variables

As described later, an instrumental variable (IV) approach was used to estimate the impact of EFC on college outcomes. Like other regression models, IV models can also include control variables. However, because IV models require a great deal of statistical power but some of the analyses were based on relatively small sample sizes, a carefully selected set of factors were included as control variables. In addition to demographic characteristics (gender, race/ethnicity, and age at the time of the interview), variables were included if they were significantly associated with both years in EFC and one or more of the three college outcomes. Most controls—reading proficiency, educational aspirations, highest completed grade, ever in special education, number of foster care placements, number of school changes, ever placed in congregate care, had a living child, mental health problem, and alcohol/substance use problem—were measured at Wave 1 when participants were seventeen/eighteen years old. The persistence and degree completion analyses, which were limited to youth who had enrolled in college, included two additional control variables: age the youth first enrolled in college and college type/selectivity.

Statistical Analyses

The main questions examined in this chapter are causal in nature: Does EFC cause changes in the chance of enrollment, persistence, and degree completion? Short of a randomized controlled trial study, it is tricky to estimate the true impact of a treatment or a policy. Therefore, sophisticated statistical methods are needed to try to get an accurate estimate of the impact of EFC. Two types of analyses were conducted. The first type is a linear probability model (LPM).[2] LPMs are similar to logistic regression models, except LPMs express the effect of a predictor as a percentage rather than an OR.

One problem with LPMs, particularly when the goal is to estimate causal impact, is that they may not sufficiently control for potential confounding. That is, if youth who stayed in EFC for different amounts of time also differ in other important ways that affect their college outcome, and if those other differences are not fully controlled in the regression model, estimates can be biased. We may wind up with an incorrect estimate of the role that EFC plays in college outcomes. The estimate might be too large or small compared to the true impact of the policy.

Fortunately, the design of the Midwest Study, when combined with a rigorous data analysis method, can be exploited to address the problem of unmeasured confounding. A unique feature of the Midwest Study is that it is a natural experiment: Illinois permitted foster youth to remain in care until age twenty-one while youth in the other two states youth exited by age eighteen, with few exceptions. Thus, depending on the state a youth happened to reside in, they either did or did not have an EFC option. We can exploit this by using an advanced statistical method called an instrumental variable (IV) approach to arrive at more accurate estimates of the impact of EFC, even if all of the relevant confounding factors are not included as control variables.

IV models are complex, but in a nutshell they identify a variable that is strongly related to EFC and that only influences the three college outcomes through its impact on the amount of time youth spend in EFC. This variable is called an "instrument." Following a previous analysis (Courtney & Hook, 2017), the instrument used in this chapter is the state in which youth lived while in foster care. The particular type of IV model used in this chapter is called a two-stage least squares (2SLS) model. As the name implies, a 2SLS model involves running two regression models. In the first stage, the association between the state of residence and the amount of time youth remain in EFC is estimated. This estimated association is then used in the second stage to predict the likelihood of the college outcome. In other words, the genius of an IV approach is that it uses the association between state and time in EFC, which may not be plagued by unmeasured confounding, as a stand-in for time in EFC, which is likely plagued by unmeasured confounding. Using the state–EFC association helps us get a more accurate estimate of the true impact of EFC.

There are several assumptions of IV models, but two are particularly important. First, it is assumed that the instrument (state) is strongly related to time in EFC. This can be tested empirically by examining the association between state and EFC. The second assumption is called the *exclusion restriction*, which states that the instrument only affects the outcome through its influence on the intervention. In other words, it is assumed that the state youth live in affects their likelihood of enrolling, persisting, and completing college only because it influences how much time they stay in care past their eighteenth birthday. If the state influences youths' likelihood of achieving these college outcomes in other ways, then the plausibility of the exclusion restriction assumption is dubious. The exclusion restriction cannot be proven definitively, but like a legal case, evidence can be examined that supports or refutes its plausibility. The first part of the next section will review evidence for and against the two IV model assumptions.

Two additional variations of the 2SLS models were run to check whether the results were consistent with the original 2SLS models. The Technical Appendix at the end of this chapter gives a more detailed explanation of IV models, IV assumptions, and the robustness checks.

Findings

Examining Assumption 1: Strong Relationship between the Instrument and the Treatment

The first IV assumption is that the state of residence is strongly predictive of the amount of time youth spend in EFC. Figure 9.1 displays the proportion of youth who were still in care in each state from about age 16.5 to age 21. On

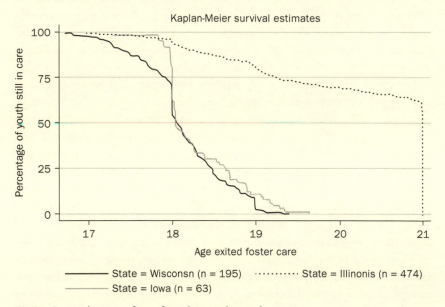

FIG. 9.1 Survival curves of age of exit, by state ($n = 732$)

average, youth in Illinois (20.3 years) exited care about full two years later than youth in Iowa (18.3 years) and Wisconsin (18.3 years; both $p < .001$). The trends for Wisconsin and Iowa follow a roughly similar pattern: a gradual decline in foster care exits up to age eighteen, a sharp drop at age eighteen, and a precipitous decline as the remaining youth leave care. This was not surprising, given that the de facto foster care age limit for these two states was age eighteen. However, it can be seen that 45.1 percent of youth in Wisconsin and 39.7 percent of youth in Iowa were in care on or after their eighteenth birthday. This high percentage is due to policies that allowed youth to remain in care under special circumstances. Under federal law, young people could remain in care past age eighteen up to their nineteenth birthday (and states can claim reimbursement under Title IV-E of the Social Security Act) if they were expected to finish high school before age nineteen. Additionally, in Wisconsin youth who were pregnant or were parents were permitted to remain in care past age eighteen. However, by age nineteen, effectively all youth had exited care in Wisconsin (only 2.5% were still in care), and nearly all youth had left care in Iowa (9.5% were still in care).

A markedly different trend was observed for youth in Illinois, where a state policy that was in effect since the late 1990s permitted youth in care on their eighteenth birthday to remain in care up to age twenty-one (Peters, 2012). Almost 70% of Illinois youth remained in care past their twentieth birthday (69.2%), and more than half were still in care on their twenty-first birthday (53.8%). Figure 9.1 depicts a clear and strong association between the instrument and treatment. Moreover, in all four 2SLS models presented in Tables 9.3 and 9.4, the F-statistic in the first stage models were well above the recommended value of 10 (Angrist & Pischke, 2009) and were statistically significantly ($p < .001$). These results indicate that the instrument in sufficiently strong and satisfies the first IV model assumption.

Examining Assumption 2: Exclusion Restriction

Comparison of Youth-Level Differences across States. The first step in assessing the plausibility of the exclusion restriction is to compare state differences in youth characteristics. In the IV models, it is assumed that state influences college outcomes only through its influence of increasing EFC participation for youth in Illinois relative to the other two states. In this section, we check for evidence to the contrary. In particular, we would be especially concerned if youth in Illinois were different from youth in the other two states in ways that would make them more ready to enroll in college, persist, and complete a degree. For example, if we found that Illinois youth had stronger academic backgrounds and encountered fewer risks than youth in the other two states, we might worry that these between-state differences in the youth, and not EFC, might be driving differences in college outcomes.

Table 9.1
Descriptive Statistics of Sample Control Variables, by State

	Illinois (n = 474)	Wisconsin (n = 195)	Iowa (n = 63)	p
Male (%)	46.0	55.9	44.0	.054
Race/ethnicity (%)				<.001
White	20.0	34.4	77.7	
African American	67.3	42.6	4.8	
Hispanic	7.6	10.8	9.5	
Other race	5.1	12.3	7.9	
Age at baseline interview (Mean/SD)	18.0 (.3)	17.6 (.3)	17.7 (.3)	<.001
Highest completed grade (%)				.009
Tenth grade or lower	34.3	41.2	28.6	
Eleventh grade	51.2	52.1	65.1	
Twelfth grade	14.6	6.8	6.4	
Reading level, standardized (mean/SD)	−.81 (1.15)	−.93 (.94)	−.32 (.90)	<.001
Ever in special education (%)	45.7	46.7	63.5	.029
Education aspirations (%)				.119
High school credential or less	10.5	16.2	11.7	
Some college	13.9	12.6	21.7	
College degree or more	75.7	71.2	66.7	
Number of school changes (mean/SD)	2.94 (1.88)	2.06 (2.06)	3.44 (1.80)	<.001
Number of foster care placements (mean/SD)	6.2 (5.9)	4.8 (5.4)	5.8 (6.0)	.010
Ever in congregate care (%)	60.9	51.8	77.8	.001
Had a living child (%)	14.2	9.3	4.8	.002
Mental health problem (%)	66.7	68.2	85.7	.009
Substance use problem (%)	26.1	18.7	37.1	.010
Among participants in the degree completion sample (n = 329)				
Age first enrolled in college (mean/SD)	19.5 (1.4)	20.0 (1.7)	19.8 (1.8)	.018
College selectivity (%)				.013
Two-year college	77.8	69.1	88.5	
Minimally selective four-year college	10.4	23.5	0.0	
Selective four-year college	11.8	7.4	11.5	

Table 9.1 compares youth in the three states on factors included in the regression analyses. In a few areas, youth in Illinois were found to significantly differ from their counterparts in ways that might *negatively affect* their higher education outcomes. Compared to foster youth in Wisconsin, Illinois foster youth had more foster care placements ($p < .01$) and were more likely to have ever been in congregate care ($p < .05$). Additionally, Illinois youth were significantly more likely than youth in the other two states to have a child (both $p < .05$) and had lower reading proficiency scores than Iowa youth ($p < .01$). In contrast, Illinois youth were less likely than Iowa youth to have been in special education, to have reported mental health problems, and to have ever been in congregate care (all

$p < .05$). Thus, in a few respects, youth in Illinois appear to have been different from youth in the other two states in ways that may have disadvantaged them in going to college and succeeding there. There was no evidence suggesting that Illinois youth had a distinct, consistent advantage over youth in Iowa and Wisconsin.

Comparison of State-Level Differences across States. State-level differences, such as statewide college enrollment rates, may also affect college outcomes of foster youth. For example, if a greater percentage of students in Illinois enroll in college than in the other two states, we might question whether these state differences, not EFC, are causing foster youth in Illinois to have higher enrollment rates than in the other two states. As a second check of the plausibility of the exclusion restriction, differences in several state-level factors related to college entry, persistence, and completion were investigated. This information came from a variety of publicly available data sources. Nearly nine in ten youth in the Midwest Study sample (89%) had first attended college in the state they resided in, and most youth (about 74%) enrolled in two-year colleges. To the extent possible, data were obtained from the years that were closest to when most participants in the Midwest Study completed high school (2002–2003) and enrolled in college (2004–2008).

As displayed in Table 9.2, there were several state-level differences that likely *disadvantaged* Illinois youth compared to one or both of the other states. Illinois high school graduation rates were about five to ten percentage points lower than in the other two states. Furthermore, Illinois high school graduates were slightly less likely than their counterparts in Wisconsin and Iowa to enter college soon after graduating. Differences between states in college retention rates in two-year colleges were modest. However, although not displayed in the table, retention rates in four-year colleges were lower in Illinois than in both other states. For example, in 2008, 72.8 percent of Illinois college students returned for a second year, which was about five percentage points lower than students in Wisconsin (78.6%) and Iowa (78.0%). In terms of degree completion, the percentage of two-year college students who completed a degree in three years was markedly lower in Illinois colleges than in the other two states. Although not displayed, six-year bachelor's degree completion rates were similar in Illinois and Wisconsin (59.6% and 58.0% in 2008, respectively), although Iowa's graduation rates were somewhat higher (62.7% in 2008).

Although secondary and postsecondary outcomes mostly favored Iowa and Wisconsin over Illinois, some state-level financial benefits may have favored college outcomes in Illinois over the other two states. The cost of tuition in public two-year colleges was lower by roughly $1,000 in Illinois than in the other two states. Additionally, the average amount of state need-based financial aid was more generous in Illinois than in Wisconsin, with qualifying low-income

Table 9.2

Comparison of State-Level Outcomes and Resources

	Illinois	Wisconsin	Iowa
High school graduation rate[a] (%)			
2002	75.9	85.8	85.3
2003	80.3	86.3	85.8
2004	79.4	86.7	86.6
College entry rates among recent high school graduates[b] (%)			
2004	55.2	57.0	61.6
2006	60.4	61.0	60.9
2008	57.4	59.1	64.3
College retention rates at two-year colleges[c]			
2007	59.0	56.5	59.0
2008	58.8	58.2	58.1
2009	60.9	61.2	59.0
Degree completion rates by 150% of expected time in two-year colleges[c]			
2004	28.5	35.9	39.1
2006	27.3	37.2	38.8
2008	26.8	35.6	38.0
Average cost of in-state tuition at two-year colleges[d]			
2004	$1,949	$2,793	$2,880
2006	$2,250	$3,168	$3,137
2008	$2,520	$3,521	$3,418
Average expenditure of state need-based financial aid[e]			
2003	$2,489	$1,922	$2,829
2004	$2,355	$2,092	$2,933
2005	$2,198	$2,067	$2,985

[a] State public high school graduation rates for 2002, 2003, and 2004 were obtained from the Common Core Data (CCD) managed by the Institute for Education Sciences. CCD's graduation rates are estimates of the percentage of entering freshmen who graduated within four years. The 2003 high school graduation rate for Wisconsin was not reported, so the rates in 2002 (85.8%) and 2004 (86.7%) were averaged to estimate a rate for 2003 (86.3%).

[b] State averages for the proportion of public high school graduates who enter college within a year after graduation were obtained from multiple years of the *Digest of Education Statistics*.

[c] Rates of college retention and degree completion were computed using the IPEDS Trend Generator data system available on the National Center of Education Statistics website.

[d] Average tuition costs were obtained from multiple years of the *Digest of Education Statistics*.

[e] Average student expenditures on state need-based financial aid were obtained from the National Association of State Student Grant and Aid Programs (NASSGAP) online search tool. Information was obtained for Illinois' Monetary Award Program, Wisconsin's Tuition Grant, and Iowa's Tuition grant.

students in Illinois receiving a few hundred dollars more in aid than youth in Wisconsin. However, Iowa had the most generous aid program by several hundred dollars.

The Illinois Department of Children and Families (DCFS) also funded the Community College Payment Program (CCPP), which was only available to young people who were still in foster care and who were enrolled in Illinois community colleges. The CCPP provided funding for up to four semesters of tuition, fees, books, and supplies that were not covered by federal financial aid grants. As a condition of receiving the CCPP, Illinois foster youth were required to complete the federal FAFSA. Most likely, many foster youth would have qualified for a Pell Grant, and because the maximum amount of the Pell Grant for each year was well above the cost of in-district community college tuition and fees,[3] it is unclear how much extra financial support the CCPP actually contributed to foster youth in Illinois. It may be more accurate to view this program as a supplemental or safety net program for foster youth if other types of aid fell through, rather than as a program that disbursed significant amounts of college aid. However, by requiring foster youth to apply for federal aid, the program could have induced some youth to gain access to federals funds that they would have otherwise not applied for. To my knowledge, Wisconsin and Iowa did not have tuition waiver programs for foster youth that were operating at a time that would apply to Midwest Study participants. There may have been other state-level differences in financial aid available to foster youth such as in ETV amounts, but evidence of this was not found.[4]

In summary, there were several indications that Illinois lagged behind its neighboring states in educational attainment, which would have likely *disfavored* Illinois foster youth in terms of entering, persisting in, and completing college. Yet, the low cost of tuition, the slightly more generous state need-based aid program (relative to Wisconsin), and the DCFS-funded award that supplemented federal financial aid may have made the cost of attendance particularly manageable for youth in Illinois EFC. Overall, however, we did not find evidence of a consistent, distinct advantage for Illinois over the other two states that would drive up postsecondary education outcomes. In fact, some of the observed differences appear to *disadvantage* Illinois, which could lead to an underestimation of the estimated benefit of EFC.

Descriptive Comparisons of College Outcomes by Amount of Time Spent in EFC

Before moving to the IV model results, let us first examine a few graphs that display differences in college enrollment, persistence, and degree completion rates between youth who spent differing amounts of time in EFC. These trends give a basic picture of how EFC is related to college outcomes.

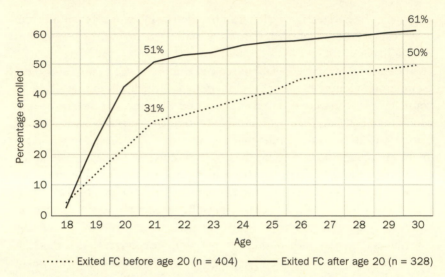

FIG. 9.2 Cumulative proportion of participants who had ever enrolled in college, by care status at age 20

Figure 9.2 displays the cumulative percentage of youth who had ever enrolled in college across ages. To make it easier to visualize these statistics, study participants were separated into two groups: youth who exited foster care before their twentieth birthday and youth who exited foster care on or after their twentieth birthday. By age twenty-one, there was a twenty-percentage-point difference in college enrollment rates ($p < .001$). About half of the youth who stayed in care after age twenty had enrolled in college, compared to less than one-third of youth who exited care before age twenty. By age thirty, the enrollment rate gap narrowed to eleven percentage points but was still statistically significant ($p = .002$).

Figure 9.3 shows that there were no significant differences by care status in one-semester persistence rates ($p = .578$), but youth who stayed in care past age twenty were significantly more likely than youth who left before age twenty to have persisted through two consecutive semesters ($p = .043$). The difference in three-semester persistence rates was not statistically significant ($p = .233$).

Differences in degree completion rates are displayed across ages in Figure 9.4. Beginning around age twenty-three, degree completion increased more sharply for the youth who had remained in care past age twenty than for youth who had left care before age twenty. By age thirty, the proportion of youth who had completed a degree was significantly greater for youth in care after their twentieth birthday than for youth who exited before age twenty (10.6% vs. 5.5%, $p = .012$).

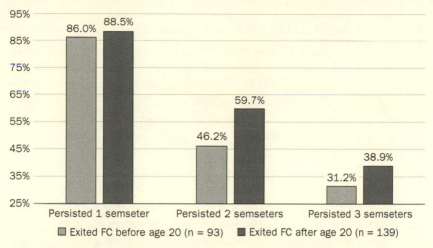

FIG. 9.3 Rates of college persistence among youth who first enrolled before age 21, by persistence duration and foster care status at age 20

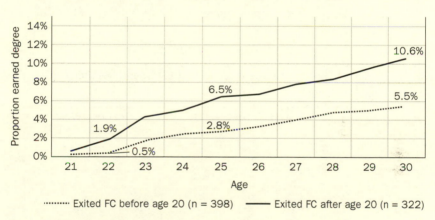

FIG. 9.4 College degree completion across ages, by foster care status ($n = 720$)
NOTE: The sample excludes 12 individuals who became deceased during the study period.

The graphs suggest that youth who remained in care past age twenty had higher rates of college enrollment (by age twenty-one and by age twenty-nine/thirty), of two-semester persistence by age twenty-one, and of degree completion by age twenty-nine/thirty. Although promising, these graphs do not control for possible differences between these two groups of youth that could affect their likelihood of attaining the college outcomes. For that, we turn to regression analyses to more rigorously evaluate the role of EFC.

Regression Analyses That Estimate the Impact of EFC

Table 9.3 displays findings from the LPM and IV regression models examining college enrollment. It shows the estimated effect on enrollment for each additional year in EFC (B), the standard error, and the *p*-value. Asterisks are used to display the level of statistical significance. EFC estimates displayed in the table are proportions and can be converted to percentages by multiplying by 100. For example, the proportion .077 in Model 1 means that each extra year youth spend in EFC is expected to increase their probability of enrolling in college by age twenty-one by 7.7% (.077 * 100 = 7.7%). Models 1–3 are the results of the LPM models that control for an increasing number of potential confounders. Model 4 displays the results of the more rigorous 2SLS model with all of the control variables. Models 5 and 6 display the results of the supplemental IV models that use a different estimation procedure (Model 5) and a different instrument (Model 6; see the Technical Appendix at the end of the chapter).

For college enrollment by age twenty-one, the results are fairly consistent across the three LPMs that add successive sets of control variables. The estimates change little in the more rigorous IV models. In Model 4, it is estimated that each year in care past age eighteen increases the probability of enrolling in

Table 9.3

The Relationships between Years in Care Past Eighteenth Birthday and College Enrollment

	Enrolled in College by Age 21 (n = 713)			Enrolled in College by Age 29/30 (n = 702)[c]		
	B	Standard error[d]	p	B	Standard error[d]	p
LPM MODELS						
Model 1	.077***	.014	<.001	.045**	.014	.001
Model 2[a]	.092***	.015	<.001	.057***	.016	<.001
Model 3[a,b]	.082***	.015	<.001	.045**	.015	.004
IV MODELS						
Model 4: 2SLS[a,b]	.109***	.024	<.001	.028	.025	.251
Model 5: LIML[a,b]	.109***	.024	<.001	.028	.025	.250
Model 6: 2SLS County Groups[a,b]	.088***	.021	<.001	.016	.022	.466

NOTE: *p < .05 **p < .01 ***p < .001.
[a] Controls included gender, race/ethnicity, age at Wave 1.
[b] Controls included reading proficiency, educational aspiration, highest completed grade, number of foster care placements, history of congregate care, has a living child, mental health problem, substance use problem, ever incarcerated.
[c] Excluded 12 youths who were deceased by the end of the Midwest Study.
[d] The standard errors in the LPM models are robust standard errors.

college by age twenty-one by about eleven percentage points. The probability of enrolling in college by age twenty-one is expected to be more than thirty percentage points higher for youth who stayed in care until age twenty-one versus youth who left care by age eighteen.

The columns on the right investigate the probability that youth enrolled in college by age twenty-nine/thirty. The estimates are fairly stable and statistically significant in the LPM models; each year in care is estimated to increase the probability of enrolling in college by age twenty-nine/thirty by about five percentage points. However, in the more rigorous IV models, the estimates of the relationship between years in care past age eighteen and enrollment decrease considerably to under 3 percent and are no longer statistically significant. These results suggest that more time in EFC increases the probability of enrolling in college by age twenty-one but not by age twenty-nine/thirty.

Table 9.4 displays results for influence of EFC on the outcomes of persistence and degree completion. These analyses include just Midwest Study participants who had enrolled in college. In all three LPMs, years in care past age eighteen was found to significantly increase the expected probability of persistence. However, in the more rigorous IV models, the estimates decrease and are no longer statistically significant. Time that youth spent in EFC was not

Table 9.4
The Relationships between Years in Care Past Eighteenth Birthday and College Persistence and Degree Completion

	Two-Semester Persistence by Age 21 (n = 228)			Two-/Four-Year Degree Completion by Age 29/30 (n = 319)[c]		
	B	Standard error[d]	p	B	Standard error[d]	p
LPM MODELS						
Model 1	.060*	.026	.022	.011	.017	.526
Model 2[a]	.078*	.032	.017	.009	.019	.649
Model 3[a,b]	.080*	.033	.015	.007	.020	.726
IV MODELS						
Model 4: 2SLS[a,b]	.068	.056	.224	−.045	.029	.121
Model 5: LIML[a,b]	.017	.053	.743	−.045	.029	.119
Model 6: 2SLS County Groups[a,b]	.024	.049	.618	−.029	.027	.278

NOTE: *$p < .05$.
[a] Controls included gender, race/ethnicity, age at Wave 1.
[b] Controls included reading proficiency, educational aspiration, highest completed grade, number of foster care placements, history of congregate care, has a living child, mental health problem, substance use problem, ever incarcerated, age first enrolled in college, college selectivity.
[c] Excluded 12 youths who were deceased by the end of the Midwest Study.
[d] The standard errors in the LPM models are robust standard errors.

significantly associated with degree completion among college entrants in any of the models that were examined.

As mentioned, the results in Table 9.4 include just Midwest Study participants who had enrolled in college. A supplemental analysis was run to see whether EFC was related to degree completion among all youth in the Midwest Study who were not missing data on the control variables and who had not died ($n = 709$). In the 2SLS model, the variable, months in care, was not significantly associated with the probability of completing a degree ($B = -.005$, $SE = .012$, $p = .663$).

Chapter Summary

This chapter examined the impact of state EFC policy differences on three college outcomes. Results find that EFC had a positive impact on college enrollment by age twenty-one; more time spent in foster care past age eighteen increased the likelihood that youth enrolled in college by their twenty-first birthday. We did not find evidence that EFC significantly increased the expected probability of college persistence or degree completion. The positive impact on enrollment by age twenty-one and the lack of a statistically significant impact on persistence are consistent with the findings of two recent studies of California foster youth (Courtney et al., 2018; Okpych et al., 2019).

When interpreting the findings of the IV models, it is important to keep in mind that the benefit of EFC only applies to foster youth whose time in care after age eighteen is influenced by state EFC policy (Angrist et al., 1996). The findings do not apply to youth whose time in EFC is unaffected by state EFC policy. For example, some foster youth are adamant about leaving care at age eighteen whether or not their state has EFC. Consequently, the finding about EFC boosting enrollment rates does not apply to youth whose time in EFC is unmoved by state policy.

There are two limitations of the analyses in this chapter that are important to note. First, although an effect of EFC was found for these three particular states during this particular historical time, we cannot assume that the impact will be the same in other states and in other historical times (called "generalizability" in research). Because states vary in the makeup of their foster youth population, child welfare policy, other policies and programs targeting postsecondary education of foster youth, and in other relevant ways, the impact of EFC may differ regionally. Second, although state was a very strong predictor of time in care past age eighteen, it is not possible to definitively rule out the exclusion criterion. Using publicly available data, several between-state comparisons were presented of factors that could conceivably influence between-state college outcomes (e.g., college entry rates, average cost of college, etc.). But certainly other factors could be at play as well. If between-state differences other than EFC policy influenced foster youths' college outcomes, this would mean that the instrument is not entirely exogenous and the estimates of the impact of EFC could be off. However, the fact that the findings reported here are consistent with those in other rigorous analyses of EFC in another state and at a different time supports the conclusions.

Technical Appendix: Instrumental Variable Models

The use of instrumental variables (IV) is an econometric approach to estimate causal effects in the presence of potential endogeneity (Greene, 2011). To provide a more rigorous assessment of the relationship between EFC and the college outcomes, two-stage least squares (2SLS) IV models were estimated for each of the three outcomes. In IV models, the predicted values for years in care after age eighteen from the first-stage equation is used in the second-stage equation to predict the expected probability of the college outcome. LPMs with robust standard errors were estimated in the second stage of the IV models because violations of assumptions of the functional form of the outcome could lead to biased estimates in IV probit and IV logit models (Elwert & Winship, 2014). LPMs are commonly used with binary outcomes, including in analyses evaluating education outcomes such as college persistence and degree completion (e.g., Bielby et al., 2013).

IV models estimate the local average treatment effect (Greene, 2011). That is, the results do not apply to never-takers (i.e., foster youth who would not participate in EFC regardless of differences in state policy) and always-takers (i.e., foster youth who would always participate in EFC regardless of state policy differences). Rather, the results pertain to foster youth whose college outcomes can be influenced by variations in state policy that lead to differences in time spent in EFC.

There are two primary assumptions of an IV approach (Angrist et al., 1996; Bielby et al., 2013). The first assumption is that the instrument (state) is related to the treatment (time in care past the eighteenth birthday). It can be tested empirically by examining the correlation between state and years in EFC, as well as the model fit statistic in the first stage of the IV model. A second major assumption of IV models is the exclusion restriction, which states that the instrument is only related to the outcomes through the treatment. Violations of this assumption would occur if factors associated with state, other than the amount of time that youth spend in care after age eighteen, affect the three college outcomes. State differences in youth-level characteristics or state-level characteristics could bias the estimated impact of extended care in the IV models. The exclusion restriction assumption cannot be empirically verified, because the universe of potential factors that could be related to state and the outcomes of interest has not been measured (Bielby et al., 2013).

Although the exclusion restriction assumption cannot be empirically confirmed, three steps were taken to assess the plausibility of the assumption. First, between-state differences in youth-level characteristics relevant to postsecondary education outcomes were examined. Factors that were found to differ significantly between states informed the selection of control variables. Second, between-state differences in several state-level factors relevant to postsecondary education outcomes were examined. These include measures of secondary and postsecondary outcomes, tuition costs, and need-based financial aid programs.

As a third step to address possible violations of the exclusion restriction, we ran two additional IV models as robustness checks. The first supplemental IV models used county groups as the instrument, instead of the state (Model 6). This was done to help break potential state-level confounding. If results from the county group IV models are consistent with results from the state IV models, this increases our confidence in the state IV models. The county group variable had five categories: Cook County in Illinois, other urban counties in Illinois, rural counties in Illinois, a group for Wisconsin state, and a group for Iowa state. Work by Peters (2012) suggests that regional variation in child welfare courts and advocacy in Illinois is a critical driver of county variation in the amount of time that youth remain in care past age eighteen. Consistent with this finding, youth in Cook County (IL) spent an average of 2.6 years in care past age eighteen, which was greater than the amount of time in EFC for youth in Illinois urban counties (1.6 years) and Illinois rural counties (1.5 years). There were neither substantive nor empirical reasons to separate county groups within Wisconsin or Iowa. For Wisconsin, average years in care past age eighteen were comparable for Milwaukee County (0.3 years), other urban counties (0.2 years), and rural counties (0.2 years). For Iowa, average years in care past age eighteen were comparable for urban counties (0.3 years) and rural counties (0.4 years).

The second supplemental IV models were estimated using limited information maximum likelihood (LIML; Model 5). LIML performs well when sample sizes are small; simulation studies indicate that LIML produces estimates that can be more consistent and reliable than 2SLS estimators in these circumstances (Sovey & Green, 2011). It was examined whether the LIML models reached similar estimates as the 2SLS models.

Part III

Recommendations

10

Policy and Practice Recommendations to Increase College Enrollment and Completion

The findings from this book bring to light some of the factors that contribute to the chances that foster youth attain postsecondary success. Recall that, collectively, the obstacles that stand between foster youth and a college degree were depicted in this book as a broken ladder. This chapter provides recommendations to address different parts of the broken ladder. It is important to keep in mind that supports for youth with care histories are appreciably better now than they were a few decades ago. In the mid-1990s, there was no federally funded extended foster care (EFC), no ETVs, no campus support programs for foster youth, no federal law to minimize unnecessary school changes, and modest federal funding for independent living services. Foster youth who aspired to go to college had to largely rely on their own will and might. Today, EFC is available in most states, ETVs can help stave off college costs, there is more funding for independent living services, and a small but growing number of college campuses house CSPs. The ladder into and through college has improved, but there are still broken parts that need fixing. The remainder of this chapter provides policy and program recommendations that add stability to the ladder. These recommendations are offered with a measure of humility. There is still a lot to learn, but I believe the recommendations are good starting points to tackling areas that demand attention and where there is potential to have an impact, if addressed with purpose.

The recommendations in this chapter are separated into two sections, which align with two key postsecondary education goals: getting foster youth into college and helping foster youth remain in and complete college. The recommendations speak to three systems that have sustained contact with foster youth during this window of time: child welfare, secondary education, and postsecondary education.

A red ribbon that runs through the recommendations is the central importance of relationships. Simply put, foster youth need to feel important. They need to feel valued. They need people to genuinely care about them, want them to succeed, and be willing to fight for them. Why are relationships so primary? First, many of the supports intended to help foster youth are delivered *through* relationships they have with caseworkers, teachers, counselors, advocates, mentors, college staff, and others. Relationships are the channel through which supports and resources flow. Second, many foster youth have been hurt by other people and have accumulated a healthy distrust of getting close to others. They have learned to survive as a lone wolf. But new relationships are an opportunity for foster youth to rewrite the script that they expect to play out. Every college-aspiring foster youth needs to have a relationship with at least one person, and ideally several people, who can be competent, compassionate guides.

Recommendations to Promote College Enrollment

College Guidance and Planning

A first target area centers on the process of selecting and enrolling in colleges. The proposed recommendations in this area are about building structures to ensure that foster youth are provided with high-quality, hands-on guidance with the college search, application, and selection process. Without this help, foster youth may fail to enroll in college or may make critical mistakes that could later be detrimental (e.g., not applying for ETVs, attending an expensive school resulting in crippling student loan debt when more affordable options are available). Another possibility is that, without structured guidance, students may enroll in a college where their chances of finishing are lower than at other colleges. Keeping the measurement limitations in mind, it was estimated that about one in three Midwest Study participants who went to college enrolled in an institution that was less selective than where they likely could have gotten into. Research on the general college student body suggests that this undermatching could hurt students' chances of graduating (e.g., Alon & Tienda, 2005; Melguizo, 2008). In chapter 8, we saw that foster youth who had similar academic and other background characteristics had different chances of succeeding in college depending on the type of school in which they enrolled. Failing to provide foster youth with enough structured support means that some will not go to college, others will make costly mistakes, and still others will enroll in colleges where their chances of success are lower.

The first recommendation is for child welfare departments to institute a mandatory annual training on postsecondary education for child welfare workers whose caseload includes a youth age sixteen years old or older. California has recently passed such a law (John Burton Advocates for Youth, 2020). Child welfare workers are the frontline staff who work directly with youth, and they can literally open up new worlds of possibility to foster youth through their advising and referrals to programs. Concretely, they are responsible for facilitating the creation of case plans that involve youths' education goals. But if education is not prioritized, conversations around college will not be purposeful and may not even happen. The purpose of the training is not to make caseworkers experts in college advising. Rather, it is to help them appreciate the power they have to shape the educational trajectories of foster youth and to equip them with essential knowledge of the college planning process and locally available education resources for foster youth. The goal of the training is to enable caseworkers to provide clear, specific, and robust case planning around postsecondary education.

A second recommendation pertains to the transitional independent living plan (TILP) meetings that occur every six months for youth in care ages sixteen or older. TILP meetings should be used as a mechanism to formalize action steps that link youth with college advising and information. Prioritizing college planning is warranted both because most foster youth plan on going to college and because higher education is so consequential to their future economic well-being. A brief standardized assessment of youths' college plans and knowledge should be a required part of the first TILP meeting. Specific college goals developed in the TILP can be guided by benchmarks used by high school guidance counselors that spell out the timing and sequence of tasks needed to apply for admission to college. For example, identifying prospective colleges and taking standardized tests typically occur in the junior year, visiting colleges and narrowing the list of schools that students will apply to take place in the summer after junior year, and college admissions applications and financial aid applications are completed in the fall of senior year. Having a formal timetable with tasks outlined in the TILP will ensure that students do not miss critical deadlines that could affect their ability to gain admission to college or get financial aid. It is important that the TILP goals be specific and actionable; for example, ensuring that foster youth register for a FAFSA pin by the start of their senior year.

Although the TILP can be used as a tool to map out college planning goals, it is unrealistic to expect child welfare workers to serve as college advisors. Rather, caseworkers should be responsible for ensuring that foster youth are connected to other professionals and resources to meet the college planning goals in the TILP. For youth who aspire to go to college, child welfare departments could require at least one professional to be designated as a person who will provide college advising; this professional, who would meet with the youth regularly and would attend the six-month case review meetings, need not be part of the welfare department staff. High school guidance counselors and other school personnel are prime professionals to take on this role, especially if the foster youth has an existing relationship with them and they are invested in the young person's success. However, child welfare workers may need to rely on other professionals. Youth-serving organizations that specialize in providing educational support for foster youth are potential partners. Child welfare departments could contract with local organizations to provide college advising to all high school age foster youth who are interested in pursuing higher education, drawing on Chafee funds.

A bolder alternative would be for child welfare departments to develop an in-house college advising capacity. This would entail creating academic specialist workers who provide college planning to high-school-age foster youth. Additionally, these workers would develop strong working relationships with local colleges in which foster youth in the jurisdiction commonly enroll. This may require child welfare departments to recruit professionals with prior college advising experience or to provide training on college advising. For youth who remain in EFC and enroll in college, academic specialists could also serve in a supportive role to promote college success. For example, the specialists could link youth to CSPs and help youth navigate and complete applications for aid (e.g., ETVs, state tuition waivers, federal student aid, scholarships). While the academic specialist position is outside the bounds of the types of services child welfare departments usually provide, it is entirely consistent with the goals of EFC and Chafee: to prepare youth to live on their own. We need to start thinking boldly and creatively about ways to achieve these goals, which may mean breaking from our usual ways of doing things.

Another set of recommendations pertains to the timing and types of colleges to which youth apply. When possible, foster youth should be encouraged to enter college soon after completing their secondary education. In chapters 6 and 7, it was found that early college entry significantly increases youths' likelihood of persisting in college and earning a degree, in part because later life circumstances and demands may pull youth away from college. Moreover, and as discussed in more detail in the next section, the late teenage years and early twenties are a time when considerable supports are available to foster youth. Some of these supports are age-limited and are not available to foster youth who delay entry into college by a few years. Foster youth should also be encouraged to apply to several colleges, and not just two-year schools, "safe" schools, and schools they are familiar with. A constrained college search may be selling foster youth short and ultimately hinder their ability to succeed. Instead, foster youth should be encouraged to apply to a few "reach" schools (colleges above their qualifications), a few match schools (colleges aligned with their qualifications), and a few safety net schools (colleges below their qualifications). Although there are many factors to consider when determining which colleges would be a good fit for a given foster youth, their options should not be limited. Foster youth need to be given good advice about the types of colleges where students are more likely to succeed (e.g., those with higher retention rates and more plentiful resources to ensure student success). Ideally, the college will have a CSP in which the student can enroll. The overriding goal is not to get them into just any college, but into one where they have a good chance of succeeding.

Navigating Application Logistics

Deadlines are critical. Oftentimes, college applications, FAFSA, ETV, state tuition waivers, and scholarships are all on different timetables. Furthermore, it is unrealistic to expect foster youth—on their own—to comprehend the esoteric language and complete sometimes complicated administrative steps of the applications. Managing the logistical steps is vital, because nontrivial proportions of foster youth fail to receive need-based grants such as Pell Grants and ETVs that they qualify for (John Burton Advocates for Youth, 2015; Courtney et al., 2016). Gross and colleagues (2019) found that foster youth were less likely than low-income first-generation students to apply for federal financial aid (49% vs. 75%). Further, about 40 percent of former foster youth in the study received no aid of any kind for college, which was significantly lower than the proportion of low-income first-generation students who received no aid (24%) (Gross et al., 2019). In a recent California study, about 42 percent of foster youth who went to college received an ETV (Okpych et al., 2020).

The first time around, each foster youth needs a competent guide to explain and walk them through the administrative steps. The various deadlines, order of operations, and required documents need to be laid out and completed alongside the youth. This will both ensure the paperwork is completed correctly and on time, and make the process far less intimidating in subsequent years.

Another recommendation is to link the ETV application to the FAFSA application. Currently, completing the FAFSA and applying for an ETV (through the state) are distinct application processes that sometimes have different application windows. For example, in Washington State a foster youth could complete a FAFSA as early as October but must wait three months until the ETV application becomes available. Having different application windows and sets of applications increases the chances that foster youth may miss aid for which they are eligible. Linking ETV applications to the FAFSA would require states to realign their application timeline to that of the federal aid timeline. It would also require the FAFSA to automatically direct applicants to their state's ETV screening webpage based on an existing FAFSA question about the applicants' history of foster care involvement. This synchronization would streamline and simplify the application process.

States could also enact laws that require completion of the FAFSA as a mandatory TILP planning goal for all college juniors who express interest in enrolling in college. This would assure that youth complete a FAFSA, whether or not they end up enrolling in college. It is far better to err on the side of completing an unused financial aid application than for youth to enroll in college and not receive grants they would have qualified for.

Another task is to work to ensure that ETV disbursements are made in a timely fashion to colleges, so that students do not need to deal with the fallout of late payments. Anecdotally I have heard stories of foster youth panicking after receiving a large tuition bill because their ETV did not come on time; in some cases, they incurred several hundreds of dollars in late fees. Adjusting the ETV disbursement schedule may require administrative maneuvering, but this is a worthwhile effort if it avoids unnecessary trouble. In a similar vein, states should establish simple, streamlined processes for verifying a youth's foster care status (e.g., a verification hotline) so that they are not denied or delayed funding that they rightfully deserve.

Increasing Academic Preparedness

As we saw earlier in the book, one of the most influential set of factors predicting college enrollment are measures of academic proficiency and preparedness. This is an especially challenging area because many youth in care attend primary and secondary schools that are underresourced, and their histories of maltreatment and placement and school mobility compound educational setbacks. We need to fight to improve the quality and resources devoted to our secondary schools so that equitable outcomes are attainable. Additionally, increasing academic preparedness involves two distinguishable but interrelated tasks. The first is to provide academic support to help youth catch up in their grade-level skills and content knowledge. The second task involves cultivating academic habits needed to succeed in college.

Why are academic habits important? One reason is that there are major differences between the routines and skills that are effective in high school and those needed to succeed in an academically rigorous college environment. Even students who developed effective habits in high school will find that college classes move at a faster pace, the material is harder, and there is typically no one who individually intervenes when students fall behind. There is also a shift in where most learning takes place. In high school, the classroom is the learning hub that is supplemented by outside work, but in college much more learning takes place outside of class. This shift is not intuitive, and often students will rely on the study habits they learned in high school to handle college work. Moreover, effectively organizing one's time is crucial in college. This includes big-picture planning for the entire semester (e.g., mapping out due dates for assignments and exams and budgeting extra time to prepare for them) and day-to-day planning. It is important to remember that students are transitioning from high school, where days are highly structured, to college, where days are mostly unstructured. In a recent study of foster youth in California, one of the most commonly stated difficulties with the transition to college is organizing one's time to finish all of one's responsibilities (63% of college students said this was a difficulty) (Courtney et al., 2018). We cannot expect foster youth to learn college-level skills on the fly after starting college. Rather, these skills need to be taught, modeled, and practiced beforehand so they enter college poised to adapt to new learning demands.

To close grade-level gaps and cultivate college academic habits, linking youth to programs that will supplement their high school education is critical. Chafee funding should prioritize programs and services that support secondary education completion and promote readiness for postsecondary education. A principal component of these programs should be regular, consistent, and high-quality tutoring to help foster youth succeed in their current classes. A second component should target habits and skills needed in college. An interactive, hands-on curriculum that allows youth to practice the skills by working through actual problems will be much more beneficial than a traditional didactic format of an instructor lecturing to students. In these classes, it will also be important to include youth with care histories who are currently in college. Often the messenger matters: having a foster youth tell her story about how learning time management skills saved her butt in college will hit home more than an adult going through a bullet point list of the advantages of creating a study schedule.

In addition to programs and services funded by Chafee dollars or other child welfare funds, foster youth will also benefit from programs funded through federal education dollars such as the Upward Bound program. It is recommended that foster youth be given priority registration for programs that target broader populations of underrepresented college students. Other education policies have been modified to acknowledge the special circumstances of foster youth, such as being granted independent student status on the FAFSA. Some colleges have also changed their course registration and housing policies to give priority to youth with care histories. These changes recognize the precarious situation that foster youth are in and the need to ensure they do not miss out on these services.

These programs not just increase foster youths' academic proficiency and habits but also change their self-beliefs and future outlooks. Some youth are never told that they are college material; in some cases, they were told the opposite. These messages certainly need to be challenged by professionals across fields, but a counter-narrative also needs to be instilled in foster youth to enable them to withstand negative narratives they may encounter. An important role of academic readiness programs is to cultivate a mindset in which foster youth know that they are capable of going to college, they do belong there, and their efforts will pay off.

Making Smart Use of Administrative Data

Administrative data are an untapped resource that can help inform college advising and the allocation of resources. First, publicly available data from IPEDS can be easily accessed to obtain information on postsecondary education institutions, such as one-year retention rates, expenditures on student support services, and degree completion rates. Child welfare departments can prepare summaries of data from nearby colleges to help inform the college advising process.

Child welfare agencies could also learn a lot from NSC data. At present, most child welfare departments do not have accurate information on where foster care alumni enroll in college and how they fare once they enroll. For a modest fee, child welfare departments can purchase NSC records for a cohort of older youth who were in foster care several years earlier. These records provide departments with valuable, actionable information. First, they identify the colleges in which foster youth most commonly enroll. This can inform where child welfare departments should dedicate resources and time to building partnerships, coordinating services (e.g., assigning a liaison to the college), and advocating for programs (e.g., campus-based programs). Second, NSC data on college outcomes (e.g., persistence and completion) can also be used to identify colleges where foster youth have particularly successful outcomes. Updating these data every couple of years would provide child welfare departments with up-to-date information that could be used to inform college advising, directing them to colleges that have a track record of high success rates for foster youth. Importantly, NSC data could also be disaggregated to identify specific subgroups of foster youth. For instance, child welfare departments may be particularly concerned about college outcomes among parenting foster youth, young people with behavioral health problems, or youth with involvement in the criminal justice system. Many of these data elements are available in existing child welfare administrative records. Administrative data would shed light on the colleges that are best able to serve young people with special circumstances and challenges. Ideally, child welfare administrative records would be supplemented by data on youths' educational history and performance (e.g., scores on state proficiency tests, high school course taking, and GPA), which would help child welfare departments better foster youths' academic qualifications to colleges.

To supplement the bird's-eye view provided by administrative data, state child welfare agencies could use their ongoing NYTD surveys to gather information on early college experiences of foster youth in their state. Under federal law, states are required every three years to interview a new sample of seventeen-year-olds in foster care and then conduct follow-up interviews at ages nineteen and twenty-one. Considerable time and resources are used to contact NYTD participants, and states could increase the value of these efforts by adding a few supplemental questions specific to young people in college. These supplemental questions could be changed with each cohort based on the interests and priorities of the child welfare agencies. In one cycle, pregnant and parenting youth may be of interest, and in the following cycle perceptions of a change in ETV procedures may a pressing concern, for instance.

A fourth recommendation at the state level is to develop an integrated data system that links primary and secondary education data, postsecondary education data, and child welfare data. Some states such as Colorado, California, and Texas are moving in this direction. Such a system will provide a powerful tool for tracking students with foster care backgrounds through the education system. It will also help outreach efforts of colleges, CSPs, and other supports to accurately identify students with care histories.

Using Extended Foster Care

This book adds to the existing literature that participating in extended foster care increases youths' chances of enrolling in college by age twenty-one. At the time this book was written, twenty-eight states plus the District of Columbia had approved EFC laws (C. Heath, personal communication, June 23, 2019). Getting foster youth into college is important in its own right. Completing some college, even if a degree is not earned, has been found to have employment benefits for foster care alumni (Okpych & Courtney, 2014). Moreover, as postsecondary programs and supports are strengthened, EFC can serve as an important on-ramp into college. EFC ensures that foster youth have a roof over their head, food on the table, electricity and water, and clothes on their back. To date, studies have not found that EFC had a statistically significant impact on increasing the odds of persistence or degree completion. However, it may be that the resources afforded by EFC are a necessary but insufficient ingredient to helping foster youth persist in college. EFC is necessary in that it helps meet youths' basic needs so that they can attend college. But it does not directly address other factors that play a big role in persistence, such as academic support, and many youth will need additional support outside of what EFC typically provides to help them acclimate to college and meet academic requirements. However, if EFC can get foster youth in the door, other programs discussed later, such as CSPs, can address those barriers.

Recommendations to Promote College Persistence and Completion

Compared to the outcome of getting foster youth enrolled in college, it is much more difficult to promote persistence to degree completion. Being admitted to college is a one-time event, and most foster youth first enroll in two-year colleges that do not have a competitive admission process, do not require standardized test scores (e.g., the SAT or ACT), and admit students on an ongoing basis. In contrast, persisting in college is an arduous journey. It stretches over years, demands sustained effort, and requires youth to maintain an acceptable level of academic performance. There is greater chance for life events and emergencies to derail progress, for motivation to wane, and for other opportunities to arise. We have seen that the after the first few semesters of college is a critical drop-off point for foster youth. This means that support structures need to be put in place early. Ideally, we want foster youth to leave their first year of college with credits under their belt and a good GPA, with a feeling of confidence that they can finish, and with the knowledge that they have or are developing the skills that will get them there. After the first year, the rest of college will not be easy, but it will be more familiar and manageable.

Accurately Identifying College Students with Foster Care Histories

One of the challenges faced by postsecondary education institutions is accurately identifying students with foster care backgrounds. As discussed in the book's introduction, a more basic question that precedes this is a definitional one: How should we define students with foster care backgrounds? The definition is important because it will determine the number of students who are counted, and it could be very narrow or quite broad.

Question 53 in section 2 of the FAFSA is a decent start. It reads: "At any time since you turned 13, were both of your parents deceased, were you in foster care, or were you a dependent or ward of the court?" However, one problem with the question is that it also identifies youth who never spent a day in foster care—students with no living parent—and thus does not exclusively pick out students who were in foster care. Second, not all foster youth who enroll in college complete a FAFSA. Third, even if youth complete a FAFSA, they may choose not to self-identify, not understanding the implications that doing so has on their financial aid eligibility. Thus, the information available to colleges from the FAFSA is not a precise identifier of foster youth.

One recommendation to improve a college's ability to identify foster youth is to add a question (or a few questions) to its admission application. If a college does not want to limit itself to a specific definition for students with foster care histories, it can add three simple questions. Because the first question has a "skip" instruction, most applicants will only answer the first question.

1 Were you ever in foster care?
   • If No, skip the next two questions.
2 What was the most recent age you were in foster care? If you are still in foster care now, write your current age.
3 In total, how much time in years and months did you spend in foster care?

The information from these three questions will allow colleges to identify students based on the age they were last in care and how much time they spent in care.

As discussed earlier, a second way of identifying college students with care histories is to create a state administrative data system that combines child welfare data and higher education data. Such a data system would accurately identify students enrolled in colleges in the state who had been in foster care in that state. A limitation is that it would not identify the small percentage of out-of-state college students who were in foster care in another state. However, if this administrative data system were combined with college application questions, it would create a very precise tool for identifying students with foster care histories.

Staving Off Economic Hardships and Unmanageable Work Demands

An important finding in this book is that economic hardships and work demands are significant impediments to degree completion for foster youth. These findings echo the self-report reasons for dropping out of college among foster youth in California (Courtney, Okpych, Park, Harty, et al., 2018). Gross and colleagues (2019) also found that, compared to their peers, foster youth have greater concerns about having the resources to pay for college, are more likely to work more than twenty hours per week, and use a significantly greater percentage of their income to cover the remaining cost of college after grants. Ensuring that foster youth can meet basic needs and pay for college without working excessively is a key aim. When financial strain is not hanging over students' heads, they are able to focus in class, devote time to studying, not worry about their next meal, and sleep better at night.

EFC is an important tool to staving off economic hardships and bouts of homelessness (Courtney, Okpych, & Park, 2018). It is recommended that states allow youth to reenter EFC if they had already decided to leave. That is, if a youth stays in care past their eighteenth birthday but then decides to leave, states should allow youth to reenter foster care if they change their mind, up to age twenty-one. A recent study in California found that a nontrivial proportion of youth (about 11%) left care after age eighteen but later decided to return (Courtney et al., 2016). As is the case with most older teenagers, young people at this age seek more autonomy and independence. Some foster youth may be able to make it on their own, but many will realize that life is more expensive and difficult than they expected. These youth should be able to resume extended care if they want to until they reach the state's age limit.

A few states have enacted laws that allow youth to remain in care past age twenty-one under certain circumstances. For example, foster youth in Connecticut can remain in care up to age twenty-three so long as they are enrolled in an approved postsecondary education institution. Extending care beyond age twenty-one for youth enrolled in higher education is a good idea for at least two reasons. First, it is not reasonable to expect foster youth to have completed their college degree by their twenty-first birthday. A higher age limit gives foster youth a more realistic window of time in which to finish their degree. Second, cutting off support at age twenty-one can undermine the investments that have already been made up to that point. If a youth was halfway to finishing a degree but had to drop out because of the loss of EFC benefits, this is an opportunity lost. Had she been able to remain in care for a few more years, she could have left college with a degree and all of the benefits that accompany it.

Receiving an ETV has been found to increase the odds of persistence (Okpych et al, 2020); however, the maximum amount a youth can receive has been $5,000 since the ETV program's inception in the early 2000s. Because the cost of college, supplies, and living expenses has considerably increased in the last seventeen years, the buying power of the ETV has greatly depreciated (Okpych, 2012). The full $5,000 ETV amount would have covered more than half of the cost of tuition, room, and board for an in-state student attending a public four-year college in 2003 (average cost was $9,951; College Board, 2011), but the voucher covers less than one-quarter of the cost in 2018 (average cost was $21,370; College Board, 2019). This is particularly problematic in states that do not offer other sources of funding such as tuition waivers. It is past time to adjust the ETV funding formula. For example, ETVs could be adjusted on an annual basis to keep pace with the rising cost of college, similar to the way Pell Grants are adjusted.[1] For example, in the first year the ETV was implemented (2002–2003), the Pell Grant maximum was about $1,000 below the ETV maximum ($4,000). Since that time, the maximum Pell Grant amount has increased by more than 52 percent to its current maximum of $6,095. If the ETV had been adjusted at the same rate, the current ETV maximum would be $7,619. Thus, although the ETV is an important resource for foster youth, it is losing its relevance as it covers an increasingly small proportion of college expenses. Increasing the size of the ETV grant would require Congress to amend previous laws to increase the ETV limit and to change the amount allocated to the program from being a set amount to one that adjusts for increasing costs.

Building on the previous point, another recommendation is to relax the satisfactory academic progress (SAP) requirement for the ETV voucher. The first few semesters are a time of huge adjustment for foster youth. Many are first-generation students and are underprepared academically; they may struggle at first to meet the minimum GPA and credit accumulation requirements. Relaxing the academic progress requirement fulfills more closely the intent of the ETV, which is to remove barriers to postsecondary education. California recently passed a law that built leniency and corrective action into the SAP requirement (Senate Bill 150). This 2019 law permits foster youth to continue receiving an ETV for up to four semesters. However, if a youth fails to meet the SAP criteria during the first year, they must meet with a college staff member to develop a plan to improve their grades. This plan is revisited if the student continues to fail to make SAP in the second year. Laws like SB 150 create a process where foster youth can learn from their mistakes and bounce back, rather than being a terminal foreclosure.

An additional recommendation pertains to employment. It is perfectly reasonable that some foster youth will work while they are enrolled in college. Working can build character, foster an appreciation for the value of schooling, cultivate relevant employment skills, and generate money for expenses. However, it is important that the hours are not excessive and disruptive. In agreement with Day and colleagues (2011), it is recommended that colleges prioritize federally funded work-study positions for students with care histories. Work-study is a relatively small program; about one in ten college students who receive a Pell Grant participate in it (Goldrick-Rab, 2016). But it is an important program because jobs are located on campus, do not place unreasonable time or travel demands on students, offer a flexible work schedule, and can help youth feel more connected to campus and invested in college. Importantly, earnings from work-study are not counted as income when calculating eligibility for federal financial aid. Although work-study jobs typically do not pay high hourly wages, they can provide income to supplement other sources of funding and possibly enable foster care youth to save for emergencies. Work-study positions can also continue after youth reach the EFC age limit. Some states, such as Washington, have already enacted laws that give current and former foster youth priority for work-study employment (Washington House Bill, 2005). Other states should follow their lead.

A final tool to help alleviate financial difficulties that interfere with foster youths' college success is an individual development account (IDA). IDAs are matched savings accounts used to help low-income individuals and families build assets and increase their financial literacy. In this plan, contributions made by foster youth would be matched by public and/or private funds at a predetermined rate, age limit, and maximum match limit. For example, a $3 match for every $1 deposit would leave foster youth with $1,500 if they deposited $500. The IDAs is not designed for long-term asset accumulation but rather to help build an emergency or rainy-day fund. These incidents may be minor setbacks for most college students but can be disastrous for foster youth. The IDAs could be set up so that the funds are limited to certain types of eligible expenses. Having backup money could also reduce stress about finances, enabling students to focus on their studies (Mukherjee et al., 2016). IDA accounts typically require participants to take financial literacy classes. Ideally, this training would provide a mix of general information (e.g., how credit card debt works) and hands-on budgeting guidance that is specific to youths' individual financial circumstances. Communities in more than a dozen states take part in the Jim Casey Youth Opportunity Initiative's Opportunity Passport program, which has funded IDAs for more than 5,000 foster youths since it was started in 2001. Other states, such as Washington, New York, and Texas, have either administered IDA programs for foster youth or introduced legislation to create accounts (Torres Flores & Hasvold, 2014).

Campus support programs for foster youth (CSPs) can complement the strategies in this section in a number of ways. These programs help youth navigate financial aid and complete applications, monitor their progress on meeting aid eligibility requirements, and advocate on the youths' behalf. CSPs could also administer IDA programs and be the home of work-study positions. Some CSPs also administer additional forms of financial assistance, such as scholarships, housing during academic breaks, paid summer internships, and book funds (Dworsky & Pérez, 2010; Fostering Success Michigan, 2019).

The strategies for linking foster youth to financial resources, as well as other supports such as low-cost childcare, may be particularly important for students with children. Parenting responsibilities decrease the time students have to spend on campus and to study. Having children also taxes financial resources, and difficulties arise in making childcare and transportation arrangements so parents can attend class (Duquaine-Watson, 2007). One study of college students who are parents found that extra funding for childcare and basic needs helps them remain in college, even when the grants are a modest amount (Brock & Richburg-Hayes, 2006).

Getting Those As and Bs: Promoting Academic Success in College

In some states, the combination of EFC, tuition waivers, Pell Grants, ETVs, and other funding completely cover the cost of college. However, simply having enough money will not automatically boost persistence rates. At the end of the day, foster youth need to meet certain academic benchmarks to remain in college. Failing to meet the GPA and credit completion requirements could result in losing Pell Grants, ETVs, state need-based grants, and other forms of aid, such as work-study jobs, loans, and scholarships. This can start a death spiral of financial hardships and academic difficulties that ends in dropping out.

Persistence is a prime concern because college-level work will be challenging to a large proportion of foster youth. At age seventeen, nearly three-quarters of youth in this study were reading below the level of their same-age peers. We also saw that youth in the toe-in-the-water group, who enrolled for a few semesters and never returned, had significantly lower reading scores and were more likely to have repeated a grade than youth in the other three groups. A study of foster youth in California reported that 88 percent of first-time students in two-year colleges had to take a basic skills course in math, English, or English as a second language (CA College Pathways, 2015). Consequently, strategies must be put into place that enable foster youth to do well in their classes, exceed the minimum GPA requirements, and accumulate credits that count toward graduation.

Several recommendations are offered here to increase foster youths' chances of succeeding academically. They are based on recent research findings and initiatives intended to increase the accuracy of identifying students in need of remediation, improve the instruction that is provided to these students, and use real-time data to track students' progress over time.

The first recommendation is for colleges to use multiple measures of students' academic preparedness when assessing incoming students' need for remediation. Typically, colleges rely primarily on scores from placement tests administered before students enroll. These tests offer brief assessments of proficiency in math, reading comprehension, expository writing, and English as a second language. These are high-stakes tests in that the results determine whether incoming students require remediation and how many remedial courses they must take (and pay for) in a given subject area. However, until recently, few studies have rigorously evaluated the predictive validity of these tests, other than studies carried out by the companies that developed the tests. Two important findings have come out of recent evaluations conducted by independent investigators. First, underplacement is more of a problem than overplacement, leading to students who do not need remediation to be placed in basic skills classes (for review, see Scott-Clayton & Stacey, 2015). One large study found that about one in four students who were required to take developmental education courses did not need to do so (Scott-Clayton et al., 2014). Second, other measures of students' academic proficiency (e.g., high school cumulative GPA, number of completed courses in English and math) are as good as or better at predicting students' need for remediation than the placement tests (Scott-Clayton & Stacey, 2015). Moreover, most studies find that when information from both placement tests *and* students' academic history ("multiple measures") are used, the predictive validity is even greater than when using individual measures (Kingston & Anderson, 2013; Ngo & Kwon, 2015; Scott-Clayton, 2012). Given the limited utility of placement tests alone and the severe impact they have on students' college success, it is recommended that colleges use multiple sources of information to evaluate students' readiness, rather than only results from brief placement tests. Doing so could help foster youth by ensuring they are appropriately assigned to remediation when it is needed and not placed in classes that they likely did not need. Each remedial course a student is required to take puts them a step further from completing a degree.

If and when it has been determined that a student requires remedial instruction, a second issue pertains to how best prepare them without having an inadvertent negative effect on their likelihood of remaining in college. The standard model requires students to take one or more remedial courses that they must pay for, that do not count for credit, and that often must be completed before they can take credit-bearing courses in that subject. Overall, developmental education has been found to negatively affect the likelihood of advancing to credit-bearing courses, the number of completed credits, and the attainment of a credential (Valentine et al., 2016). A growing body of research suggests that alternative course structures are more effective in ensuring that students pass credit-bearing courses and persist in college than traditional remediation (for review, see Bettinger et al., 2013). One promising alternative approach is the co-requisite course model, in which students enroll in a credit-bearing class in tandem with a noncredit class that provides them with extra instruction and support. This approach allows students to build basic skills alongside a credit-bearing course, rather than before it. Although more research is needed, existing evaluations of the co-curricular model have shown it to have a positive impact on credit-bearing course completion and college persistence (e.g., Hern & Edgecombe, 2012; Hu et al., 2016; Jenkins et al., 2010; Jenkins et al., 2009).

A third target area involves identifying foster youth who are struggling early in their first semester. The first time that students typically appear on college radars is when they fail to meet the SAP requirement for financial aid (Bailey et al., 2015). By this time, students may already have one foot (or both feet) out the door. Bailey and colleagues (2015) recommend that colleges set up early warning tools that provide feedback to students early enough to allow effective intervention. For example, student-friendly software programs can be created that provide roadmaps for students on their path to achieving their college objectives, and automated messages can be sent to students when instructors notice that students are falling off track (e.g., missed class, missed assignments, low grades). Such a real-time data system alerts students, instructors, and other staff with access to the system (e.g., potentially CSP staff) that it may be time to intervene.

Even without a warning system, CSPs can play an important role in identifying early signs that students are struggling. CSPs are more targeted, and they may be more feasible to implement than some of the larger, systemic changes discussed earlier. For instance, redesigning a remedial education program will not happen overnight, and in the meantime, foster youth need to be able to succeed within the existing system. The regular contact that CSP staff have with foster youth puts them in a good place to detect problems before they become insurmountable. In other words, CSP staff can serve as the early detection system and then intervene appropriately. A proactive approach will benefit foster youth who may not ask for help on their own or may not recognize the problem.

Finally, supplemental learning will be needed for some classes. As discussed earlier, the pace and rigor of college courses make it easy for foster care youth to fall behind, and the unspoken expectation is that the onus is on the student to learn the material they are struggling with. This means that students should be strongly encouraged to participate in supplemental learning activities. Tutoring is a primary resource. Many schools have tutoring centers with both scheduled appointments and walk-in hours. It is not enough, however, to simply notify foster youth that they can go to the tutoring center. More proactive and hands-on approaches will need to be taken, particularly if students feel self-conscious about needing tutoring. CSPs can play a helpful role in this manner. For example, CSP staff can schedule and attend the first tutoring session with the student during the first week of classes. This can be a standard procedure done with all CSP participants, so the activity is a normative part of getting oriented to college and trying out available resources. It can also be instituted as a standard procedure for classes that are notoriously difficult. Certainly, other forms of supplemental learning, such as instructor office hours, review session, TA meetings, group study session, and reading hours, are also available on campuses. Again, what is important is that proactive measures are taken to engage foster youth early on so these services will scaffold their success, instead of having to bail them out.

Helping Youth Find Their Village of Support

The first two sets of recommendations in this section pertained to meeting youths' financial and material needs and putting processes and practices in place that support their academic success. But the key to increasing persistence is not just material and skill based: it is fundamentally relational. It is about successfully engaging youth and sustaining engagement. Foster youth need supportive people to help them navigate college, normalize difficulties, keep them in the game when they want to quit, and cultivate a feeling that they belong. They will need someone to model and teach them skills to be successful in college. Foster youth need problem solvers and connectors—people adept at sniffing out a problem and linking them to what they need. Youth need someone who will check in with them on a regular basis, hold them accountable, and guide them back on track if they slip. Youth need to be given the opportunity to develop sustained, reliable, dependable relationships with people who genuinely care about them and have the knowledge and skills to guide them and advocate for them. Some of these relationships may be with professionals such as therapists, advisors, faculty, or CSP staff, whereas others may be with friends, roommates, and classmates. In many cases, these relationships will not occur automatically or easily, and sometimes they will only form after a long and hard battle. But it will be this village that supports and sustains them during the long, arduous expedition through college.

CSPs may be an effective way of building a village within the college community. The programs provide a sense of stability, consistency, and safety after years of bouncing around from place to place. One of the striking features of CSPs is the close family-like or community-like bond that frequently emerges. Indeed, in studies that have examined CSP participants' perceptions of the program, the sense of family that develops among participants and staff is one of the commonly stated benefits (Dworsky & Pérez, 2010; Miller et al., 2017). CSPs create an opportunity for young people with similar backgrounds and experiences to form a community of support. This can help allay some of the culture shock of starting college during the first critical year when the dropout risk is high. CSP students who are in their sophomore, junior, and senior years are living proof that persistence is possible, and they can help guide and sustain new students through their first year of college. The CSP community also plays an important role in helping youth to solidify a positive and affirming identity.

One challenge is that, at present, most college campuses do not have a CSP. This is especially true in two-year colleges. In schools without CSPs, other supports on campuses will need to be identified, such as an Extended Opportunity Program and Services (EOPS) program, or other individuals will need to serve as a bridge to campus and community resources. This could be a designated professional who currently works on campus. In all of California's community colleges, an administrator on campus is designated as a liaison to assist foster youth with accessing financial aid, academic support, and other tasks. A liaison model may be a viable alternative for campuses where there are too few foster care students to justify creating a full-fledged CSP. Additionally, the academic specialist within child welfare departments or other professionals in youth-serving organizations can use their relationship with the youth and with people on campus to ensure that foster care students are connected to communities, groups, and organizations. For all postsecondary education institutions, professionals also need to learn about special circumstances that foster youth face and how these might affect their work with them. For example, it is important that financial aid counselors are conversant in the funding sources that are specifically available to foster youth.

Dealing with the Ramifications of Trauma and Instability

An important finding from this book is that high avoidant attachment imperils foster youths' chances of persisting in college and completing a degree.[2] Some foster youth may be particularly resistant to efforts to build relationships and being in a position where they need to depend on others. Even if youth are not at the very high end of avoidant attachment, most have experienced trauma and relational instability in their lives and have some level of distrust of relationships. It is important to recognize this for what it is—a survival strategy that helped them endure perilous relational situations. What may come across as disinterest or resistance is really the result of accumulated trauma and loss. Professionals need to be trained to think in this framework.

Addressing attachment avoidance among college students with care histories is a relatively new area of research, and more work needs to be done. An important question is whether youth high in avoidant attachment can become more open to relying on others and whether certain interventions can promote this openness. Youth high in avoidant attachment have grown accustomed to inhabiting a world of relationships in limbo, and they have learned to detach themselves from feelings of sadness, fear, shame, and anger associated with fractured relationships. When these feelings are not processed, individuals remain perpetually on-guard (Boss, 2006). There are strong evidence-based treatment models for treating adolescents and adults with histories of trauma, such as trauma-focused cognitive-behavioral therapy (Lancaster et al., 2016). Psychotherapy may help foster youth find meaning in past trauma, reconstruct beliefs about their identity and relationships, regulate affect, and provide opportunities to practice and build skills in connecting with others. Mikulincer and colleagues (2015) point out that "trauma victims are implicitly searching for a security provider when they experience threats and face painful memories. It is possible that providing experiences of security within the therapeutic setting can counteract the regulatory deficits reviewed here and reestablished the healing role of attachment security. To this end, therapists should also identify and foster other sources of security in the client's life (e.g., family members, friends, a religious community) that can facilitate and support the healing process" (p. 92).

CSPs can be a source of security for former and current foster youth (Dworsky & Pérez, 2010). Their close-knit, family-like atmosphere may help youth let down their guard with invested staff and with peers who have shared experiences of loss and trauma. Peers provide emotional support and encouragement during tough times, and they hold each other accountable for working toward their academic goals. It may be easier for youth high in avoidant attachment to let down their guard in relationships with peers who have also grown up in the system and who have shared experiences of loss and trauma. This can be a powerful alternative for youth who have developed a distrust of professionals who have cycled in and out of their lives and are perceived as just "doing their job," rather than having a genuine interest in their well-being (Greeson et al.,, 2015). Peer support groups may be an important on-ramp for youth with a high degree of emotional guardedness. Additionally, the one-on-one relationships that youth develop with CSP staff over the course of weeks and months can help restore trust if those relationships are consistent, genuine, and reliable. There may also be specific program features, components, or activities that work effectively with students who are high in avoidant attachment, but more research is needed to identify and test those elements.

A third intervention strategy involves normalizing hardships encountered in college and using support. For example, difficulties can be framed as road-blocks that are normal and expected, not as reflections of a personal deficit. Seeking help from others can be framed as a move of strength that will aug-ment youths' own efforts, rather than as a sign of inadequacy, incapability, or weakness. If clear messages can be frontloaded before the start of college, and youths are connected to specific individuals to assist with problems, then fos-ter youth may be more likely to use these resources.

Fighting for Stable Funding for CSPs

Readers will notice that CSPs have been referenced frequently in the recom-mendations for addressing barriers to persistence and degree completion. If CSPs are developed and operated properly, I believe they can have a powerful positive impact on foster youths' chances of completing college. The fact that CSPs target foster youth makes them efficient; they reach the specific subgroup of students they are intended to reach and are built to meet the specific needs of these students. CSPs can also serve as a one-stop shop for meeting a wide variety of problems that can arise in college, which helps eliminate the bureau-cratic runaround. CSPs are poised to deal with students' special circum-stances, such as pregnant and parenting students, mental health and substance use issues, housing gaps, difficulty accessing Medicaid-eligible health provid-ers, and a full gamut of emergencies that can spring up. These special circum-stances may not affect all program participants, but they are highly disruptive when they arise, potentially undermining the academic, financial, and logisti-cal supports that are in place. Perhaps most importantly, CSPs are focused on engagement—connecting with youth and keeping them linked to a network of peers and resources that can help them through graduation.

Although they are promising interventions, a major challenge is that no reli-able source of public funding exists to support CSPs. As reported in the study by Geiger and colleagues (2018), most CSPs survive by patching together a com-bination of funding from a variety of sources. Since these programs are typi-cally small with just a small handful of paid staff, this means that one of the main hats the program director must wear is that of fundraiser. This takes the director away from concentrating time and effort on effectively running and improving the program and creates an atmosphere of uncertainty. Funding may be secure for the next few years, but if a major funder backs out, the survival of the program is in jeopardy. Instability is not good for students who have experienced the rug being pulled out from under them time and again.

Gross and associates (2019) also underscore the value of CSPs and recognize the problems of inadequate funding and the lack of CSPs in two-year colleges. They urge educators and decision makers to consider forming private–public partnerships to help establish CSPs in community colleges. This is a fair suggestion, but I argue that we need to go further. A reliable source of public funding needs to be established to fund CSPs, which will require legislative action. The optimal route would be for Congress to establish a separate fund expressly for CSPs, similar to the amendment that funds the ETV program. This would ensure that, according to some designated formula, states are provided funding each year for CSPs on the campuses where foster youth in their state commonly enroll.

Another option is to amend current laws to give states more flexibility to use existing funds to support CSPs. Although states can use their Chafee funding to help pay for CSPs, the funding will likely be inadequate and more importantly will harm the other dozen independent living areas that Chafee funding is also designated for (e.g., housing, employment support). Another option is to permit states to use unspent ETV funds to supplement the cost of CSPs. A maximum of $60M is slated for the ETV program, but only about $43M is used each year. The roughly $17M dollars could be appropriated to fund CSPs.

The option of using existing funds is not ideal, both because this funding amount is likely to be insufficient and because it could fluctuate from year to year and decrease over time. For example, if ETVs were adjusted to keep pace with the rising cost of college (as suggested earlier), more of the $60M allotment would be used up, leaving little funds for CSPs. Thus, establishing a distinct funding stream for CSPs is the best option. This is prudent for many reasons, but let me name just two. First, postsecondary education attainment is a core outcome that child welfare should be trying to promote for the young people in its care. Most youth in care want to go to college, and we know that helping them earn a degree will improve their economic security. They will be healthier, happier, contribute to the economy, and be less reliant on government support. Second, EFC and ETVs reduce financial barriers to college, but they do not address the academic and day-to-day obstacles to graduation. Funding CSPs is smart because it will maximize the benefits of other programs that we are already funding.

Limitations of This Study

The Midwest Study offers a valuable opportunity to investigate long-term college outcomes of a representative sample of foster youth. The findings presented in this book, however, are not without limitations and caveats, and several are noted. The first limitation pertains to the generalizability of the findings. The study included a representative sample of young people in three Midwestern States during a specific time in history, and outcomes may be different in states with differing foster youth populations, polices, and contexts.

A second set of limitations pertain to features of the NSC data. In addition to issues of undercoverage and blocked records that were discussed earlier in the book, a limitation of NSC data is that they do not contain information on the specific courses that youth enrolled in and their credit accumulation over time. This data would provide a more precise measure of progress toward a credential than simply enrollment across semesters. Had this information been available, it would have been possible to examine the extent to which youth enrolled in basic education classes, as well as the proportion of youth who made it past these developmental prerequisites.

A third set of limitations pertains to shortcomings of some of the variables. In terms of outcome, this book focused on two-year and four-year degree completion. It did not include completion of vocational certificates in part because the types of courses and the shorter time it takes to complete a certificate make them substantively different from postsecondary degrees. Since few youth completed vocational certificates in NSC data, it was not possible to analyze this as a separate outcome. In terms of predictors, data available from administrative sources would help with some measures, such as youths' academic background (e.g., number and types of schools attended, cumulative high school GPA, timing and reason for involvement in special education) and foster care history (e.g., age of entry, number of years in care). This would have also allowed for a more rigorous assessment of college match. It is also not possible to empirically test the exclusion restriction of the exogenous predictor in the bivariate probit models (college prep activities) and the instrument in the IV models (state). Finally, the decision rules used to create enrollment groups were described in detail; however, a degree of subjectivity was involved in creating those rules.

In addition to these limitations, there were several findings that were unexpected or surprising. These are explored in the Appendix. One finding that I discuss here is that this study did not find the three college outcomes to significantly differ by race or ethnicity. The only exception is that youth who identified as Hispanic were less likely than youth who identified as White to persist through three semesters. The lack of significant differences in this study contrasts with findings in national studies of college students, which report that

Black and Hispanic students have lower rates of enrollment, persistence, and degree completion than White students (Chen et al., 2019; NSC, 2018). One possible explanation for the nonsignificant differences has to do with the heightened vulnerability that is associated with being in foster care. Economic and educational differences that vary starkly by race and ethnicity in the general population, such as poverty, quality of schooling, and family history of college attendance, may not be as large among youth in care. Most foster youth come from disadvantaged backgrounds, and most foster youth have experienced loss and trauma. These adverse experiences cut across race and ethnicity, and may result in smaller disparities in college outcomes between White, Black, and Latino/a foster youth. Another possibility is that there *are* differences in college outcomes by race and ethnicity, but this study was underpowered to detect those differences. The lack of significant findings is not to say that college experiences are the same for foster youth from different racial and ethnic backgrounds. On the contrary, Black and Latino/a students experience overt and subtle forms of racism, in combination with the stigma associated with being in foster care (e.g., Lane, 2017; Perez & Romo, 2011; Whitman, 2016). This calls for CSPs, other foster-youth-serving organizations, and the child welfare and education systems at large to be intentional about listening to the experiences of youth of color, and being willing to engage in more race-conscious and affirming practices (Whitman, 2016).

Closing Thoughts

This concluding chapter provided several recommendations to make the college ladder for foster youth sturdier and more climbable. One point I hope to convey is that there is no silver bullet to getting more foster youth into and through college. It is a complex, multifaceted challenge that defies simple solutions. But there are some good ideas about how to get there, and I am confident that many more good ideas will arise in the future. What we need to do now is make sensible changes to our policies, to how we use data, to how we collaborate across professions, and to how we include, engage, and serve youth. And then we need to put in the hard work.

Appendix: Comments on Nonsignificant Predictors

There were several factors that were not found to significantly predict college outcomes in expected ways. One finding is the diminishing role that academic performance played in enrollment to persistence to degree completion. One reason is that the reading proficiency assessment and high school math/English

GPA were gathered when youth were seventeen years old, and as the college out-comes of interest become more distant, these measures lose their predictive power. They become more like historical artifacts and less like a current, vital, and accurate gauge of participants' academic proficiency. This is particularly true for youth who had a later start at college. Current barriers such as the need to work and economic hardships figure more largely in their ability to persist and finish. It is also important to recognize limitations in the measures. The reading proficiency assessment was intentionally brief and not as comprehen-sive as other assessments. No assessments of participants' math proficiency and other relevant skills were collected at baseline. The high school grades measure may not have been as strong of a predictor, because it only included informa-tion from youths' English and math grades in their most recent high school marking period, rather than their cumulative high school GPA. Additionally, self-reported grades are less reliable then grades taken from administrative rec-ords (Kuncel et al., 2005). Information was not available on the type of classes students were enrolled in (e.g., basic, regular, honors, AP) or the quality/competitiveness of the school they attended, which are other important factors to consider when assessing the role of high school grades.

Contrary to expectations, maltreatment was not significantly related to any of the outcomes, including in the results of supplemental analyses that exam-ined different types of maltreatment separately (i.e., physical abuse, sexual abuse, and neglect). Maltreatment may affect college outcomes to the extent to which it increases youths' emotional and behavioral problems and alcohol/substance use problems, and these latter factors were more direct predictors of college outcomes. As with baseline academic factors, none of the maltreatment history or foster care history characteristics predicted college completion. More-over, it is important to keep in mind that this study includes just youth in foster care, and foster youth experience maltreatment at higher rates than young people in the general population. This means that the study is assessing differ-ences in degrees of maltreatment among youth who have already have high rates of maltreatment. If the sample included youth who had not been in foster care (with lower rates of maltreatment), we may have seen that maltreatment does indeed affect college outcomes.

The presence of mental health problems was also not significantly associated with the odds of entering college, persisting, or completing a degree. The most common mental health problems that adolescents in foster care report are depressive disorders and PTSD (Havlicek et al., 2013). Although these condi-tions can interfere with daily functioning, they may not have been as disruptive or pervasive as the effects of alcohol/substance use problems and the con-stellation of behavioral problems that are correlated with substance use. Additionally, the measures used to capture mental health problems (i.e., positive screen for depression/PTSD symptoms, psychiatric hospitalization, psychotropic drug use) may cast a broad net that does not differentiate between discomforting versus debilitating levels of mental health severity. The measures may not have been acute enough to capture severe problems that would cause college success to suffer.

Likewise, youths' involvement with special education may not have been measured with enough acuity to capture associations with future outcomes. For example, information was not available about the reasons youth were placed in special education (e.g., ADHD, learning disability, speech production disorder, emotional problems); the severity of the disorder; whether it was a past or current issue; and the type, quality, and duration of services and accommodations youth received. Another explanation is that many youth in this study may have been placed in special education because of emotional or behavioral problems, rather than for a learning disability or some other reason. In one study of eighth-grade students in Chicago public schools who were in foster care, 45 percent were receiving special education services, and among the children in special education about 40 percent were classified as having an emotional or behavior disorder (Courtney et al., 2004). Youth who had been in special education were more likely than those who had not been in special education to have baseline mental health problems, alcohol/substance use problems, prior school expulsions, and higher delinquency scores (all $p < .05$). Thus, special education may have been a marker of psychological and behavioral problems for a large proportion of youth with special education histories, which explains why special education did not independently explain college outcomes after these other markers of emotional and behavioral problems were included in the regression models.

Appendix A

Statistics in Plain Language

Explanation of Prediction, Regression, and Statistical Significance

In everyday language, "predict" is used to mean anticipating something that will happen in the future. It has a different meaning in statistics, and it is used in a type of analysis called a regression. In regression analysis, we assess how much different predictors impact an outcome of interest. For example, we may want to assess whether students' high school grades at age 18 influences their likelihood of enrolling in college by age 20. In this example, high school grades is the *predictor*, and college enrollment is the outcome. The results of the regression analysis will tell us how strong the relationship is between the predictor and outcome and whether the relationship is *statistically significant* (more on this later).

Providing a detailed explanation of regression analysis is beyond the scope of this book, but there are some critical things to point out. First, one of the really useful things about regression is that we can examine several factors at once. More specifically, we can estimate the relationship between a predictor and an outcome *after accounting for the influence of other predictors*. This gives us a more precise estimate of how the predictor is expected to influence the outcome. In statistics terminology, we *control for* other predictors. This is important because analyzing predictors by themselves often leads to misleading conclusions. For example, say that we found in a simple regression model that

Table A.1
Fictitious Example Demonstrating the Importance of Statistical Controls

	How Much an Extra School Change Affects the Probability of Enrolling in College	p
Without controlling for reading scores	6.1%	.011
After controlling for reading scores	3.0%	.046

each additional high school change decreased youths' probability of enrolling in college by 6.1% (see Table A.1). From this basic analysis, we may be tempted to conclude that school changes hurt youths' chances of enrolling in college. However, the problem is that students who change schools a lot may be different in important ways from students who change school less frequently, and these differences also affect the chances of enrolling in college. To get a purer estimate of the influence of school changes, we can control for other predictors by adding them to our regression model. We can then see if our estimate of the relationship between school mobility and college enrollment changes after the new predictors are added. In this example, we add a measure of students' reading scores, because students who changed schools frequently read at lower grade levels than students who changed schools less frequently. In effect, "controlling for" students' reading score means that we compare students who are the same in terms of their reading score but differ in the number of school changes they experienced. Without getting into the math, this statistically removes the influence of the reading score differences, because we are comparing students who are the same in their reading scores. In the Table A.1 results, we see that the effect of each school change is only about 3%, not 6%. Thus, without controlling for reading score, we would have overestimated the role of school changes.

A second important use of regression analyses is to make *inferences*. A fact of life in research is that we seldom have data for everyone we are interested in (e.g., all foster youth in the United States). Instead, we usually have to collect data from a sample of individuals. For example, we may be interested in the population of 1,500 foster youths in New Jersey, but we only have enough time and money to collect data from 120 youths. Even though a sample may just be a small percentage of the larger population, if the sample was well selected, it would actually be a good representation of the larger population of interest. That is, when calculating the percentage of New Jersey foster youth who went to college, the percentage we get from our sample data can be an accurate estimate of the percentage we would get if we had data on all 1,500 youths. The jump from using sample data to estimate (i.e., approximate) things about the larger population is call inference. We are inferring characteristics of an unseen population based on the data we have from a representative sample. Inference also applies to regression analyses. We use associations in our sample to make inferences about associations in the population of interest.

A third concept in regression analysis, which is related to inference, is *statistical significance*. Statistical significance is the degree of confidence that an association found in our sample between a predictor and an outcome truly exists in the population. Because a sample is a subset of the larger population, there is always the chance that the predictor–outcome relationship we observe is a peculiarity of particular group of individuals we happened to include in our sample.

A relationship between a predictor and an outcome is deemed to be statistically significant if it passes a high statistical bar. We examine the p-value that is calculated for the predictor–outcome relationship, and if the p-value is small enough, we conclude that a predictor is statistically significant. P-values can range from 0 and 1. The smaller the p value the better, and p values have to be below .05 for us to say that a predictor is "statistically significant". The $p < .05$ cutoff is a common benchmark in research.

So what does a p-value tell us? A p-value is the probability of finding a predictor–outcome relationship that is as extreme (or more extreme) as the one observed in our sample if in reality there was no association between the predictor and outcome. For example, let's say that in our sample of 120 youths that the college enrollment rate for females (57%) was higher than the college enrollment rate for males (47%), and this difference was statistically significant ($p = .02$). If the college enrollment rate had been the same for males and females

Table A.2
Three Conventional p-value Cutoffs

p-value Cutoff	Number of Asterisks	Interpretation
$p < .05$	*	Read as "the p-value is less than point-o-five." This indicates a p-value less than .05 but greater than .01. When a p-value is less than .05, this means that it would be *quite rare* (less than 1 in 20) to get an association this strong by sheer chance.
$p < .01$	**	Read as "the p-value is less than point-o-one." This indicates a p-value less than .01 but greater than .001. When a p-value is less than .01, this means it would be *very rare* (less than 1 in 100) to get an association this strong by sheer chance.
$p < .001$	***	Read as "the p-value is less than point-zero-zero-one." This is used when the p-value is less than .001, which means it would be *extremely rare* (less than 1 in 1,000) to get an association this strong by sheer chance.

in the population, what the $p = .02$ means is that if we drew samples of 120 foster youths again and again from the population, then we would find a 10-percentage-point difference in college enrollment rates *by sheer chance* in only about 2% of the samples. [Note that we get the 2% by changing the p-value from a proportion to a percentage $(.02 \times 100 = 2\%)$]. Two percent is very rare, and it is below the p-value cutoff of 5% (i.e., .05). This means that in research, we are willing to acknowledge that an association is something we should pay attention to only if it is very unlikely to have found it by sheer chance.

In the regression tables in this book, next to each predictor you will either see a p-value or a symbol (an asterisk) that represents a p-value cutoff. Asterisks help us quickly spot results that are statistically significant. The more stars, the greater the statistical significance (i.e., the less likely it would be to find this outcome by sheer chance). There are three conventional levels of statistical significance that are flagged (see Table A.2).

A fourth level is also used in this book when p-values are close to but slightly above the .05 p-value cutoff. These results are denoted by a hat ($^\wedge$) and signify estimates that have a p-value that IS less than .10. P-values that are between .05 and .10 are called *marginally statistically significant*.

Appendix B

Making Sense
of Odds Ratios

If "odds ratio" is an unfamiliar term to you, you are in good company. There is no real need to understand what it is in everyday life, but it is important when trying to make sense of certain types of regression analyses. Binary logistic regression is used when the outcome can take one of two categories (e.g., enrolled vs. not enroll). Odds ratios (ORs) tell us something about how each predictor is expected to be associated with the outcome. This appendix will walk you through how to interpret ORs with a few examples.

Here are a few quick points to stick in your brain from the start. An OR tells us whether a predictor increases or decreases the likelihood that the outcome will occur. ORs can range from 0 to infinity, and 1.0 is the center point. When an OR is exactly 1.0, a predictor has no influence on increasing or decreasing the likelihood of the outcome. When an OR is above 1.0, the predictor increases the likelihood of the outcome. When an OR is less than 1.0, the predictor decreases the likelihood of the outcome.

Some Light Math: From Percentages to Odds Ratios

To start with, we will review a few different mathematical ways to express the likelihood of something occurring. Follow along in Table B.1 where we look at differences between males and females in the likelihoods of enrolling in college. The most familiar way of expressing a likelihood is as a *percentage*. We get a percentage by taking the number of people who experienced an outcome,

Table B.1
The Math behind Odds Ratios

Unit	How to Calculate	For Females	For Males
Percentage	$\dfrac{\text{\# enrolled}}{\text{total \#}} \times 100$	$\dfrac{233}{377} \times 100 = \mathbf{61.8\%}$	$\dfrac{169}{355} \times 100 = \mathbf{47.6\%}$
Odds	$\dfrac{\text{\# enrolled}}{\text{\# not enrolled}}$	$\dfrac{233}{144} = \mathbf{1.62}$	$\dfrac{169}{186} = \mathbf{0.91}$
Odds Ratio	$\dfrac{\text{odds of group 1}}{\text{odds of group 2}}$	Odds ratio of females to males: $\dfrac{1.62}{0.91} = \mathbf{1.78}$	

dividing that by the total number of people, and then multiplying by 100. This will give us a number between 0–100. In the example, we see that 233 of the 377 females enrolled in college, which equals an enrollment rate of about 62%. For males, 169 of the 355 Midwest Study participants enrolled in college, which works out to an enrollment rate of about 48%. From these two numbers (62% vs. 48%) it is plain to see that a greater percentage of females enrolled in college than males.

We can also express these likelihoods as *odds*. When switching to odds, the likelihood of enrollment does not change; we are just moving to a different unit. Odds are calculated by taking the number of youth who *did* experience the outcome and dividing it by the number of youth who *did not* experience the outcome. Note that if the number of students who experience the outcome is the same as the number of students who do not experience the outcome, we get 1.0. Thus, the odds of 1.0 is the exact middle point: 50% of the students experienced the outcome and 50% did not. When odds are greater than 1.0, it means that more youth experienced the outcome than not. Conversely, when the odds are less than 1.0, it means that more youth did not experience the outcome than did. We see these two cases for females and males. For females, 233 enrolled and 144 did not enroll, which equals an odds of 1.62. Since it is more common for females to enroll than not enroll, the odds are above the middle point of 1.0. Conversely, for males, 169 enrolled and 186 did not enroll. Since it was more common for males to not enroll than to enroll, the odds are below the middle point of 1.0 (i.e., it is 0.91).

We are getting close to ORs. The final step is to *compare the odds of one group to the odds of another group*. When we divide the odds of one group by the odds of another group, we get an OR. Thus, if we wanted to compare the odds of enrolling for females versus males, we would divide 1.62 by 0.91, which would give us 1.78. Since females are more likely than males to enroll, the OR is above 1.0.

ORs have similar properties as odds; if the odds of enrolling for females is the same as the odds of enrolling for males, then the OR would be 1.0. This would happen, for example, if the odds for females were 1.3 and the odds for males were also 1.3. We would also get an odds ratio of 1.0 if the odds were 0.6 for males and 0.6 for females. With 1.0 as the middle point, if we see an OR that is greater than 1.0, then the outcome is more likely for the first group than it is for the reference group. Conversely, if the OR is less than 1.0, then the odds are less likely for the first group than for the reference group. In our example, we find an OR of 1.78. This means that the odds of enrolling in college are greater for females than for males. We can be more specific than this in our interpretation. Since an OR of 1.0 would mean the odds are the same for males and females, 0.78 above 1.0 means that the odds of enrolling are 78% greater for females than for males.

Interpreting ORs: Examples

The following tables examine differences between males and females in the likelihood of enrolling in college. Table B.2 gives a few examples for how to

Table B.2
Interpreting Odds Ratios

Strength of Association	Example Odds Ratio	Example Interpretation
Odds ratio is greater than 1.0	1.91	The odds of enrolling in college is 91% greater for females than for males.
Odds ratio is much greater than 1.0	3.66	The odds of enrolling in college for females is about 3.7 times the odds of enrolling in college for males. Equally: the odds of enrolling in college for females is about 2.7 times greater than the odds of enrolling in college for males.
		Note: when we use "greater" in the interpretation, we have to subtract 1.0 from the odds ratio (i.e., 3.7−1.0 = 2.7). Recall that the OR would be 1.0 if the odds of the outcome were the same for both groups, so we are looking for differences over and above 1.0.
		Note: Technically we could also say that the odds are 266% greater for females than for males, but this is awkward. When ORs are larger than 2.0, we typically do not use the percentage interpretation.
Odds ratio is less than 1.0	0.77	The odds of enrolling in college for females are about 33% less than the odds of enrolling in college for males.
		Note: 33% was calculated by subtracting 0.77 from 1.0 (i.e., the OR when there is no group differences): 1.0−0.77 = .33. Convert this proportion to a percentage by multiplying by 100 to get 33%.

Table B.3
Making Sense of Odds Ratios and *p*-values in Logistic Regression Analyses

Predictor	Odds Ratio	p	How to Interpret
Male (reference: Female)	0.64*	.012	The first thing we check is the *p*-value, which is less than .05. This means that there is a statistically significant association between the predictor (gender) and the outcome (enrollment). Next, we see that the OR is below 1.0. This means that the odds of enrolling are lower for males than for females. Specifically, the odds of enrolling are about 36% less for males than for females.
Reading score	1.60***	<.001	The *p*-value is much lower than the cutoff of .05, so this relationship is statistically significant. Next, we see that the odds ratio is above 1.0, which means that having a higher reading score increases the likelihood of enrolling. Specifically, a 1-unit increase in reading score is associated with a 60% increase in the odds of enrolling.
Ever in special education	1.04	.830	First, the *p*-value is not below .05 (it is not even close to .05), so there is no statistically significant relationship between ever being in special education and the likelihood of going to college. It is tempting to try to interpret the OR, but resist! No statistically significant relationship was found between being in a special education classroom and the expected odds of enrolling in college.
Number of college prep activities (0–4)	1.15^	.052	The *p*-value is slightly above the .05 cutoff. Strictly speaking, the OR is not statistically significant at *p* < .05. However, it is pretty close, and researchers sometimes describe *p*-values that fall between .05 and .10 as *marginally* statistically significant. Specifically, there was a marginally statistically significant association between college prep activities and enrollment. Each additional activity that youth took part in increased the expected odds of enrollment by 15%.

interpret ORs of different values. Table B.3 gives examples of how to interpret ORs for different types of predictors and different *p* values. All of the numbers in Tables B.2 and B.3 are fictitious. Spend some time reviewing these tables. Getting familiar with OR interpretations will help a lot when reviewing the tables in chapters.

As a final note about ORs, some of the predictors do not involve comparing two groups of people. For example, one predictor examined in this book is the number of school changes a youth experienced, which could range from 0 to 5 or more. In this case, the OR expresses the change in odds of enrollment for a *one-unit change in the predictor*. For example, an OR of 0.93 would be interpreted as the following: each additional school change decreases the expected odds of enrolling by 7%.

Appendix C

What Is Multivariable Regression and Why Do We Need It?

Why do we need regression models that have more than one predictor (i.e., *multivariable* regression models)? Are not the results from bivariate models sufficient? The simple answer is no. The main problem with bivariate regression models (i.e., a regression model with just one predictor) is that they can yield misleading conclusions. Let's take a hypothetical example of a bivariate regression model showing that youth who worked are more likely than youth who did not work to enroll in college. This may lead us to conclude that working has a positive impact on getting into college, and we may even recommend trying to get more high-school-aged youth jobs because this will increase their chances of going to college. However, these results may be wrong: it may be that it is not having a job that causes youth to enroll, but rather enrollment is influenced by the characteristics of youth who tend to work. For example, youth who work may do better in school, be less likely to get in trouble, and so forth. It may be these other characteristics, and not the job itself, that makes them more likely to go to college.

For a moment, let us imagine that we were able to compare working and non-working youth who were *exactly* the same in terms of their grades, how much they got into trouble, and all of the other relevant characteristics that could influence their likelihood of going to college. The only thing that differed between the youth was whether or not they had worked. Would this help us to get a more accurate estimate of the role that having a job has on youths' likelihood of enrolling in college? Yes it would. The reason is because all of the other relevant characteristics *are the same* between youth, so it could not be differences in these characteristics that are causing their college enrollment chances to differ. The only distinguishing characteristic is their employment status. Thus, by making youth similar on all other relevant characteristics, we are able to isolate the effect of employment on enrollment.

This is precisely what multivariable regression attempts to do. The models do not actually line up working and nonworking youth who are exactly the same on all other relevant characteristics. Rather, the regression analysis does this *statistically* by removing the effects of the other characteristics when estimating the relationship between employment and the odds of enrollment. What is calculated is the estimated role that having a job plays on youths' odds of college enrollment, after adjusting for the influence of reading scores, delinquency scores, school expulsions, gender, and all of the other predictors included in the regression model. These other predictors are called *control variables*. In short, multivariable regression models help us arrive at a more accurate estimate of the actual association between a predictor and an outcome. In practice, how well a regression model improves the accuracy of our estimate depends on whether we have (a) included measures for all of the relevant characteristics and (b) accurately measured and modeled these characteristics. Although no regression model is perfect, a well-built multivariable model gives us more confidence in the accuracy of our estimates than does a simple bivariate regression model.

Appendix D

Description of Study Predictors

Table D.1
Description of Study Measures

Measure	Description
YOUTH CHARACTERISTICS AT AGE 17/18 (WAVE 1)	
DEMOGRAPHIC CHARACTERISTICS	
Gender	Binary measure (male, female)
Race/ethnicity	Four-category measure (White, African American, Hispanic, and other race)
State	Three-category measure of the state in which a youth was in foster care (Illinois, Wisconsin, and Iowa)
ACADEMIC HISTORY	
High school math and English grades	Youth were asked to report their grades in math and English in their most recent marking period (A, B, C, or D or lower). A composite measure was created by averaging the two grades. An additional measure was created by classifying youth into one of three GPA tertiles (bottom, middle, or top).
Reading proficiency	The Wide-Range Achievement Test: Third Edition (WRAT3) was used to provide a brief assessment of reading proficiency (Wilkinson, 1993). In this standardized assessment, youth were asked to read aloud a list of words that increased in difficulty until they mispronounced 10 consecutive words. Raw scores were converted to an age-based standardized scale similar to the IQ scale (mean = 100, SD = 15). Youths' reading scores were then standardized so that a 1-unit change represents a 1 standard deviation change in reading proficiency.

(continued)

Table D.1 (*continued*)

Measure	Description
Highest completed grade	Youth reported the highest grade they had completed at the time of their interview, which was used to create a three-category variable (tenth grade or lower, eleventh grade, and twelfth grade or higher).
Grade repetition	A binary variable (yes, no) captured whether the youth reported ever repeating a grade.
Special education	A binary variable (yes, no) indicated if the youth was ever placed in a special education classroom.
School expulsion	A binary variable (yes, no) captured whether the youth had ever been expelled from school.
College preparatory activities	Youth were asked if they had participated in several activities and trainings intended to prepare them to go to college, including SAT preparation, assistance with college applications, assistance with financial aid/loan applications, and participation in college fairs. A count variable was created ranging from 0–4. Cronbach's alpha for these four items was .73, indicating acceptable internal reliability.

FOSTER CARE HISTORY CHARACTERISTICS AND MALTREATMENT HISTORY

Ever placed in congregate care	A binary variable (yes, no) indicated whether youth had ever been placed in a congregate care setting (i.e., group care, residential treatment center, or childcare institution).
Number of foster care placements	Youth were asked about (a) the number of foster care homes they had been placed in and (b) the number of group homes/residential treatment centers they had been placed in. Both variables were top coded at 20 and summed to create a measure of the total number of foster care placements (range 1–40).
Number of school changes	Youth were asked about the number of times they had to change schools because of a foster care placement change or a family move (0, 1, 2, 3, 4, or 5 or more).
Maltreatment	The Lifetime Experiences Questionnaire (Rose et al., 2000) was used to assess the youths' histories of neglect (9 items), physical abuse (7 items), and sexual abuse (2 items). To create a maltreatment measure, a count of affirmative responses to the 18 different instances of maltreatment was calculated, and youth were then classified into tertiles: low maltreatment, medium maltreatment, and high maltreatment. The Cronbach's alpha for these items was .86, indicating high internal reliability. The three types of maltreatment—neglect, physical abuse, and sexual abuse—were analyzed separately, but statistically significant associations with the three college outcomes were not found.

Table D.1 (*continued*)

Measure	Description

Mental health problem	Binary variables (yes, no) indicated the presence of a mental health problem if any of the following criteria were met: (1) positive screen for depression symptoms, (2) positive screen for PTSD symptoms, (3) youth received psychological or emotional counseling in the past year, (4) youth received medication for emotions in the past year, (5) youth spent one or more nights in a psychiatric hospital since their last interview. Depression and PTSD were both included because they are two of the most prevalent mental health disorders among foster care youth (Havlicek et al., 2013) and because symptoms of these disorders were assessed at all five interview waves. Depression and PTSD were screened using the Composite International Diagnostic Interview (CIDI), a brief structured interview designed for nonclinicians to assess behavioral health problems (World Health Organization, 1998). The other three criteria (counseling, medication, and hospitalization) came from three survey items.
Alcohol or substance use problems	Binary variables (yes, no) indicated the presence of a substance or alcohol use problem if any of the following criteria were met: (1) positive screen for alcohol abuse or dependence symptoms, (2) positive screen for substance abuse or dependence symptoms, (3) attended an alcohol/substance use treatment program in the past year. The presence of symptoms of alcohol use and substance use problems was screened using the CIDI and was assessed at all five interview waves. A separate survey item asked youth about their participation in treatment programs for alcohol or substance use problems.
Economic hardships	Economic hardship measures were available for Waves 2 through 5. Six items asked youth about economic hardships experienced in the past 12 months: not having enough money to buy clothing, not having enough money to pay rent, being evicted because of an inability to pay rent, not having enough money to pay utility bills, having their telephone services cut off because of an inability to pay the bill, and not having enough money to pay for gas or electricity. The original response options included "often true," "sometimes true," and "never true." Each of the six variables were dichotomized (no hardship vs. sometimes/often experienced hardship). The six binary items were then summed to create a count of the number of economic hardships the youth encountered in the past year (range 0–6). The Cronbach's alphas ranged from .73 to .79 at each wave.
Food insecurity	Food insecurity was assessed in Waves 2 through 5 using the USDA's measure of food insecurity (Bickel et al., 2000). Five items asked youth if they had experienced each of the following during the past 12 months: had to cut the size of meals because they were not able to afford more, did not eat for a whole day because they did not have

(*continued*)

Measure	Description
	enough money for food, had to eat less than they should because they did not have enough money, often worried about running out of food, and sometimes or often were not able to afford to eat balanced meals. Following the USDA's coding strategy, participants were classified as being food insecure (yes, no) if they answered affirmatively to at least two of the five items.
Delinquency score	Respondents were asked more than a dozen questions taken from the National Longitudinal Study of Adolescent Health (Resnick et al., 1997) that asked them about the frequency in which they engaged in delinquent behaviors in the past 12 months (e.g., vandalism, stealing, fighting, threatening to use a weapon, and selling drugs). Ten of these items were asked during all of the interview waves. These ten items, along with an additional binary item asking if participants if had been incarcerated since the previous interview wave, were used to create delinquency scores. For each of the ten items, the response set included $0 =$ never, $1 =$ one or two times, $2 =$ three or four times, and $3 =$ five or more times. The binary item of past incarceration was coded as 0 if the participant had never spent time in jail and 3 if they had spent time in jail. Delinquency scores were calculating by taking the average of the ten delinquency items and one incarceration item (range 0–3). Cronbach's alphas at each ranged from .71 to .85.
Parental status	Binary variables (yes, no) indicated if youth had a living child in their pre-entry and post-entry periods. A second pair of variables indicated if youth had a child who resided with them.
Employment status	Youth were asked about the number of hours they were currently working at each interview wave, which was used to create a four-category measure of employment status (not employed, 1–19 hours/week, 20–34 hours/week, and 35 or more hours/week). Data on employment between interview waves were not consistently gathered across waves, so current employment status was used.
Social support	Measures of social support were created using 18 items from the Medical Outcomes Study's Social Support Survey (Sherbourne & Stewart, 1991). Four types of support were assessed: emotional/informational (8 items, e.g., someone to confide in and listen to their problems, to provide advice and information), tangible (4 items, e.g., someone to take to the doctor if sick, help prepare meals if were unable to cook, help with daily chores if sick), positive social interaction (3 items, e.g., someone to relax with, have a good time with, distract from problems), and affectionate (3 items, e.g., someone to hug you, shows love and affection, make you feel wanted). The response options were $0 =$ none of the time, $1 =$ a little of the time, $2 =$ some of the time, $3 =$ most of the time, and $4 =$ all of the time. Average social support scores were calculated ranging from 0–4. Cronbach's alphas at each of the five interview waves were above .90.

Measure	Description
Educational aspirations	A survey item at each interview wave asked respondents about the highest level of educational attainment they aspired to complete. The original response set included 0 = below high school, 1 = graduate from high school, 2 = some college, 3 = graduate from college, 4 = more than college, and "other." The "other" write-in responses were recoded into existing categories when possible. For the regression analysis of predictors of college entry, a three-category pre-entry variable was constructed: high school degree or less, some college, graduate from college or more. For the analyses of college persistence and completion, which included only college entrants, a three-category pre- and post-entry variable was used: some college, graduate from college, more than a college degree.

YOUTH CHARACTERISTICS OF SPECIAL INTEREST

Avoidant attachment	Avoidant attachment was assessed at Wave 1 using 11 items from the Experiences in Close Relationships-Revised (ECR-R) instrument (Fraley et al., 2000). Seven ECR-R items for avoidant attachment were not administered due to time constraints. See chapter 8 for more information.
Years in care past age 18	A measure of the number of years youth spent in care past age 18 was created from child welfare discharge records (range 0–3 years). Youth who exited care before age 18 were coded as 0.

IMPORTANT DATE VARIABLES

Date of secondary credential completion	The date participants earned their secondary credential (i.e., high school diploma, GED, or alternative credential) was calculated from Midwest Study interviews. After examining youths' secondary completion status at each of the five interview waves, 589 of the 732 participants had earned a secondary credential (80.5%). Respondents who completed the Wave 2 interview and had earned a high school diploma by that time provided the month and year in which their diploma was earned (n = 375, 63.7% of the secondary credential holders). For the other 214 youths, the date of their secondary credential attainment had to be estimated. The interview at which a youth's secondary completion status changed from no credential to credential was identified. Next, the median date between the current interview and the previously completed interview was identified. For youth who reported earning a high school diploma, June 15 of the year closest to the median date was used, since high school graduations typically occur in May or June. For youth who reported earning a GED, the median date between the two interview waves was used.
Date of college enrollment	The exact date when youth first entered college was available for all 331 participants in the NSC data (82% of college entrants), but specific dates were not available for the 71 youths identified via Midwest Study data. For these 71 youths, a college entry date was created by identifying

(*continued*)

Table D.1 (*continued*)

Measure	Description
	the two waves in which their status changed from not enrolled to enrolled and then taking the median date between the two interview waves. Because the overwhelming majority of students in the NSC records first enrolled in either the fall or spring semesters, their college start date was designated as the fall or spring semester start date closest to the median date.
Date of college completion	Specific graduation dates were available from NSC records for most of the 80 youths who had earned a postsecondary credential (n = 69, 86.3%). For the 11 youths who reported earning a college degree based on self-report information from Midwest Study interviews, the median date between the two Midwest Study interview dates in which their college degree status change was identified. The May 15 that was closest to the median date was used as the completion date, because most graduations in the NSC data occurred in May. Checks were also made to ensure that the completion dates for these 11 youth were reasonable (e.g., completion of a four-year degree occurred at least four years after their college entry date).

INSTITUTIONAL CHARACTERISTICS

Measure	Description
College type/ selectivity	A measure of institution type/selectivity classified the college into one of three categories: two-year college, minimally competitive four-year college, and competitive four-year college. The four-year college rankings were based on data from *Barron's Profiles of American Colleges*. See chapter 3 for more information.
Sector and control	Institutions were classified as public, private nonprofit, or private for-profit based on data contained in the NSC file. Few youth attended private colleges (especially private nonprofit colleges), so this variable was not included in regression models due to failure of some models to converge.
Size	Using IPEDS, institutional size is the count of the institution's total undergraduate enrollment in the fall term. Institutions were classified into four categories (less than 2,500, 2,500–5,000, 5,001–10,000, and more than 10,000).
Tuition	A continuous IPEDS measure was used for the average in-state tuition and required fees for undergraduate students.
Percent of students receiving Pell Grants	An IPEDS measure reported the percentage of first-time undergraduate students in the fall who were receiving a Pell Grant, a federal need-based grant for low-income students.
Percent of part-time students	An IPEDS measure captured the percentage of first-time undergraduate students in the fall who were attending college on a part-time basis (typically less than 12 credits per semester).
Retention rate	Institutional retention rate was an IPEDS measure of the percentage of full-time students who had first enrolled in the previous fall and then had enrolled in the institution in the current fall. For four-year

Measure	Description
	institutions, this measure pertains to first-time students seeking to complete a bachelor's degree. For two-year institutions, this measure pertains to all degree- and certificate-seeking students who either returned in the fall or successfully completed their certificate program by the fall.
Expenditures on instruction	Using IPEDS, this measured the average dollar amount spent per full-time enrolled student on instructional expenditures, which includes expenses for general academic instruction, vocational and remedial education, and services related to instruction (e.g., information technology).
Expenditures on academic support services	Using IPEDS, this measured the average dollar amount spent per full-time enrolled student on academic support services, which includes expenses for academic administration (e.g., deans), libraries and museums, course and curriculum development, and audio/visual and information technology support for instruction.
Expenditures on student services	Using IPEDS, this measured the average dollar amount spent per full-time enrolled student on student services, which includes expenses for admissions, registrar activities, activities intended to develop students' emotional and physical well-being (e.g., guidance, counseling), and activities intended to promote their social and cultural development outside of the classroom (e.g., student activities, intramural athletics, student organizations, cultural events, and school newspapers).

Acknowledgments

This book grew out of a project that spanned about five years, which included completing my doctoral dissertation and then converting it to a book. First and foremost, it is by the grace and strength of God that this book was written. Many people played important roles, and I would like to convey my deep gratitude to them. I am forever grateful for the support from my family. I want to thank my wife Rachael for not kicking me out of the house when I first told her that I was thinking about applying to doctoral programs. Moving to a cold, windy city that her California blood was not cut out for was a great sacrifice. Thank you for all of your words of encouragement during the lows and the celebrations during the highs. To my two daughters Olivia and Noelle, thank you for taking care of all of the basics while I was writing this book: fruit snacks for energy and walks around the block to take a break from writing. When you get older and misbehave, reading this book will be your punishment. Thank you to my mother Rebecca, sister Alysa, and brother Matt. Even though you were hundreds of miles away, I still felt your love from a distance.

I would like to thank Mark Courtney for being a supportive teacher and mentor during my years as a doctoral student at the University of Chicago. You have been a great role model of what a scholar can be, were there at the right moments for last-minute pep talks, and have taught me many things big and small. Thank you for pushing back on my ideas and always challenging me to think deeper, broader, and more critically. I am also greatly indebted to those who were part of my dissertation as committee members (Yoonsun Choi, Andy Zinn, and Camille Farrington) and readers (Curtis McMillen and Harold Pollack). My work was stronger, shaper, and more compelling with your guidance and feedback.

I want to thank the gracious support from the Doris Duke Fellowship for the Promotion of Child Well-Being. It has been an honor to be connected to a vibrant community of scholars who are passionate about reducing child maltreatment and its repercussions. Thank you, Debbie Raucher and Alexia Everett, for serving as my Doris Duke policy mentors and helping keep my work grounded and policy relevant. I am also grateful to the National Academy of Education/Spencer Foundation for their generous support of my dissertation work. It was an honor to exchange ideas and receive feedback from so many experts in the education field.

I would like to thank my new academic family at the University of Connecticut's School of Social Work for being supportive as I took on the task of writing this book. Finally, I would like to thank all of the youths I have worked with over the years in many different roles. You are too many to name but not too many to forget.

Notes

Introduction

1   This description was given by a young woman who was part of a research study of foster youth enrolled in a four-year college in a southern state.

2   Most qualitative studies recruit participants through convenience sampling, which usually gets participants who are easy to find. This can result in a sample that does not capture the full range of experiences of foster youth in college. See the end of chapter 2 for a discussion on this topic.

3   As reviewed in chapter 5, some quantitative studies of predictors of college outcomes include studies by Courtney and Hook (2017); Day, Dworsky, & Feng, (2013); Villegas et al. (2014), and Salazar (2012).

Chapter 1   Framework for the Book

1   In some cases, at the discretion of the judge, youth were permitted to stay in care past age eighteen under certain circumstances. For example, some states made exceptions for pregnant or parenting youth, or young people who were close to finishing high school. A small handful of other states, such as New York, Illinois, and Washington, DC, had policies that allowed youth to remain in care up to their twenty-first birthday. But by and large, adolescents in care who had not returned home and were not adopted had to leave care by their eighteenth birthdays.

2   Other sources of funding, such as dollars contributed by the state, can be used to supplement the FCIA funding.

3   The original ETV age limit was twenty-three years, but it was raised to twenty-six years of age under the 2018 Family First Prevention Services Act.

4   The "independent student" status also applies to students who were ever a dependent or a ward of the court since turning thirteen and who had no living parent (biological or adoptive) since turning thirteen.

5   This only applies to states that have enacted an extended foster care law, or states providing services to youth who aged out that are comparable to what would be provided had the state enacted an extended care law.

6 The maximum amount for the ETV Program remains at $60M. The funding allocated for the Chafee program will increase by $3M (2.1%) to $143M in fiscal year 2020.

7 Parker and Sarubbi (2017) found that twenty-eight states offer tuition assistance programs for students with foster care histories; the award amount and age limit differ by state. A more recent report found that thirty states have tuition waivers at the time this book was written (University of Washington, 2020).

Chapter 2 Description of the Midwest Study

1 For participants who did not have NSC data, their college entry date and degree completion date were estimating using information from all five Midwest Study interviews. The median semester between interview waves was used to estimate the semester of first enrollment and semester of degree completion. For example, if a youth indicated for the first time in their Wave 3 interview that they had enrolled in college, then the fall semester closest to the middle between their Wave 2 and Wave 3 interviews was designated as their first enrollment date. If a youth stated in their Wave 4 interview that they earned a two-year degree, then their degree conferral date was designated as the spring semester in the middle of their Wave 3 and Wave 4 interviews.

Chapter 3 Exploring College Outcomes

1 Retention is a term that is similar to persistence, but there is an important difference. Retention means that a student continues to remain enrolled for a specified period of time *at the same institution*. Persistence does not have the "same institution" restriction; as long as a student continues to remain enrolled at any college from one marking period to the next, be it at the college they started at or a different college, they are considered as persisting.

2 Youths with no NSC data were included in the third panel if they had enrolled in college at least six years before their last Midwest Study interview.

3 As a sensitivity analysis, BPS persistence and degree completion rates were standardized so that the gender and race/ethnicity distribution of the BPS sample matched the gender and race/ethnicity distribution of the Midwest Study sample. This standardization changed the college outcomes only slightly for the BPS sample. The two-semester persistence rate dropped less than a half-percentage point to 76.9 percent, and the six-year credential status rates were as follows: no credential (59.3%), certificate (14.6%), two-year degree (10.1%), and four-year degree (16.0%).

4 As an additional check, the BPS estimates were standardized to match the gender and age of first enrollment distributions of the Midwest Study sample. For the persistence analysis, the age of first enrollment categories used for standardization included 19 years old or younger, 20 years old, 21 to 24 years old, and 25 to 29 years old. The degree completion age categories were 19 years old or younger, 20 years old, and 21 to 24 years old. Age categories were used rather than individual ages due to sparse data. The estimates changed only slightly with this alternate standardization. The persistence rate was 77.1 percent, and the completion rates were as follows: no credential (57.2%), certificate (15.8%), two-year degree (10.4%),

and four-year degree (16.7%). All differences between Midwest Study and BPS students were statistically significant after standardization ($p < .001$).

Chapter 4   College Enrollment Patterns

1 Stopout contrasts with *dropout*. The latter occurs when students leave school and do not return. A dropout becomes a stopout when the student reenrolls in college.

2 For example, researchers must decide which enrollment characteristics to use and which to exclude when forming the groups. They must also make decisions about the specific analytic methods to use to generate results. In analyses of latent groups and trajectories, multiple solutions are produced (e.g., a solution with two groups, another with three groups, etc.) that the researcher must evaluate and select from. This involves considering both statistical criteria and substantive considerations.

3 More than 500 students from the atD sample could be linked to the Community College Student Report.

4 The one exception to the four-semester rule were youths who enrolled in consecutive semesters in a two-year college and completed a certificate in less than four semesters (n = 3).

5 The Toe-in-the-water group was less likely than the Buffet group to have completed just tenth instead of eleventh ($p = .030$) or twelfth grade ($p = .011$). Additionally, Toe-in-the-water students were more likely to have repeated a grade than students in all three groups (all $p < .05$), more likely to have been expelled than Consistently enrolled students ($p = .007$) and Boomerang students ($p = .029$), and more likely to have been in special education than Consistently enrolled students ($p = .001$).

6 Compared to Consistently enrolled youth, Toe-in-the-water youth were more likely to be unemployed ($p = .029$) or employed full-time ($p = .001$) than to be employed just part-time. Similarly, compared to Boomerang youth, Toe-in-the-water youth were more likely to be unemployed ($p = .033$) or employed full-time ($p = .021$) than to be employed just part-time. Additionally, compared to Buffet youth, Toe-in-the-water youth were less likely to be unemployed than employed part-time ($p = .033$).

Chapter 5   Predictors of College Enrollment

1 The first NYTD cohort (2011 cohort) had the following national response rates: 54% at age 17, 26% at age 19, and 24% at age 21 (National Data Archive on Child Abuse and Neglect, 2014). The second NYTD cohort (2014 cohort) had the following national response rates: 69% at age 17, 37% at age 19, and 33% at age 21 (NDACAN, 2019). The response rates for age 19 and age 21 are the number of completed surveys among the baseline population of youth who were eligible to participate in the NYTD.

2 In the Gross and colleagues' (2019) analyses of NPSAS:16 data, they compared two groups: a group of students with foster care backgrounds who were in years one through five of college versus a group of students without foster care backgrounds who were in years one through five in college. The sampling issue has to do with students who were in their second to fifth years of college. These students are the ones who stayed in college past freshman year. They are likely a high-performing subgroup of students from their freshman cohort. When comparing two groups of

students, a problem arises if the two groups have different dropout rates. For example, image that only 20% of foster youth freshmen made it to years 2–5, whereas 50% of the non-foster youth freshman made it to years 2–5. This would be an unequal comparison. The remaining foster youth would be the all-stars of their starting class, while the remaining non-foster youth would be less exceptional. This could lead to inaccurate conclusions when comparing the two groups, like finding that the two groups are not all that different on a characteristic like college GPA. However, if dropout rates were similar between the two groups (e.g., for both groups 50% of freshman made it to years 2–5), then substantial differences may have been found. The key point is that the differing dropout rates distort the comparison between the two groups. The issue of differences in dropout rates is called differential attrition in research, and it can lead to biased findings. Given that multiple studies show that foster youth are less likely to persist in college than their peers (see Day et al., 2011; Frerer et al., 2013; John Burton Advocates for Youth, 2017; Okpych & Courtney, 2018), it is likely that differential attrition was at play in the analyses conducted by Gross and colleagues (2019). The magnitude of the problem depends on (a) the proportion of their sample comprised of students in years 2–5 and (b) how different the dropout rates were for foster youth versus non-foster youth. The chapters in the book that analyze NPSAS:16 data need to be interpreted with this limitation in mind.

3   Factors that were not marginally statistically significant ($p < .10$) predictors of enrollment, either by age 21 or age 29/30, include number of school changes, history of maltreatment, parental status at age 17, social support, and presence of a mental health problem.

4   Statistical note: checks were performed to ensure that the omitted variables did not become statistically significant when other covariates were entered into the model (i.e., suppression effects). No suppression effects were found for the variables omitted from the multivariable model presented in Table 5.2.

5   Delinquency and alcohol/substance use are more direct measures of underlying behavioral problems and substance use issues, whereas school expulsion and congregate are placement are more indirect proxies of these phenomena.

6   The coefficient for a predictor in logistic regression models is typically presented as log odds. However, odds ratios are more interpretable than log odds. Log odds can be converted to odds ratio by taking the exponent of the log odds.

7   Note that a third (uncommon) outcome was also possible: the youth died before they enrolled in college and before they turned 21. For these youth, their estimated date of becoming deceased was used as the time they exited the risk set.

8   Statistical note: Time is modeled continuously as the number of days from age 17.5 to the date of the youths' twenty-first birthday. Ties (i.e., college entries occurring on the same day) are handled using the Efron method, which provides accurate beta estimates in the presence of ties (Hertz-Picciotto & Rockhill, 1997).

9   Statistical note: The proportional hazards assumption (PHA) is a main assumption of Cox regression models, which states that hazard functions (determined by the values of model predictors) are proportional over time (Kleinbaum & Klein, 2012). Taking gender as an example, if we find a hazard ratio of .75, indicating that the rate of entry is 25% lower for males than females at a given time, the assumption is that this proportional difference is the same across the observation period (e.g., age 17.5 to age 21). The hazard rates for males and females can increase or decrease over the observation period, but it is assumed that they move together so

that the 25% difference in rates is present at any given age. This constancy is what makes the estimated HRs valid, since they provide a single summary estimate of the influence of covariates over the whole observation period. When the PHA is not met, a model assuming proportionality is not appropriate and alternative models should be considered (Kleinbaum & Klein, 2012). Violations of the PHA were assessed by a global test of the PHA using Stata's phtest command, visual inspection of graphs (e.g., Kaplan-Meier Curves for time-invariant covariates with few categories), and inclusion of interaction terms between time-varying covariates and a function of time (Kleinbaum & Klein, 2012). Both individual predictors and the overall regression model (in models with multiple predictors) were tested for violations of the PHA. In the multiple imputation context, which was the method used to address missing data, the PHA must be tested on individual imputed datasets (White & Royston, 2009). A random sample of 10 imputed datasets were used to inspect violations of the PHA. When college enrollment was examined up to age 29/30, the PHA was consistently violated in the overall model ($p < .0001$). Several variables were found to violate the PHA in all of the 10 imputed datasets when examining outcome up to age 29/30, and unsuccessful corrective steps were taken to try address the violation. While it is possible to use alternative models that do not assume proportionality (e.g., an Extended Cox model), these models are sensitive to correctly specifying the functional form of observation time, and interpretation of the coefficients are more complicated (Kleinbaum & Klein, 2012). Instead of using an alternative modeling strategy, only enrollment up to 21 years of age was investigated.

10 Statistical note: In the Cox model examining enrollment by age 21, the PHA was assessed using a similar approach to the one described in the previous endnote. Two predictors were found to violate the PHA in each of the 10 imputed datasets that were analyzed: special education and grade repetition. Examination of the survival curves indicated that youth who were in special education enrolled in college a slightly faster rate than their peers soon after age 17.5, but then lagged behind their peers through the rest of the observation period to age 21. Thus, the rate of enrollment was not proportionate throughout the observation period. A similar pattern was observed for grade repetition. Due to these violations, grade repetition and special education were not included in the Cox models. A third variable that was found to be in violation of the PHA in some of the 10 imputed datasets was the race/ethnicity variable. In particular, between ages 17.5 and 18.5 African American youth enrolled in college at a slower rate than their peers, but their rate dramatically increased in relation to other youth. The race/ethnicity variable is substantively important and was thus retained in the Cox model presented in Table 5.3, but the coefficient (particularly for African American youth) should be interpreted with caution.

11 An interaction term (gender × parental status) was included in the Cox model to assess whether the rate of college enrollment significantly differed for male parents versus female parents. The interaction term was not statistically significant ($HR = 0.85, p = .637$).

Chapter 6   Predictors of College Persistence

1 Studies by Barnow and colleagues (2015) and Courtney and Hook (2017) each investigated predictors of educational attainment among foster youth that

included postsecondary education outcomes. However, neither study focused exclusively on persistence among youth in college. Rather, the outcome measures were broader and included secondary education outcomes. Barnow and colleagues (2015) investigated the following ordered outcome: (1) no HS diploma/GED, (2) completed a GED, (3) completed HS diploma, (4) completed a postsecondary certificate/two-year degree, and (5) completed a four-year degree. Courtney and Hook (2017) investigated the following ordered outcome: (1) no HS diploma/ GED, (2) HS diploma/GED, and (3) completed 1+ years of college. In both studies, ordinal logistic regression was used to evaluate the odds of moving into higher levels of education. Neither study was an investigation of college persistence among foster youth in college, but rather a broader investigation of secondary and postsecondary education attainment.

2 The following predictors were not found to be statistically significantly related to persistence. Background characteristics: male, age at baseline interview, state, number of college preparatory activities, and maltreatment. Pre-entry factors: educational aspirations, parental status, marital status, social support, and mental health problem. Institutional characteristics: institutional size, % of students receiving a Pell Grant, in-state tuition cost, expenditure of instruction, and expenditures on student support services.

3 In this model, the main effect coefficient for male was $OR = 1.39, p = .364$. The main effect coefficient for parent was $OR = 2.15, p = .102$.

4 Similar results were found for pre-entry resident parents (i.e., parents who were living with all of their children). The interaction term (male $\times$ pre-entry resident parent) suggested a significantly worse effect for males than for females ($OR = 0.14$, $p = .010$). In this model, the main effect coefficient for male was $OR = 1.12, p = .739$. The main effect coefficient for resident parent was $OR = 1.74, p = .217$.

Chapter 7 Predictors of Degree Completion

The content of this chapter was originally published in this journal article, "Barriers to Degree Completion for College Students with Foster Care Histories: Results from a 10-Year Longitudinal Study," by N. J. Okpych and M. E. Courtney, 2018, *Journal of College Student Retention*, https://doi.org/10.1177/1521025118791776. The material is reproduced with permission from *JCSR*.

1 Only two statistically significant differences ($p < .05$) were found between youth identified by NSC records and youth identified by Midwest Study data. Compared with college students identified by the Midwest Study interviews, youths identified by NSC records were less likely to report post-entry alcohol/substance use problems (32.4% vs. 49.7%, $p = .008$) and were less likely to be working 1 to 19 hours (vs. 35+ hours) after entering college ($OR = 0.20, p = .025$). It is important to note that nearly three dozen variables were assessed, and these differences may have been due to sheer chance. Nevertheless, we included a dummy variable in the regression analyses to control for the data source that identified the participants as college students.

2 Youth background predictors that were not statistically significant in the bivariate models were gender, race/ethnicity, age at baseline, state, educational aspirations, highest completed grade, reading level, ever in special education, number of

college preparatory activities, ever in congregate care, number of school changes, and maltreatment.

3 The pre-entry and post-entry measures that were not statistically significant in the bivariate models were parental status (pre- only), marital status (pre- only), social support (post- only), employment status (pre- only), delinquency score (pre- and post-), mental health problems (pre- and post-), alcohol/substance use (pre- and post-), economic hardships (pre- only), and food insecurity (pre- only).

4 Institutional predictors that were not statistically significant in bivariate regression models were size, percentage of students receiving Pell Grant, expenditures on instruction, and retention rate.

5 Although not displayed in Table 7.1, supplemental analyses investigated different versions of the parental status variables. As reported earlier, odds of earning a degree among youth who were parents after entering college were about 60% lower than for youth who were not parents. The relationship was less pronounced and not statistically significant when only custodial parental status was examined ($OR = 0.57, p = .236$).

6 Youth working full-time were more likely than youth who worked 1–19 hours per week ($OR = 8.54, p = .003$) and youth who worked 20–34 hours per week ($OR = 2.55, p = .011$) to report needing to work as a dropout reason. Additionally, youth working full-time were significantly more likely than youth working 20–34 hours per week ($OR = 2.30, p = .022$) and marginally significantly more likely than youth working 1–19 hours per week ($OR = 3.71, p = .053$) to say needing to work was a barrier to going back to college.

Chapter 8 The Role of Avoidant Attachment on College Persistence and Degree Completion

The content of this chapter was originally published in the journal article: "The Role of Avoidant Attachment on College Persistence and Completion among Youth in Foster Care," by N. J. Okpych and M. E. Courtney, 2018, *Children and Youth Services Review, 90*, 106–117. The material is reproduced with permission from *CYSR*.

1 I ran bivariate ordinary least squares (OLS) regression models to examine the associations between Wave 1 measures of youths' demographic characteristics, academic history, foster care history, and other risk and promotive factors.

2 Recall that as an OR moves closer to 1.0, this indicates a weakening of the association between the avoidant attachment and the outcome. For example, a change in the odds ratio from 0.71 to 0.76—in which the OR is moving closer to 1.0—between Model 2 and Model 3 indicates a weakening in the relationship between avoidant attachment and the odds of persistence.

Chapter 9 Impact of Extended Foster Care on College Outcomes

The content of this chapter was originally published as a journal article: "The Relationship between Extended Foster Care and College Outcomes for Foster Care Alumni," by N. J. Okpych and M. E. Courtney, 2020, *Journal of Public Child Welfare, 14*(2): 254–276. The material is reproduced with permission from *JPCW*.

1   For participants whose college outcomes came from the Midwest Study data (i.e., they did not appear in NSC data), their college outcomes were observed until age twenty-five/twenty-six (the last Midwest Study interview).
2   Robust standard errors were estimated in the LPMs.
3   For example, the average cost of Illinois in-state tuition and fees for the 2003–2004 school year was $2,686, and the maximum Pell Grant award amount for the same year was $4,050.
4   The Education and Training Voucher (ETV) program was operating around the time Midwest Study participants enrolled in college, but data were not available on the percentage of applicants who received ETVs and the award amounts across states. Simmel and colleagues (2013) accessed data needed to calculate the average ETV amount per eligible youth broken down by state for the fiscal year of 2009. The average allocated ETV amounts for foster youth were quite similar in Illinois ($1,396), Wisconsin ($1,456), and Iowa ($1,355).

Chapter 10   Policy and Practice Recommendations to Increase College Enrollment and Completion

1   Gross and colleagues (2019) point out that the real dollar value of Pell Grants has also decreased over the years. In 1975, a Pell Grant covered 79% of the cost of attendance at a four-year college, but in recent years it has covered just 29% of college costs (p. 154). It is certainly true that Pell Grants have lost their buying power over the years, and this supports the need to ensure that the ETV amount does not remain fixed, and that foster youth apply for multiple sources of aid that could more adequately cover the cost of attendance.
2   This section is taken from Okpych and Courtney (2018b).

References

Adelman, C. (2005). *Moving into town—and moving on: The community college in the lives of traditional-age students*. U.S. Department of Education.

Adelman, C. (2006). *The toolbox revisited: Paths to degree completion from high school through college*. U.S. Department of Education.

Adoption and Foster Care Analysis and Reporting System (AFCARS). (2019). *AFCARS Report #26*. https://www.acf.hhs.gov/cb/resource/afcars-report-26

Ainsworth, M. S. (1979). Infant–mother attachment. *American Psychologist, 34*(10), 932.

Allison, P. D. (2009). Missing data. In R. E. Millsap & A. Maydeu-Olivares (Eds.), *The Sage handbook of quantitative methods in psychology* (pp. 72–89). Sage.

Alon, S., & Tienda, M. (2005). Assessing the "mismatch" hypothesis: Differences in college graduation rates by institutional selectivity. *Sociology of Education, 78*(4), 294–515.

Ammon, B. V., Bowman, J., & Mourad, R., (2008). Who are our students? Cluster analysis as a tool for understanding community college student populations. *Journal of Applied Research in the Community College, 16*(1), 29–41.

Angrist, J. D., Imbens, G. W., & Rubin, D. B. (1996). Identification of causal effects using instrumental variables. *Journal of the American Statistical Association, 91*(434), 444–455.

Angrist, J. D., & Pischke, J. S. (2009). *Mostly harmless econometrics: An empiricist's companion*. Princeton University Press.

Astin, A. W. (1977). *Four critical years: Effects of college on beliefs, attitudes, and knowledge*. Jossey Bass.

Azur, M. J., Stuart, E. A., Frangakis, C., & Leaf, P. J. (2011). Multiple imputation by chained equations: What is it and how does it work? *International Journal of Methods in Psychiatric Research, 20*(1), 40–49.

Bahr, P. R. (2010). The bird's eye view of community colleges: A behavioral typology of first-time students based on cluster analytic classification. *Research in Higher Education, 51*(8), 724–749.

Bailey, T. R., Alfonso, M., Scott, M., & Leinbach, T. (2004). *Educational outcomes of occupational postsecondary students* (Contract Number ED-00-CO-0023). U.S. Department of Education.

Bailey, T. R., Jaggars, S. S., & Jenkins, D. (2015). *Redesigning America's community colleges*. Harvard University Press.

Barban, N., & Billari, F. C. (2012). Classifying life course trajectories: A comparison of latent class and sequence analysis. *Journal of the Royal Statistical Society: Series C (Applied Statistics), 61*(5), 765–784.

Barnow, B. S., Buck, A., O'Brien, K., Pecora, P., Ellis, M. L., & Steiner, E. (2015). Effective services for improving education and employment outcomes for children and alumni of foster care service: Correlates and educational and employment outcomes. *Child and Family Social Work, 20*(2), 159–170.

Barth, R. (1986). Emancipation services for adolescents in foster care. *Social Work, 31*(3), 165–171.

Barth, R. (1990). On their own: The experiences of youth after foster care. *Child and Adolescent Social Work Journal, 7*(5), 419–440.

Batsche, C., Hart, S., Ort, R., Armstrong, M., Strozier, A., & Hummer, V. (2014). Post-secondary transitions of youth emancipated from foster care. *Child and Family Social Work, 19*(2), 174–184.

Bean, J. P. (1980). Dropouts and turnover: The synthesis and test of a causal model of student attrition. *Research in Higher Education, 12*(2), 155–187.

Beath, K. J., & Heller, G. Z. (2009). Latent trajectory modeling of multivariate binary data. *Statistical Modeling, 9*(3), 199–213.

Belasco, A. S., & Trivette, M. J. (2016). Aiming low: Estimating the scope and predictors of postsecondary undermatch. *Journal of Higher Education, 86*(2), 233–263.

Bettinger, E. P., Boatman, A., & Long, B. T. (2013). Student supports: Developmental education and other academic programs. *Future of Children, 23*(1), 93–115.

Bhattacharya, J., Goldman, D., & McCaffrey, D. (2006). Estimating probit models with self-selected treatments. *Statistics in Medicine, 25*(3), 389–413.

Bickel, G., Nord, M., Price, C., Hamilton, W., Cook, J. (2000). *Guide to measuring household food security*. U.S. Department of Agriculture, Food and Nutrition Service, Office of Nutrition, Analysis and Evaluation.

Bielby, R. M., House, E., Flaster, A., & DesJardins, S. L. (2013). Instrumental variables: Conceptual issues and an application considering high school course taking. In M.B. Paulsen (Ed.), *Higher education: Handbook of theory and research* (Vol. 28, pp. 263–321). Springer Netherlands.

Borden, V. M. H. (2004). Accommodating student swirl: When traditional students are no longer the tradition. *Change: The Magazine of Higher Learning, 36*(2), 10–17.

Boss, P. (2006). *Loss, trauma, and resilience: Therapeutic work with ambiguous loss*. W. W. Norton.

Bowen, W., Chingos, M., & McPherson, M. (2009). *Crossing the finish line: Completing college at America's public universities*. Princeton University Press.

Bowlby, J. (1973). *Attachment and loss: Vol. 2. Separation: Anxiety and anger*. Basic Books.

Braxton, J. M., Doyle, W. R., Hartley III, H. V., Hirschy, A., Jones, W. A., & McLendon, M. K. (2013). *Rethinking college student retention*. Jossey-Bass.

Brock, T., & Richburg-Hayes, L. (2006). *Paying for persistence: Early results of a Louisiana Scholarship Program for low-income parents attending community college*. MDRC.

Bryan, J., Moore-Thomas, C., Day-Vines, N. L., & Holcomb-McCoy, C. (2011). School counselors as social capital: The effects of high school college counseling on college application rates. *Journal of Counseling & Development, 89*(2), 190–199.

Cabrera, A. F., Burkum, K. R., La Nasa, S. M., & Bibo, E. (2012). Pathways to a four-year degree: Determinants of degree completion among socioeconomically disadvantaged students. In A. Seidman (Ed.) *College student retention: Formula for success* (2nd ed., pp. 167–211). Rowman & Littlefield.

Cabrera, A. F., Nora, A., & Castaneda, M. B. (1992). The role of finances in the persistence process: A structural model. *Research in Higher Education, 33*(5), 571–593.

Carter, D. F., Locks, A. M., & Winkle-Wagner, R. (2013). From when and where I enter: Theoretical and empirical considerations of minority students' transition to college. In M. Paulsen (Ed.), *Higher education: Handbook of theory and research* (Vol. 28, pp. 93–149). Springer Netherlands.

Caspi, A., Bem, D. J., & Elder, G. H. (1989). Continuities and consequences of interactional styles across the life course. *Journal of Personality, 57*(2), 375–406.

Child Trends Databank. (2018). *Foster care.* https://www.childtrends.org/?indicators =foster-care

Chen, X., Elliott, B. G., Kinney, S. K., Cooney, D., Pretlow, J., Bryan, M., Wu, J., Ramirez, N. A., & Campbell, T. (2019). *Persistence, retention, and attainment of 2011–12 first-time beginning postsecondary students as of spring 2017* (First Look) (NCES 2019-401). U.S. Department of Education, National Center for Education Statistics. https://nces.ed.gov/pubs2019/2019401.pdf

Cicchetti, D. (2016). Socioemotional, personality, and biological development: Illustrations from a multilevel developmental psychopathology perspective on child maltreatment. *Annual Review of Psychology, 67*, 187–211

Clemens, E. V., Lalonde, T. L., & Sheesley, A. P. (2016). The relationship between school mobility and students in foster care earning a high school credential. *Children and Youth Services Review, 68*, 193–201.

Cohen, S., Underwood, L. G., & Gottlieb, B. H. (Eds.). (2000). *Social support measurement and intervention: A guide for health and social scientists.* Oxford University Press.

Cohodes, S., & Goodman, J. (2012). *First degree earns: The impact of college quality on college completion rates.* Working Paper. Harvard Kennedy School.

College Board. (2011). *Trends in college pricing 2011: Tuition and fee and room and board charges over time—unweighted.* http://trends.collegeboard.org/college_pricing /report_findings/indicator/Tuition_and_Fee_Room_and_Board_Unweighted

College Board. (2019). *Average published charges by sector over time.* https://trends .collegeboard.org/college-pricing/figures-tables/average-published-undergraduate -charges-sector-2018-19

Collins, N. L., & Feeney, B. C. (2004). Working models of attachment shape perceptions of social support: Evidence from experimental and observational studies. *Journal of Personality and Social Psychology, 87*(3), 363.

Courtney, M. E. (2009). The difficult transition to adulthood for foster youth in the US: Implications for the state as corporate parent. *Society for Research in Child Development, Social Policy Report, 23*(1): 1–20.

Courtney, M. E., Charles, P., Okpych, N. J., Napolitano, L., Halsted, K., & Courtney, M. E. (2014). *Findings from the California Youth Transitions to Adulthood Study (CalYOUTH): Conditions of foster youth at age 17.* Chapin Hall Center for Children at the University of Chicago.

Courtney, M. E., Dworsky, A., Brown, A., Carey, C., Love, C., & Vorhies, V. (2011). *Midwest evaluation of adult functioning of former foster youth: Outcomes at age 26.* Chapin Hall Center for Children at the University of Chicago.

Courtney, M. E., Dworsky, A., Ruth, G., Havlicek, J., Pérez, A., & Keller, T. (2007). *Midwest evaluation of adult functioning of former foster youth: Outcomes at age 21.* Chapin Hall Center for Children at the University of Chicago.

Courtney, M. E., Dworsky, A., Ruth, G., Keller, T., Havlicek, J., & Bost, N. (2005). *Midwest evaluation of adult functioning of former foster youth: Outcomes at age 19.* Chapin Hall Center for Children at the University of Chicago.

Courtney, M. E., & Hook, J. L. (2017). The potential educational benefits of extending foster care to young adults: Findings from a natural experiment. *Children and Youth Services Review, 72,* 124–132.

Courtney, M. E., & Okpych, N. J. (2017). *Memo from CalYOUTH: Early findings on the relationship between extended foster care and youths' outcomes at age 19.* Chapin Hall Center for Children at the University of Chicago.

Courtney, M. E., Okpych, N. J., Charles, P., Mikell, D., Stevenson, B., Park, K., Kindle, B., Harty, J., & Feng, H. (2016). *Findings from the California Youth Transitions to Adulthood Study (CalYOUTH): Conditions of foster youth at age 19.* Chapin Hall Center for Children at the University of Chicago.

Courtney, M. E., Okpych, N. J., & Park, S. (2018). *Report from CalYOUTH: Findings on the relationships between extended foster care and youths' outcomes at age 21.* Chapin Hall Center for Children at the University of Chicago.

Courtney, M. E., Okpych, N. J., Park, K., Harty, J., Feng, H., Torres-Garcìa, A., & Sayed, S. (2018). *Findings from the California youth transitions to adulthood study (CalYOUTH): Conditions of youth at age 21.* Chapin Hall Center for Children at the University of Chicago.

Courtney, M. E., Piliavin, I., Grogan-Kaylor, A., & Nesmith, A. (2001). Foster youth transitions to adulthood: A longitudinal view of youth leaving care. *Child Welfare, 80*(6), 685–717.

Courtney, M. E., Terao, S., & Bost, N. (2004). *Midwest evaluation of adult functioning of former foster youth: Conditions of youth preparing to leave state care.* Chapin Hall Center for Children at the University of Chicago.

Crisp, G., Taggart, A., & Nora, A. (2015). Undergraduate Latina/o students: A systematic review of research identifying factors contributing to academic success outcomes. *Review of Educational Research, 85*(2), 249–274.

Crosta, P. M. (2014). Intensity and attachment: How the chaotic enrollment patterns of community college students relate to educational outcomes. *Community College Review, 42*(2), 118–142.

Curry, S. R., & Abrams, L. S. (2015). Housing and social support for youth aging out of foster care: State of the research literature and directions for future inquiry. *Child and Adolescent Social Work Journal, 32*(2), 143–153.

Davidson, J. C., & Wilson, K. B. (2016). Community college student dropouts from higher education: Toward a comprehensive conceptual model. *Community College Journal of Research and Practice, 19,* 1–14.

Day, A., Dworsky, A., & Feng, W. (2013). An analysis of foster care placement history and post-secondary graduation rates. *Research in Higher Education Journal, 19,* 1–17.

Day, A., Dworsky, A., Fogarty, K., & Damashek, A. (2011). An examination of post-secondary retention and graduation among foster care youth enrolled in a four-year university. *Children and Youth Services Review, 33*(11), 2335–2341.

Day, A., Riebschleger, J., Dworsky, A., Damashek, A., & Fogarty, K. (2012). Maximizing educational opportunities for youth aging out of foster care by engaging youth voices in a partnership for social change. *Children and Youth Services Review, 34*(5), 1007–1014.

de los Santos Jr., A., & Wright, I. (1990). Maricopa's swirling students: Earning one-third of Arizona state's bachelor's degrees. *Community, Technical, and Junior College Journal, 60*(6), 32–34.

Deutsch, S. A., Lynch, A., Zlotnik, S., Matone, M., Kreider, A., & Noonan, K. (2015). Mental health, behavioral and developmental issues for youth in foster care. *Current Problems in Pediatric and Adolescent Health Care, 45*(10), 292–297.

Donders, A. R. T., van der Heijden, G. J., Stijnen, T., & Moons, K. G. (2006). Review: A gentle introduction to imputation of missing values. *Journal of Clinical Epidemiology, 59*(10), 1087–1091.

Duquaine-Watson, J. M. (2007). "Pretty darned cold": Single mother students and the community college climate in post-welfare reform America. *Equity and Excellence in Education, 40*(3), 229–240.

Dworsky, A., & Pérez, A. (2010). Helping former foster youth graduate from college through campus support programs. *Children and Youth Services Review, 32*(2), 255–263.

Dworsky, A., Smithgall, C., & Courtney, M. E. (2014). *Supporting youth transitioning out of foster care.* Urban Institute. https://www.urban.org/sites/default/files/publication/43266/2000127-Supporting-Youth-Transitioning-out-of-Foster-Care.pdf

Dynarski, S. M., Hemelt, S. W., & Hyman, J. M. (2013). *The missing manual: Using National Student Clearinghouse data to track postsecondary outcomes.* No. w19552. National Bureau of Economic Research.

Eddings, W., & Marchenko, Y. (2012). Diagnostics for multiple imputation in Stata. *Stata Journal, 12*(3), 353–367.

Eisenberg, R. (2018, October). Parents' support to adult kids: A stunning $500 billion a year. *Forbes.* https://www.forbes.com/sites/nextavenue/2018/10/02/parents-support-to-adult-kids-a-stunning-500-billion-a-year/#537d182e5c87

Elwert, F., & Winship, C. (2014). Endogenous selection bias: The problem of conditioning on a collider variable. *Annual Review of Sociology, 40*, 31–53.

Emerson, J. (2006). *Strategies for working with college students from foster care. E-source for College Transitions, 3*(4), 3–4. National Resource Center for the First Year Experience and Students in Transition. https://sc.edu/nrc/system/pub_files/ES_3-4_Feb06.pdf

Fawley-King, K., Trask, E. V., Zhang, J., & Aarons, G. A. (2017). The impact of changing neighborhoods, switching schools, and experiencing relationship disruption on children's adjustment to a new placement in foster care. *Child Abuse and Neglect, 63*, 141–150.

Fernandes-Alcantara, A. (2017). *Youth transitioning from foster care: Background and federal programs.* Congressional Research Service. https://fas.org/sgp/crs/misc/RL34499.pdf

Fernandes-Alcantara, A. (2019). *John H. Chafee Foster Care Program for Successful Transition to Adulthood.* Congressional Research Service. https://fas.org/sgp/crs/misc/IF11070.pdf

Festinger, T. (1983). *No one ever asked us . . . : A postscript to foster care.* Columbia University Press.

Fischer, M. J. (2007). Settling into campus life: Differences by race/ethnicity in college involvement and outcomes. *Journal of Higher Education, 78*(2), 125–156.

Fostering Success Michigan. (2019). *National postsecondary support map.* http://fosteringsuccessmichigan.com/campus-support

Fraley, R. C., Waller, N. G., & Brennan, K. A. (2000). An item response theory analysis of self-report measures of adult attachment. *Journal of Personality and Social Psychology, 78*(2), 350–365.

Franco, J., & Durdella, N. (2018). The influence of social and family backgrounds on college transition experiences of foster youth. *New Directions for Community Colleges, 2018*(181), 69–80.

Fraser, M. W., Galinsky, M. J., & Richman, J. M. (1999). Risk, protection, and resilience: Toward a conceptual framework for social work practice. *Social Work Research, 23*(3), 131–143.

Frerer, K., Sosenko, L. D., & Henke, R. R. (2013). *At greater risk: California foster youth and the path from high school to college.* Stuart Foundation.

Fries, L., Klein, S., & Ballantyne, M. (2014). Are foster children's schools of origin always best? School quality in birth vs. foster parent neighborhoods. *Child & Family Social Work, 21*(3), 317–327.

Geen, R. (2009). *The Fostering Connections to Success and Increasing Adoptions Act: Implementation issues and a look ahead at additional child welfare reforms.* Working Paper. Child Trends. https://eric.ed.gov/?id=ED510757

Geenen, S., Powers, L. E., Phillips, L. A., Nelson, M., McKenna, J., Winges-Yanez, N., & Swank, P. (2015). Better futures: A randomized field test of a model for supporting young people in foster care with mental health challenges to participate in higher education. *Journal of Behavioral Health Services and Research, 42*(2), 150–171.

Geiger, J. M., & Beltran, S. J. (2017a). Experiences and outcomes of foster care alumni in postsecondary education: A review of the literature. *Children and Youth Services Review, 79*, 186–197.

Geiger, J. M., & Beltran, S. J. (2017b). Readiness, access, preparation, and support for foster care alumni in higher education: A review of the literature. *Journal of Public Child Welfare, 11*(4–5), 487–515.

Geiger, J. M., Piel, M. H., Day, A., & Schelbe, L. (2018). A descriptive analysis of programs serving foster care alumni in higher education: Challenges and opportunities. *Children and Youth Services Review, 85*, 287–294.

Gillum, N. L., Lindsay, T., Murray, F. L., & Wells, P. (2016). A review of research on college educational outcomes of students who experienced foster care. *Journal of Public Child Welfare, 10*(3), 291–309.

Goldrick-Rab, S. (2006). Following their every move: An investigation of social-class differences in college pathways. *Sociology of Education, 79*(1), 61–79.

Goldrick-Rab, S. (2016). *Paying the price: College costs, financial aid, and the betrayal of the American dream.* University of Chicago Press.

Goldrick-Rab, S., Baker-Smith, C., Coca, V., Looker, E., & Williams, T. (2019). *College and university basic needs insecurity: A national #RealCollege Survey report.* https://hope4college.com/college-and-university-basic-needs-insecurity-a-national-realcollege-survey-report/

Goldrick-Rab, S., Harris, D. N., & Trostel, P. A. (2009). Why financial aid matters (or does not) for college success: Toward a new interdisciplinary perspective. In J. C. Smart (Ed.), *Higher education: Handbook of theory and research* (Vol. 24, pp. 1–45). Springer Netherlands.

Goldrick-Rab, S., Richardson, J., Schneider, J., Hernandez, A., & Cady, C. (2018). *Still hungry and homeless in college.* Hope Center. https://hope4college.com/still-hungry-and-homeless-in-college/

Greene, W. H. (2011). *Econometric analysis.* Pearson Education.

Greeson, J. K., Thompson, A. E., Ali, S., & Wenger, R. S. (2015). It's good to know that you got somebody that's not going anywhere: Attitudes and beliefs of older youth in foster care about child welfare-based natural mentoring. *Children and Youth Services Review, 48*, 140–149.

Gross, J. P., Geiger, J., & Stolzenberg, E. B. (2019). *Former foster youth in postsecondary education: Reaching higher.* Palgrave Macmillan.

Guiffrida, D. A. (2006). Toward a cultural advancement of Tinto's theory. *Review of Higher Education, 29*(4), 451–472.

Haber, M. G., Cohen, J. L., Lucas, T., & Baltes, B. B. (2007). The relationship between self-reported received and perceived social support: A meta-analytic review. *American Journal of Community Psychology, 39*(1–2), 133–144.

Hagedorn, L. S., & Prather, G. (2005). *The community college solar system: If university students are from Venus, community college students must be from Mars* [Paper presentation]. Annual Forum of the Association for Institutional Research, San Diego, CA, United States.

Hass, M., Allen, Q., & Amoah, M. (2014). Turning points and resilience of academically successful foster youth. *Children and Youth Services Review, 44*, 387–392.

Hass, M., & Graydon, K. (2009). Sources of resiliency among successful foster youth. *Children and Youth Services Review, 31*(4), 457–463.

Havlicek, J. R., Garcia, A. R., & Smith, D. C. (2013). Mental health and substance use disorders among foster youth transitioning to adulthood: Past research and future directions. *Children and Youth Services Review, 35*(1), 194–203.

Hearn, J. C. (1992). Emerging variations in postsecondary attendance patterns: An investigation of part-time, delayed, and nondegree enrollment. *Research in Higher Education, 33*(6), 657–687.

Heckman, J. J. (1977). *Sample selection bias as a specification error (with an application to the estimation of labor supply functions).* NBER Working Paper No. 172. National Bureau of Economic Research.

Hern, K., & Edgecombe, N. (2012, June). *The accelerated alternative: Findings from an analysis of Chabot College's one-semester integrated reading and writing course* [Paper presentation]. Annual Conference on Acceleration in Developmental Education, Baltimore, MD, United States.

Hertz-Picciotto, I., & Rockhill, B. (1997). Validity and efficiency of approximation methods for tied survival times in Cox regression. *Biometrics 53*(3), 1151–1156.

Hines, A. M., Merdinger, J., & Wyatt, P. (2005). Former foster youth attending college: Resilience and the transition to young adulthood. *American Journal of Orthopsychiatry, 75*(3), 381–394.

Hogan, S. R. (2018). Foster youth in higher education: Mental health and academic achievement during the first college year. *Journal of the First-Year Experience & Students in Transition, 30*(2), 65–78.

Holm, A., & Jaeger, M. M. (2011). Dealing with selection bias in educational transition models: The bivariate probit selection model. *Research in Social Stratification and Mobility, 29*(3), 311–322.

Hossler, D., Ziskin, M., Gross, J. P., Kim, S., & Cekic, O. (2009). Student aid and its role in encouraging persistence. In J. C. Smart (Ed.), *Higher education: Handbook of theory and research* (Vol. 24; pp. 389–425). Springer Netherlands.

Hu, S., Park, T., Woods, C. S., Richard, K., Tandberg, D., & Bertrand Jones, T. (2016). Probability of success: Evaluation of Florida's developmental education redesign based on cohorts of first-time-in-college students from 2009–10 to 2014–15.

http://centerforpostsecondarysuccess.org/wp-content/uploads/2016/07
/StudentDataReport2016-1.pdf

Jack, A. A. (2019). *The privileged poor: How elite colleges are failing disadvantaged students*. Harvard University Press.

Jenkins, D., Speroni, C., Belfield, C., Jaggars, S. S., & Edgecombe, N. (2010). *A model for accelerating academic success of community college remedial English students: Is the accelerated learning program (ALP) effective and affordable?* CCRC Working Paper No. 21. Community College Research Center, Columbia University.

Jenkins, D. Zeidenberg, M., & Gregory, K. (2009). *Building bridges to postsecondary training for low-skill adults: Outcomes of Washington State's I-BEST program*. Community College Research Center, Columbia University.

John Burton Advocates for Youth. (2015). *Charting the course: Using data to support foster youth college success*. https://www.scribd.com/document/334234361/Charting -the-Course-Final-pdf

John Burton Advocates for Youth. (2017). *Accelerating success: Turning insights into action for youth in California community colleges*. https://www.jbaforyouth.org/wp -content/uploads/2017/10/Accelerating-Success.pdf

John Burton Advocates for Youth. (2020*). College transitions framework: A guide for child welfare and probation agencies to embed college-going practices into policies and procedures*. https://www.jbaforyouth.org/wp-content/uploads/2020/04/College -Transitions-Framework_FINAL.pdf

Jones, M. A., & Moses, B. (1983). *West Virginia's former foster children: Their experiences in care and their lives as young adults*. Child Welfare League of America.

Kelly, J. (2015). *California weighing options to expand Chafee education grants*. https://chronicleofsocialchange.org/news-2/california-weighing-options-to -expand-chafee-education-grants.

Kids Count. (2018). Children in foster care in the United States. Annie E. Casey Foundation. https://datacenter.kidscount.org/data/tables/6243-children-in-foster -care#detailed/2/2-53/false/871,870,573,869,36,868,867,133,38,35/any/12987

Kim, Y., Ju, E., Rosenberg, R., & Farmer, E. M. Z. (2019). Estimating the effects of independent living services on educational attainment and employment of foster care youth. *Children and Youth Services Review, 96,* 294–301.

Kingston, N. M., & Anderson, G. (2013). Using state assessments for predicting student success in dual-enrollment college classes. *Educational Measurement: Issues and Practice, 32*(3), 3–10.

Klein, B., Damiani-Taraba, G., Koster, A., Campbell, J., & Scholz, C. (2015). Diagnosing attention-deficit hyperactivity disorder (ADHD) in children involved with child protection services: Are current diagnostic guidelines acceptable for vulnerable populations? *Child: Care, Health and Development, 41*(2), 178–185.

Kleinbaum, D. G., & Klein, M. (2012). *Survival analysis*. Springer New York.

Kools, S. (1999). Self-protection in adolescents in foster care. *Journal of Child and Adolescent Psychiatric Nursing, 12*(4), 139–152.

Kriegbaum, K., Villarreal, B., Wu, V. C., & Heckhausen, J. (2016). Parents still matter: Patterns of shared agency with parents predict college students' academic motivation and achievement. *Motivation Science, 2*(2), 97–115.

Kuncel, N. R., Credé, M., & Thomas, L. L. (2005). The validity of self-reported grade point averages, class ranks, and test scores: A meta-analysis and review of the literature. *Review of Educational Research, 75*(1), 63–82.

Lancaster, C. L., Teeters, J. B., Gros, D. F., & Back, S. E. (2016). Posttraumatic stress disorder: Overview of evidence-based assessment and treatment. *Journal of Clinical Medicine, 5*(11), 105.

Lane, T. Y. (2017). Tribulations and achievements: The lived experiences of African American college students formerly in foster care. *Journal of Human Behavior in the Social Environment, 27*(3), 141–150.

Lanza, S. T., & Collins, L. M. (2006). A mixture model of discontinuous development in heavy drinking from ages 18 to 30: The role of college enrollment. *Journal of Studies on Alcohol and Drugs, 67*(4), 552–561.

Lee, R. E., & Whiting, J. B. (2007). Foster children's expressions of ambiguous loss. *American Journal of Family Therapy, 35*(5), 417–428.

Lemly, A., Lockwood, C., & Tureck Lee, S. (2019, July). *Beyond the safety net: Findings from a two-year initiative to transform housing providers into college success programs* [Powerpoint slides]. John Burton Advocates for Youth. https://www.jbaforyouth .org/7-17-19-webinar/

Longwell-Grice, R., & Longwell-Grice, H. (2008). Testing Tinto: how do retention theories work for first-generation, working-class students? *Journal of College Student Retention: Research, Theory and Practice, 9*(4), 407–420.

Ma, J., Pender, M., & Welch, M. (2016). *Education pays 2016: The benefits of higher education for individuals and society.* College Board.

Marti, C. N. (2008). Latent postsecondary persistence pathways: Educational pathways in American two-year colleges. *Research in Higher Education, 49*(4), 317–336.

Mayhew, M. J., Rockenbach, A. N., Bowman, N. A., Seifert, T. A.D., Wolniak, G. C., Pascarella, E. T., & Terenzini, P. T. (2016). *How college affects students: 21st century evidence that higher education works* (Vol. 3). Jossey-Bass.

McCormick, A. C. (2003). Swirling and double-dipping: New patterns of student attendance and their implications for higher education. *New Directions for Higher Education, 2003*(121), 13–24.

McDonough, P. M. (1997). *Choosing colleges: How social class and schools structure opportunity.* State University of New York Press.

McMillen, J. C., Scott, L. D., Zima, B. T., Ollie, M. T., Munson, M. R., & Spitznagel, E. (2004). Use of mental health services among older youths in foster care. *Psychiatric Services, 55*(7), 811–817.

McMillen, J. C., & Tucker, J. (1999). The status of older adolescents at exit from out-of-home care. *Child Welfare, 78*, 339–360.

Melguizo, T. (2008). Quality matters: Assessing the impact of attending more selective institutions on college completion rates of minorities. *Research in Higher Education, 49*(3), 214–236.

Melguizo, T. (2011). A review of the theories developed to describe the process of college persistence and attainment. In J. S. Smart & M. B. Paulsen (Eds.), *Higher education: Handbook of theory and research* (Vol. 26; pp. 395–424). Springer Netherlands.

Merdinger, J. M., Hines, A. M., Osterling, K. L., & Wyatt, P. (2004). Pathways to college for former foster youth: Understanding factors that contribute to educational success. *Child Welfare, 84*(6), 867–896.

Metz, G. W. (2004). Challenge and changes to Tinto's persistence theory: A historical review. *Journal of College Student Retention: Research, Theory and Practice, 6*(2), 191–207.

Mikulincer, M., Horesh, N., Eilati, I., & Kotler, M. (1999). The association between adult attachment style and mental health in extreme life-endangering conditions. *Personality and Individual Differences, 27*(5), 831–842.

Mikulincer, M., & Shaver, P. R. (2003). The attachment behavioral system in adulthood: Activation, psychodynamics, and interpersonal processes. *Advances in Experimental Social Psychology, 35*, 53–152.

Mikulincer, M., & Shaver, P. R. (2007). *Attachment in adulthood: Structure, dynamics, and change.* Guilford Press.

Mikulincer, M., Shaver, P. R., & Solomon, Z. (2015). An attachment perspective on traumatic and posttraumatic reactions. In M. Safir, H. S. Wallach, & A. Rizzo (Eds.), *Future directions in post-traumatic stress disorder* (pp. 79–96). Springer US.

Miller, J. J., Benner, K., Kheibari, A., & Washington, E. (2017). Conceptualizing on-campus support programs for collegiate foster youth and alumni: A plan for action. *Children and Youth Services Review, 83*, 57–67.

Montgomery, P., & Lilly, J. (2012). Systematic reviews of the effects of preparatory courses on university entrance examinations in high school-age students. *International Journal of Social Welfare, 21*(1), 3–12.

Mortenson, T. G. (2012). Measurements of persistence. In A. Seidman (Ed.), *College student retention: Formula for success* (2nd ed., pp. 35–60). Rowman & Littlefield.

Morton, B. M. (2015). Barriers to academic achievement for foster youth: The story behind the statistics. *Journal of Research on Childhood Education, 29*(4), 476–491.

Morton, B. M. (2018). The grip of trauma: How trauma disrupts the academic aspirations of foster youth. *Child Abuse & Neglect, 75*, 73–81.

Mukherjee, M., McKinney, L., Serra Hagedorn, L., Purnamasari, A., & Martinez, F. S. (2016). Stretching every dollar: The impact of personal financial stress on the enrollment behaviors of working and nonworking community college students. *Community College Journal of Research and Practice*, 1–15.

Murphy, S., Elklit, A., Hyland, P., & Shevlin, M. (2016). Insecure attachment orientations and posttraumatic stress in a female treatment-seeking sample of survivors of childhood sexual abuse: A cross-lagged panel study. *Traumatology, 22(1)*, 48–55.

Myers, J. E. B. (2006). *Child protection in America: Past, present, and future.* Oxford University Press.

Nadal, K. L., Wong, Y., Griffin, K. E., Davidoff, K., & Sriken, J. (2014). The adverse impact of racial microaggressions on college students' self-esteem. *Journal of College Student Development 55*(5), 461–474.

National Center for Education Statistics. (2018). *The condition of education 2018.* https://nces.ed.gov/pubsearch/pubsinfo.asp?pubid=2018144

National Center for Education Statistics. (2019). *Immediate college enrollment rate (updated February 2019).* https://nces.ed.gov/programs/coe/indicator_cpa.asp

National Data Archive on Child Abuse and Neglect. (2014). *National Youth in Transition Database (NYTD): Outcomes file: Cohort 1 (age 17 in FY2011): Waves 1, 2, and 3.* https://www.ndacan.acf.hhs.gov/datasets/dataset-details.cfm?ID=202

National Data Archive on Child Abuse and Neglect. (2019). *National Youth in Transition Database (NYTD): NYTD outcomes survey: FY2014 cohort.* https://www.ndacan.acf.hhs.gov/datasets/dataset-details.cfm?ID=228

National Student Clearinghouse. (2018). *Snapshot report—Persistence and retention.* https://nscresearchcenter.org/snapshotreport33-first-year-persistence-and-retention/

National Student Clearinghouse. (2019a). *About the NSC*. https://studentclearing house.org/educational-organizations/studenttracker-for-educational-organizations/

National Student Clearinghouse. (2019b). *Fact sheet*. https://studentclearinghouse .info/onestop/wp-content/uploads/NSCFactSheet.pdf

National Student Clearinghouse. (2019c). *Working with our data: Coverage: Enroll- ment coverage workbook*. https://nscresearchcenter.org/workingwithourdata/

Neal, D. (2017). Academic resilience and caring adults: The experiences of former foster youth. *Children and Youth Services Review, 79*, 242–248.

Ngo, F., & Kwon, W. W. (2015). Using multiple measures to make math placement decisions: Implications for access and success in community colleges. *Research in Higher Education, 56*(5), 442–470.

Nora, A., & Crisp, G. (2009). Hispanics and higher education: An overview of research, theory, and practice. In J. C. Smart (Ed.), *Higher education: Handbook of theory and research* (Vol. 24; pp. 317–353). Springer Netherlands.

Núñez, A. M. (2014). Advancing an intersectionality framework in higher education: Power and Latino postsecondary opportunity. In M. B. Paulsen (Ed.), *Higher education: Handbook of theory and research* (Vol. 29; pp. 33–92). Springer Netherlands.

Okpych, N. J. (2012). Policy framework supporting youth aging-out of foster care through college: Review and recommendations. *Children and Youth Services Review, 34*(7), 1390–1396.

Okpych, N. J. (2015). Receipt of independent living services among older youth in foster care: An analysis of national data from the U.S. *Children & Youth Services Review 51*, 74–86.

Okpych, N. J., & Courtney, M. E. (2014). Does education pay for youth formerly in foster care? Comparison of employment outcomes with a national sample. *Children and Youth Services Review, 43*, 18–28.

Okpych, N. J., & Courtney, M. E. (2017). Who goes to college? Social capital and other predictors of college entry for foster care youth. *Journal of the Society of Social Work and Research 8*(4), 563–593.

Okpych, N. J., & Courtney, M. E. (2018a). Barriers to degree completion for college students with foster care histories: Results from a 10-year longitudinal study. *Journal of College Student Retention: Research, Theory, & Practice*. https://doi.org /10.1177/1521025118791776

Okpych, N. J., & Courtney, M. E. (2018b). The role of avoidant attachment on college persistence and college completion for older youth in foster care. *Children and Youth Services Review, 90*, 106–117.

Okpych, N. J., Courtney, M., & Dennis, K. (2017). *Memo from CalYOUTH: Predic- tors of high school completion and college entry at ages 19/20*. Chapin Hall at the University of Chicago.

Okpych, N. J., Park, S., & Courtney, M. E. (2019). The relationship between extended foster care and college outcomes for foster care alumni. *Journal of Public Child Welfare, 14*(2), 254–276.

Okpych, N. J., Park, S., & Courtney, M. E. (2019). *Memo from CalYOUTH: Early findings on the impact of extended foster care on foster youths' postsecondary education enrollment and persistence*. Chapin Hall at the University of Chicago.

Okpych, N. J., Park, S., Sayed, S., & Courtney, M. E. (2020). The roles of campus- support programs (CSPs) and education and training vouchers on college persis- tence for youth with foster care histories. *Children and Youth Services Review, 111*. https://doi.org/10.1016/j.childyouth.2020.104891.

OPRE (2011). *Multi-Site Evaluation of Foster Youth Programs (Chafee Independent Living Evaluation Project), 2001–2010*. Administration for Children and Families. https://www.acf.hhs.gov/opre/research/project/multi-site-evaluation-of-foster -youth-programs-chafee-independent-living

Ozaki, C. C. (2016). College impact theories past and present. *New Directions for Community Colleges, 2016*(174), 23–33.

Parker, E. & Sarubbi, M. (2018). *Tuition assistance programs for foster youth pursuing postsecondary education: 50-state review*. Education Commission of the States. Retrieved from https://eric.ed.gov/?id=ED573294

Pecora, P. J., Kessler, R. C., O'Brien, K., White, C. R., Williams, J., Hiripi, E., & Herrick, M. A. (2006). Educational and employment outcomes of adults formerly placed in foster care: Results from the Northwest Foster Care Alumni Study. *Children and Youth Services Review, 28*(12), 1459–1481.

Perez, B. F., & Romo, H. d. (2011). "Couch surfing" of Latino foster care alumni: Reliance on peers as social capital. *Journal of Adolescence, 34*(2), 239–248.

Perna, L. (2013). Conclusions: Improving college access, persistence, and completion: Lessons learned. in L. W. Perna & A. P. Jones (Eds.), *The state of college access and completion: Improving college success for students from underrepresented groups* (pp. 208–224). Routledge.

Perna, L., & Titus, M. A. (2005). The relationship between parental involvement as social capital and college enrollment: An examination of racial/ethnic group differences. *Journal of Higher Education, 76*(5), 485–518.

Perry, B. L. (2006). Understanding social network disruption: The case of youth in foster care. *Social Problems, 53*(3), 371–391.

Peter, K., & Cataldi, E. F. (2005). *The road less traveled? Students who enroll in multiple institutions. Postsecondary education descriptive analysis report*. NCES 2005-157. National Center for Education Statistics.

Peters, C. M. (2012). Examining regional variation in extending foster care beyond 18: Evidence from Illinois. *Children and Youth Services Review, 34*(9), 1709–1719.

Pew Research Center. (2016). *The state of American jobs*. https://www.pewsocialtrends .org/2016/10/06/1-changes-in-the-american-workplace/

Plank, S. B., & Jordan, W. J. (2001). Effects of information, guidance, and actions on postsecondary destinations: A study of talent loss. *American Educational Research Journal, 38*(4), 947–979.

Ramist, L. (1981). *College student attrition and retention*. College Board. http://research .collegeboard.org/publications/college-student-attrition-and-retention

Reilly, T. (2003). Transition from care: Status and outcomes of youth who age out of foster care. *Child Welfare, 82*(6), 727–746.

Rendón, L. I., Jalomo, R. E., & Nora, A. (2000). Theoretical considerations in the study of minority student retention in higher education In J. M. Braxton (Ed.), *Reworking the student departure puzzle* (pp. 127–156). Vanderbilt University Press.

Resnick, M. D., Bearman, P. S., Blum, R. W., Bauman, K. E., Harris, K. M., Jones, J., . . . & Ireland, M. (1997). Protecting adolescents from harm: Findings from the National Longitudinal Study on Adolescent Health. *JAMA, 278*(10), 823–832.

Riebschleger, J., Day, A., & Damashek, A. (2015). Foster care youth share stories of trauma before, during, and after placement: Youth voices for building trauma-informed systems of care. *Journal of Aggression, Maltreatment and Trauma, 24*(4), 339–360.

Rios, S. J., & Rocco, T. S. (2014). From foster care to college barriers and supports on the road to postsecondary education. *Emerging Adulthood 2*(3), 227–2387.

Roderick, M., Nagaoka, J., Coca, J., & Moeller, E. (2008). *From high school to the future: Potholes on the road to college.* Consortium on Chicago School Research.

Roderick, M., Nagaoka, J., Coca, J., & Moeller, E. (2009). *From high school to the future: Making hard work pay off.* Consortium on Chicago School Research.

Romano, E., Babchishin, L., Marquis, R., & Fréchette, S. (2015). Childhood maltreatment and educational outcomes. *Trauma, Violence, and Abuse, 16*(4), 418–437.

Rose, D. T., Abramson, L. Y., & Kaupie, C.A. (2000). *The Lifetime Experiences Questionnaire: A measure of history of emotional, physical, and sexual maltreatment.* University of Wisconsin-Madison.

Rosenberg, R., & Kim, Y. (2018). Aging out of foster care: Homelessness, post-secondary education, and employment. *Journal of Public Child Welfare, 12*(1), 99–115.

Rothman, K. J., Greenland, S., & Lash, T. L. (Eds.). (2008). *Modern epidemiology.* Lippincott Williams & Wilkins.

Salazar, A. M. (2012). Supporting college success in foster care alumni: Salient factors related to postsecondary retention. *Child Welfare, 91*(5), 139–167.

Samuels, G. M. (2009). Ambiguous loss of home: The experience of familial (im)permanence among young adults with foster care backgrounds. *Children and Youth Services Review, 31*(12), 1229–1239.

Samuels, G. M., & Pryce, J. M. (2008). "What doesn't kill you makes you stronger": Survivalist self-reliance as resilience and risk among young adults aging out of foster care. *Children and Youth Services Review, 30*(10), 1198–1210.

Schulte, M. (2015). Stopout, swirl, double-dip, and dropout: Attempting to understand student enrollment patterns. *Journal of Continuing Higher Education 63*(2), 133–135.

Scott-Clayton, J. (2012). *Do high-stakes placement exams predict college success?* Community College Research Center, Columbia University.

Scott-Clayton, J., Crosta, P. M., & Belfield, C. R. (2014). Improving the targeting of treatment: Evidence from college remediation. *Educational Evaluation and Policy Analysis, 36*(3), 371–393.

Scott-Clayton, J., & Stacey, G. W. (2015). *Improving the accuracy of remedial placement.* Community College Research Center, Columbia University.

Seidman, A. (2005). Where we go from here: A retention formula for student success. In A. Seidman (Ed.), *College student retention: What works?* (pp. 7–24). Jossey-Bass.

Seidman, A. (Ed.). (2012). *College student retention: Formula for student success.* Rowman & Littlefield.

Seita, J., Day, A., Carrellas, A., & Pugh, G. L. (2016). Assessing the help-seeking behaviors of foster care alumni within their own social networks. *Journal of Sociology, 4*(2), 1–10.

Shamsuddin, S. (2016). Berkeley or bust? Estimating the causal effect of college selectivity on bachelor's degree completion. *Research in Higher Education, 57*(7), 795–822.

Shapiro, D., Dundar, A., Huie, F., Wakhungu, P.K., Bhimdiwala, A. & Wilson, S. E. (2018, December). *Completing college: A national view of student completion rates—Fall 2012 cohort (Signature Report No. 16).* National Student Clearinghouse. Research Center. https://nscresearchcenter.org/signaturereport16/

Sherbourne, C. D., & Stewart, A. L. (1991). The MOS social support survey. *Social Science Medicine, 32*(6), 705–714.

Simmel, C., Shpiegel, S., & Murshid, N. S. (2013). Foster care alumni and funding for postsecondary education: Examining variation in state support. *Journal of Policy Practice, 12*(1), 43–61.

Skobba, K., Meyers, D., & Tiller, L. (2018). Getting by and getting ahead: Social capital and transition to college among homeless and foster youth. *Children and Youth Services Review, 94*, 198–206.

Smerek, R. E. (2010). Cultural perspectives of academia: Toward a model of cultural complexity. In J. C. Smart (Ed.), *Higher education: Handbook of theory and research* (pp. 381–423). Springer Netherlands.

Smith, J. Pender, M., & Howell, J. (2013). The full extent of student-college academic undermatch. *Economics of Education Review 32*, 247–261.

Sovey, A. J., & Green, D. P. (2011). Instrumental variables estimation in political science: A readers' guide. *American Journal of Political Science, 55*(1), 188–200.

Sroufe, L. A. (2005). Attachment and development: A prospective, longitudinal study from birth to adulthood. *Attachment and Human Development, 7*(4), 349–367.

St. John, E. P., Cabrera, A. F., Nora, A., & Asker, E. H. (2000). Economic influences on persistence reconsidered: How can finance research inform the reconceptualization of persistence models. In J. M. Braxton (Ed.), *Reworking the student departure puzzle* (pp. 29–47). Vanderbilt University Press.

Stanton-Salazar, R. D. (2011). A social capital framework for the study of institutional agents and their role in the empowerment of low-status students and youth. *Youth and Society, 43*(3), 1066–1109.

Steele, C. M. (1997). A threat in the air: How stereotypes shape intellectual identity and performance. *American Psychologist, 52*(6), 613–629.

Stephens, N. M., Fryberg, S. A., Markus, H. R., Johnson, C. S., & Covarrubias, R. (2012). Unseen disadvantage: How American universities' focus on independence undermines the academic performance of first-generation college students. *Journal of Personality and Social Psychology, 102*(6), 1178–1197.

Strolin-Goltzman, J., Woodhouse, V., Suter, J., & Werrbach, M. W. (2016). A mixed method study on educational well-being and resilience among youth in foster care. *Children and Youth Services Review 70*, 30–36.

Sullivan, M. J., Jones, L., & Mathiesen, S. (2010). School change, academic progress, and behavior problems in a sample of foster youth. *Children and Youth Services Review, 32*(2), 164–170.

Summers, A., Wood, S., Russell, J., & National Council of Juvenile and Family Court Judges, & United States of America. (2012). *Disproportionality rates for children of color in foster care, May 2012.* https://www.ncjrs.gov/App/Publications/Abstract .aspx?id=261613

Summerskill, J. (1962). Dropouts from college. In N. Sanford (Ed.), *The American college* (pp. 627–637). John Wiley and Sons.

Svoboda, D. V., Shaw, T. V., Barth, R. P., & Bright, C. L. (2012). Pregnancy and parenting among youth in foster care: A review. *Children and Youth Services Review, 34*(5), 867–875.

Terriquez, V., Gurantz, O., & Gomez, A. (2013). *California's college stopouts: The significance of financial barriers to continuous school enrollment.* University of California All Campus Consortium on Research for Diversity.

Tierney, W. G. (1999). Models of minority college-going and retention: Cultural integrity versus cultural suicide. *Journal of Negro Education 68*(1), 80–91.

Tinto, V. (1975). Dropout from higher education: A theoretical synthesis of recent research. *Review of Educational Research 45*(1), 89–125.

Tinto, V. (1987). *Leaving college: Rethinking the causes and cures of student attrition.* University of Chicago Press.

Tinto, V. (1993). *Leaving college: Rethinking the causes and cures of student attrition* (2nd ed.). University of Chicago Press.Tinto, V. (2012). Completing college: Rethinking institutional action. University of Chicago Press. Tobolowsky, B., Scannapieco, M., Aguiniga, D., & Madden, E. (2019). Former foster youth experiences with higher education: Opportunities and challenges. *Children and Youth Services Review, 104*. https://doi.org/10.1016/j.childyouth.2019.05.039

Torres Flores, Q., & Hasvold, A. (2014). Individual development accounts for foster youth. *National Conference of State Legislators Legisbrief 22*(9). http://www.ncsl .org/research/labor-and-employment/individual-development-accounts-for-foster -youth635303106.aspx

Tureck, S. (2016, June). Chafee education grants: The margin between school and survival. *Chronicle of Social Change.* https://chronicleofsocialchange.org/opinion /chafee-education-grants-margin-school-survival/18644.

University of Washington (2020). *Foster care and higher education: Tuition waivers by state.* http://depts.washington.edu/fostered/tuition-waivers-state.

Unrau, Y. A., Dawson, A., Hamilton, R. D., & Bennett, J. L. (2017). Perceived value of a campus-based college support program by students who aged out of foster care. *Children and Youth Services Review, 78*, 64–73.

Unrau, Y. A., Font, S. A., & Rawls, G. (2012). Readiness for college engagement among students who have aged out of foster care. *Children and Youth Services Review, 34*(1), 76–83.

Unrau, Y. A., Seita, J. R., & Putney, K. S. (2008). Former foster youth remember multiple placement moves: A journey of loss and hope. *Children and Youth Services Review, 30*(11), 1256–1266.

U.S. Department of Health and Human Services. (2005). *Federal foster care financing: How and why the current funding structure fails to meet the needs of the child welfare field.* Office of the Assistant Secretary for Planning and Evaluation. https://aspe .hhs.gov/report/federal-foster-care-financing-how-and-why-current-funding -structure-fails-meet-needs-child-welfare-field

Valentine, J. C., Konstantopoulos, S., & Goldrick-Rab, S. (2016). *A meta-analysis of regression discontinuity studies investigating the effects of placement into developmental education: A working paper.* Wisconsin Hope Lab. http://www.wihopelab.com /publications/

VanDerLinden, K. (2002). *Credit student analysis: 1999 and 2000.* Community College Press, American Association of Community Colleges.

Verbeke, G., Fieuws, S., Molenberghs, G., & Davidian, M. (2014). The analysis of multivariate longitudinal data: A review. *Statistical Methods in Medical Research, 23*(1), 42–59.

Villegas, S., Rosenthal, J., O'Brien, K., & Pecora, P. J. (2014). Educational outcomes for adults formerly in foster care: The role of ethnicity. *Children and Youth Services Review, 36*, 42–52.

Washington House Bill Report (2005). *House bill report ESSB 5084.* http:// lawfilesext.leg.wa.gov/biennium/2005-06/Pdf/Bill%20Reports/House/5084-S .HBR.pdf

Watt, T. T., Kim, S., & Garrison, K. (2018). The relationship between state supports and post-secondary enrollment among youth aging out of foster care: An analysis of the National Youth in Transition Database. *Child Welfare, 96*(3), 1–20.

White, I. R., Daniel, R., & Royston, P. (2010). Avoiding bias due to perfect prediction in multiple imputation of incomplete categorical variables. *Computational Statistics and Data Analysis, 54*(10), 2267–2275.

White, I. R., & Royston, P. (2009). Imputing missing covariate values for the Cox model. *Statistics in Medicine, 28*, 1982–1988.

White, I. R., Royston, P., & Wood, A. M. (2011). Multiple imputation using chained equations: Issues and guidance for practice. *Statistics in Medicine, 30*(4), 377–399.

White, T., Scott, L. D., Jr., & Munson, M. R. (2018). Extracurricular activity participation and educational outcomes among older youth transitioning from foster care. *Children and Youth Services Review, 85*, 1–8.

Whitman, K. L. (2016). Students on the margins-margins: A critical examination of research on African American foster youth in higher education. *Urban Education Research and Policy Annuals, 4*(1), 47–54.

Whittaker, J. K., del Valle, J. F., & Holmes, L. (Eds.). (2014). *Therapeutic residential care for children and youth: Developing evidence-based international practice.* Jessica Kingsley.

Wildeman, C., & Emanuel, N. (2014). Cumulative risks of foster care placement by age 18 for US children, 2000–2011. *PloS one, 9*(3), e92785.

Wilkinson, G. S. (1993). *Wide Range Achievement Test 3.* Wide Range Inc.

Wojciak, A. S. (2017). "It's complicated": Exploring the meaning of sibling relationships of youth in foster care. *Child & Family Social Work, 22*(3), 1283–1291.

Wolanin, T. R. (2005). *Higher education opportunities for foster youth: A primer for policy makers.* Institute for Higher Education Policy. http://www.ihep.org/research/publications/higher-education-opportunities-foster-youth

World Health Organization (1998). *The Composite International Diagnostic Interview (CIDI).* https://www.hcp.med.harvard.edu/wmhcidi/

Index

About the Author

NATHANAEL J. OKPYCH is an assistant professor at the University of Connecticut School of Social Work. Okpych draws on his professional experience in social work, mental health, and secondary and postsecondary education in his work that investigates ways to improve college outcomes for youth with foster care histories. He holds both a PhD in social service administration and a master's in biostatistics from the University of Chicago, a master's in social work from Rutgers University, and a master's in clinical psychology from Duquesne University.